TIPS & TRICKS
of
TRAPPING

TIPS & TRICKS
of
TRAPPING

A Classic Guide for the Modern Trapper

W. HAMILTON GIBSON

Illustrated by the Author

DOVER PUBLICATIONS, INC.
Mineola, New York

Bibliographical Note

This Dover edition, first published in 2018, is an unabridged republication of the work originally published in 1881 by Harper & Brothers, New York, under the title *Camp Life in the Woods and the Tricks of Trapping and Trap Making.*

Library of Congress Cataloging-in-Publication Data

Names: Gibson, W. Hamilton (William Hamilton), 1850-1896, author.
Title: Tips and tricks of trapping : a classic guide for the modern trapper / W. Hamilton Gibson.
Description: Mineola, New York : Dover Publications, Inc., [2018] | Includes index. | Originally published: Camp life in the woods and the tricks of trapping and trap making, New York : Harper & Brothers, 1881.
Identifiers: LCCN 2017031027| ISBN 9780486819099 (paperback) | ISBN 0486819094 (paperback)
Subjects: LCSH: Trapping. | Camping. | BISAC: SPORTS & RECREATION / Hunting.
| SPORTS & RECREATION / Outdoor Skills. | SPORTS & RECREATION / Camping. |
CRAFTS & HOBBIES / Woodwork.
Classification: LCC SK283 .G44 2018 | DDC 639/.1-dc23
LC record available at https://lccn.loc.gov/2017031027

Manufactured in the United States by LSC Communications
81909402   2020
www.doverpublications.com

TO

MY BELOVED FRIENDS,

MR. AND MRS. F. W. GUNN,

KIND INSTRUCTORS, AND PARTICIPANTS

IN THE

BRIGHTEST JOYS OF MY YOUTH,

THIS BOOK IS

AFFECTIONATELY DEDICATED BY

The Author.

PREFACE

F all the various subjects in the catalogue of sports and pastimes, there is none more sure of arousing the enthusiasm of our American boys generally, than that which forms the title of this book. Traps and Trapping, together with its kindred branches, always have been and always *will* be subjects of great interest among boys, and particularly so to those who live in the country.

It is a fact to be regretted that we have so few examples of "Boys' Books" published in this country. There are a few English works of this character, that are very excellent as far as they go, but are nevertheless incomplete and unsatisfactory to the wants of American boys, dwelling largely on sports which are essentially English, and merely touching upon or utterly excluding *other* topics which are of the *utmost* interest to boys of this country. In no one of these books, so far as the author of the present volume knows, is the subject of Traps considered to any fair extent, and those examples which are given, represent only the most common and universal varieties already known to the general public.

With these facts in mind, the author has entered with zeal-
ous enthusiasm upon the preparation of a work which shall fill
this odd and neglected corner in literature, and judging from
the reminiscences of his own boyish experiences, he feels certain that in placing such a volume within reach of the public,
he supplies a long felt want in the hearts of his boy-friends
throughout the land.

Far be it from us in the publication of this volume, to be understood as encouraging the wanton destruction of poor innocent animals.   Like all kindred sports, hunting and fishing for
example, the sport of Trapping may be perverted and carried to a
point where it becomes simple cruelty, as is *always* the case when
pursued for the mere *excitement* it brings.   If the poor victims
are to serve no use after their capture, either as food, or in the
furnishing of their plumage or skins for useful purposes, the
sport becomes heartless cruelty, and we do not wish to be understood as encouraging it under any such circumstances.   In
its *right* sense trapping is a delightful, healthful, and legitimate sport, and we commend it to all our boy-readers.

It shall be the object of the author to produce a thoroughly
practical volume, presenting as far as possible such examples
of the trap kind as any boy, with a moderate degree of ingenuity, could easily construct, and furthermore to illustrate each
variety with the utmost plainness, supplemented with the most
detailed description.

With the exception of all "clap-trap." our volume will embrace nearly every known example of the various devices used
for the capture of Bird, Beast, or Fowl, in all countries, simpli-
fying such as are impracticable on account of their complicated
structure, and modifying others to the peculiar adaptation of
the American Trapper.

Devices, which inflict cruelty and prolonged suffering, shall,
as far as possible, be excluded, as this is not a necessary quali-
fication in any trap, and should be guarded against wherever
possible.   Following out the suggestion conveyed under the

title of " The Trapper," we shall present full and ample directions for baiting traps, selections of ground for setting, and
other hints concerning the trapping of all our principal game
and wild animals, valuable either as food or for their fur. In
short, our book shall form a complete trapper's guide, embrac-
ing all necessary information on the subject, anticipating every
want, and furnishing the most complete and fully illustrated
volume on this subject ever presented to the public. In vain
did the author of this work, in his younger days, search the
book stores and libraries in the hopes of finding such a book,
and many are the traps and snares which necessity forced him
to invent and construct for himself, for want of just such a volume. Several of these original inventions will appear in the
present work for the first time in book form, and the author can
vouch for their excellence, and he might almost say, their infalli-
bility, for in their perfect state he has never yet found them to
" miss " in a single instance.

As the writer's mind wanders back to his boyish days, there
is one autumn in particular which shines out above all the rest ;
and that was when his traps were first set and were the chief
source of his enjoyment. The adventurous excitement which
sped him on in those daily tramps through the woods, and the
buoyant, exhilarating effect of the exercise can be realized only
by those who have had the same experience. The hope of success, the fears of disappointment, the continual suspense and
wonder which fill the mind of the young trapper, all combine to
invest this sport with a charm known to no other. Trapping
does not consist merely in the manufacture and setting of the
various traps. The study of the habits and peculiarities of the
different game—here becomes a matter of great importance ;
and the study of natural history under these circumstances
affords a continual source of pleasure and profit.

Among the most useful, although the most cruel, of inventions used by the professional trapper are the steel traps ; so
much so that the author would gladly omit them. But as they

are of such unfailing action, of such universal efficacy, and in many cases are the only ones that can be used, any book on trapping would certainly be incomplete without them. The scope of our volume not only embraces the arts of trapping and trap-making, but extends further into the subject of the wild life of a trapping campaign,—containing full directions for building log cabins, and shanties; boats and canoes; hints on food and cooking utensils; also full directions for the curing and tanning of fur skins,—in short, a complete repository of all useful information pertaining to the life and wants of a professional trapper.

In the preparation of the work no pains have been spared to insure clearness in general directions, and every point which would be likely to puzzle the reader has been specially covered by separate illustration. In this particular it stands unique in the list of boys' books. Every difficulty has been anticipated, and in every instance the illustrations will be found thoroughly comprehensive and complete. That the care and thoroughness which has been displayed throughout the work, and to which its pages will bear witness, may meet with the appreciation and enthusiastic approval of every boy-reader throughout the land, is the most earnest hope of

THE AUTHOR.

CONTENTS

BOOK I.

TRAPS FOR LARGE GAME.

Introduction.—THE DEAD FALL.—Honey as Bait for Bears.—THE GUN TRAP.—Peculiar Habits of the Puma.—"Baiting" for the Puma.—Caution required in Setting the Gun Trap.—Several Guns used.—Different Modes of Setting.—Various animals to which the Gun Trap is adapted.—THE BOW TRAP.—Vane and Barb for Arrows.—Best Wood for Bow.—A Second Example of Bow Trap.—Arrows Barbed and Poisoned.—THE DOWN FALL; or Hippopotamus Trap.—The terrible Harpoon used by the African Trapper.—Different Modes of Setting the Down Fall.—Modification of the Down Fall for small animals.—THE BEAR TRAP.—Various Methods of Setting.—Honey as Bait for Bear.—Bait for Puma. —THE PITFALL.—Use of the Trap in Asia as a means of defence against the Tiger.—Disposition of the Bait.—Wonderful agility of the Puma.—Niceties required in the construction of the Pitfall.—THE LOG COOP TRAP.—Various animals for which it is adapted.—Different Modes of Setting.—THE CORRALL OR HOPO of Africa.—Its Construction and Appalling Effects.—THE NET TRAP.—Its Use in the Capture of the Lion and the Tiger.—American animals to which it may be adapted.—Two Methods of Setting.—BIRD LIME.—Its Use for the Capture of the Lion and Tiger..pages 17—36.

BOOK II.

SNARES OR NOOSE TRAPS.

General Remarks.—Requisite Materials for Snaring.—THE QUAIL SNARE.—"Sucker Wire" Nooses.—Six Quail caught at a time.—HOOP NOOSES.—HORSE HAIR NOOSES.—HEDGE NOOSES.—Peculiarities of the Grouse.—Selection of Ground. —THE TRIANGLE TREE SNARE.—A Hawk captured by the device.—The Wire Noose, as arranged for the capture of the Woodchuck, Muskrat, and House Rat. —THE TWITCH-UP.—Selection of Ground for Setting.—Various Modes of Constructing the Traps.—THE POACHERS' SNARE.—Its portability.—THE PORTABLE SNARE.—Its Peculiar Advantages.—The "Simplest" Snare.—The valuable principle on which it is Constructed.—Its Portability.—Various Adaptations of the Principle.—THE QUAIL SNARE.—Its ample capabilities of Capture.—Peculiarities of the Quail.—Successful Baits.—THE BOX SNARE.—Modification in a very small scale.—THE DOUBLE BOX SNARE.—The Animals for which it is Adapted.—GROUND SNARES.—THE OLD-FASHIONED SPINGLE.—THE IMPROVED SPINGLE.—Objections to Ground Snares.—THE FIGURE FOUR GROUND SNARE.—THE PLATFORM SNARE..............................pages 39—62.

BOOK III.

TRAPS FOR FEATHERED GAME.

THE SIEVE TRAP.—THE BRICK TRAP.—THE COOP TRAP—Improved Method of Setting.—Defects of the old style.—THE BAT FOWLING NET.—Its Use in England. —How the Dark Lantern is Used by Bird Catchers.—THE CLAP NET.—Its Extensive Use in Foreign Countries.—Decoy Birds.—The "Bird Whistle" used in place of decoy.—Wonderful Skill attained in the Use of the Bird Whistle.—Selection of Trapping Ground.—The BIRD WHISTLE Described.—Its Use and Marvellous Capabilities.—THE WILD GOOSE TRAP.—Its Extensive Use in the Northern Cold Regions for the Capture of the Goose and Ptarmigan.—Tame Geese Used as Decoys.—Gravel as Bait.—THE TRAP CAGE.—A Favorite Trap among Bird Catchers.—Call Birds.—THE SPRING NET TRAP.—Rubber Elastic as Spring Power.—A SIMPLER NET TRAP.—Common Faults in many Bird Traps.—Complicated Construction an Unnecessary Feature.—Requisites of a good Bird Trap. —Hints on Simple Mechanism.—Different Modes of Constructing Hinge.—Hoop Iron Used as Spring Power.—Manner of Tempering Spring.—THE UPRIGHT NET TRAP.—A Second Method of Constructing Platform.—THE BOX OWL TRAP.— Ventilation a Desirable Feature in all Box Traps.—Tin Catch for Securing Cover in Place.—Peculiar Mode of Baiting for Birds.—Modification of Perch.— Baiting for the Owl.—Locality for Setting.—The Owl in Captivity.—Its Food.— Hints on the Care of the Bird.—THE BOX BIRD TRAP.—Cigar Box Used as a Trap.—THE PENDENT BOX TRAP.—Ventilation.—Simple Mechanism.—Care in Construction of Bearings.—THE HAWK TRAP.—A "Yankee" Invention.— Stiff-Pointed Wires Effectually Used in the Capture of the Hawk.—Owl also Captured by the Same Device.—THE WILD DUCK NET.—Its Use in Chesapeake Bay.—Manner of Constructing the Net.—Decoy Ducks.—Bait for Ducks.—THE HOOK TRAP.—Its Cruel Mode of Capture.—Peculiar Bait for Ducks.—THE "FOOL'S CAP" TRAP.—Its Successful Use in the Capture of the Crow.—Shrewdness of the Crow.—Strange antics of a Crow when Captured in the Trap.—Bird Lime the Secret of its Success.—Wonderful Tenacity of the Cap.—Different Modes of Setting.—BIRD LIME Described.—Its astonishing "Sticky" Qualities.—The Bird Lime of the Trade.—Various "Home-Made" Recipes.—Manner of Using Bird Lime.—Limed Twigs.—The Owl Used as a Decoy in connection with Bird Lime.—Bird Lime used in the Capture of the Humming Bird.—A Flower Converted into a Trap.—Masticated Wheat as Bird Lime.—Its Ready Removal from the Feathers.—Delicate Organization of the Humming Bird.—Killed by Fright.—Use of its Plumage.—Snares for the Humming Bird.—Blow Guns Successfully Used for its Capture.—Killed by Concussion.—Disabled by a Stream of Water.......................pages 65—99.

BOOK IV.

MISCELLANEOUS TRAPS.

The Common Box Trap.—Two Modes of Setting.—Animals for which it is Adapted. —A Modification of the Trap.—Another Box Trap.—The Figure Four Trap.—Its Advantages.—The Double Ender.—A Favorite Trap in New England.—Simplicity of Construction.—The Rabbit's Fondness for Salt.—Its Use as a Bait.—The Self-Setting Trap.—Animals for which it is adapted.—The Dead Fall.—Various Methods of Construction.—Animals for which it is usually Set.—Remarkable Cunning of some Animals.—The Precautions which it Necessitates.—Bait for the Muskrat.—Various Baits for the Mink.—Skunk Baits.—A Fox Entrapped by a Dead Fall.—Slight Modification in the Arrangement of Pieces.—Live Duck used as Bait.—Another Arrangement for the Dead Fall.—Trap Sprung by the Foot of the Animal.—The Figure Four Trap.—Applied to the Dead Fall.—The Garotte.—Its Singular Mode of Capture.—Its Common Victims.—The Bow Trap.—An oddity of the Trap Kind.—Its Singular mechanism.—The Mole Trap.—A Much-needed Contrivance.—Subterranean Mode of Setting.—Its Unfailing Success.—A Fish Trap.—A Section of Stove Pipe used as a Trap.—Its Various Victims.—Adjustment of Bait.—Curious Mode of Capture..pages 103—121.

BOOK V.

HOUSEHOLD TRAPS.

A Chapter Dedicated to Pestered Housekeepers.—The Domestic Cat as a Household Trap.—The Rat.—Its Proverbial Shrewdness and Cunning.—The Barrel Trap.—Its unlimited Capabilities of Capture—Other Advantages.—"Baiting" for Rats.—A Second Form of Barrel Trap.—Various other Devices adapted to the capture of the Rat.—The Steel Trap.—Hints on Setting.—Necessary Precautions.—The Box Dead Fall.—The Board Flap.—The Box Pit Fall. —Animals for which it may be set.—Its Extensive Capabilities of Capture.—Its Self-Setting Qualities.—The principle Utilized for the Capture of the Muskrat.— The Cage Trap.—The Jar Trap.—A Preserve Jar Converted into a Mouse Trap.—Its Complete Success.—Bowl Traps.—Two Methods.—Fly Paper.— Recipe for Making.—Fly Trap...............................pages 125—136.

BOOK VI.

STEEL TRAPS AND THE ART OF TRAPPING.

General Remarks.—Advantages of the Steel Trap.—Its extensive use in the business of Trapping.—Hints on the Selection of Traps.—Requisites of a Good Steel Trap.—The Newhouse Trap.—Various sizes.—Rat Trap.—Muskrat Trap.— Mink Trap.—Fox Trap.—Otter Trap.—Beaver Trap.—" Great Bear Tamer."—Small Bear Trap.—Hints on Baiting the Steel Trap.— The Staked Pen.—Old Method of Baiting.—Its Objections.—Advantages of the New Method.—The Spring Pole.—Its Service to the Trapper.—The Sliding Pole.—Advantages of its Use in the Capture of Aquatic Animals.— The Clog.—Objections against Securing the Steel Trap to a Stake.—Method of Attaching the Clog.—The Grappling Iron.—The Season for Trapping.— Best condition for Furs.—The Art of Trapping.—Antiquity of the Sport.— Necessary Qualifications for Successful Trapping.—The Study of Natural History a source of pleasure and profit.— The Professional Trapper's most serious

Obstacles.—Marvellous Cunning of many Animals.—Necessity of the Study of
their Habits.—"Practical Natural History."—Trapping Without Bait.—Runways or By-paths.—How Utilized by the Trapper.—How Detected.—Favorable
Localities for the Setting of the Steel Trap.—Natural Advantages.—Entrapping
animals through their Sense of Smell.—Remarkable Power of Scent Baits.—
Their great value in the Capture of the Beaver.—Caution in Handling the Steel
Trap.—Effect of the Touch of the Hand.—Buckskin Gloves a Necessary Re-
quisite.—MEDICINES, OR SCENT BAITS.—Their Great Importance in the Art of
Trapping.—CASTOREUM or BARKSTONE—How Obtained.—Castoreum Composi-
tion.—Recipe for Making.—How Used.—MUSK—ASSAFŒTIDA.—OIL OF RHOD-
IUM.—FISH OIL.—Its General Use in the Capture of Aquatic Animals.—Valuable
Recipe for its Manufacture. — OIL OF SKUNK. — How Obtained. — How
Eradicated from Hands or Clothing.—OIL OF AMBER.—OIL OF AMBERGRIS.
OIL OF ANISE. — Its General Use as a "Universal Medicine." —SWEET
FENNEL.—CUMMIN—FENUGREEK—LAVENDER — COMPOUND MEDICINE —THE
TRAIL— Its Object and Value.— Various Modes of Making. — HOW TO
TRAP.—General Remarks.—THE FOX.—Its Scientific Classification.—The
Various American Species.—The Red Fox. — The Cross Fox. — Why so
Named.—The Black or Silver Fox.—The Great Value of its Fur.—The
Prairie Fox.—The Kit or Swift Fox.—The Gray Fox.—Similarity in the General
Characteristics of the Various Species.—Food of the Fox.—Its Home.—Its con-
summate Craft.—Instances of its Cunning. — Baffling the Hounds.— How to Trap
the Fox.—Preparation of the Trap.—Adverse Effect of Human Scent.—Necessity of handling Trap with Gloves.—The "Bed."—"Baiting" the Bed Necessary.—Precautions in Setting the Trap.—The "Tricks of the Trapper" Illustrated.—How to Proceed in case of Non-Success. —The Scent-Baits Utilized.—
Various Modes of Setting the Trap.—The Baits Commonly Used.—The Dead
Fall as a Means of Capture.—Common Mode of Skinning the Fox.—Directions
for Stretching Skin.—THE WOLF.—The Various Species.—Fierce Characteristics of the Wolf.—Its Terrible Inroads among Herds and Flocks.—The Gray
Wolf.—The Coyote or Common Prairie Wolf.—The Texan Wolf.—Home of the
Wolf.—Number of Young.—Cunning of the Wolf.—Caution Required in Trap-
ping.—How to Trap the Wolf.—Preparation of Trap.—Various Ways of Setting
the Trap.—Use of the Trail and Scent Baits.—"Playing Possum."—The Dead
Fall and "Twitch-up" as Wolf Traps.—Directions for Skinning the Wolf and
Stretching the Pelt.—THE PUMA.—Its Scientific Classification.—Its Life and
Habits.—Its Wonderful Agility.—Its Skill as an Angler.—Its Stealth.—Various
Traps Used in the Capture of the Puma.—The Gun Trap.—The Bow Trap.—
The Dead Fall.—Trap for Taking the Animal Alive.—Log Coop Trap.—The
Pit Fall.—Bait for the Puma.—The Steel Trap.—Common Mode of Setting.—
Selection of Locality for Trapping.—How to Skin the Puma.—Directions for
Stretching the Pelt.—THE CANADA LYNX.—Description of the Animal.—Its
Life and Habits.—Its Food.—Its Peculiar Appearance when Running.—Easily
Killed.—The Dead Fall as a Lynx Trap.—Peculiar Manner of Construction for
the Purpose.—The Gun Trap.—The Bow Trap.—The Twitch-up.—Young
of the Lynx.—Value of its Fur.—The Steel Trap.—Various Methods of Setting.
—Directions for Skinning the Animal and Stretching the Pelt.—THE WILD CAT.
—Its Resemblance to the Domestic Species.—Its Strange Appetite.—Its Home.
—Number of Young.—Haunts of the Wild Cat.—Its Nocturnal Marauding ex-
peditions.—Its Lack of Cunning.—How to Trap the Wild Cat.—An Entire Colo-
ny Captured.—Ferocity of the Wild Cat.—The Twitch-up.—Its Common Use in
the Capture of the Wild Cat.—Other Successful Traps.—Various Baits for the
Wild Cat.—Directions for Skinning the Animal, and Stretching the Pelt.—THE
BEAR.—The Various American Species.—The Grizzly.—Its Enormous Size and
Power.—Its Terrible Fury.—Description of the Animal.—Food of the Grizzly.
—The Black Bear or Musquaw.—Its General Description.—Bear Hunting.—
Danger of the Sport.—Food of the Bear.—Its Fondness for Pigs.—Honey Its
Special Delight.—The Cubs.—The Flesh of the Bear as Food.—"Bears'
Grease."—Hybernation of the Bear.—Traps for the Bear.—The Dead Fall.—Pit-

fall.—Giant Coop.—Gun Trap.—The Steel Trap.—The Clog and Grappling-Iron.
—Their Advantages.—How to Trap the Bear.—Various Methods of Adjusting
Traps.—Natural Advantages.—Honey as Bait.—Other Baits.—Scent Baits.—
Skinning the Bear.—Directions for Stretching the Pelt.—THE RACCOON.—Classi-
fication—Cunning and Stealth of the Animal.—Characteristic Features.—The
" Coon Chase."—How the Raccoon is Hunted.—The " Tree'd Coon."—Varied
Accomplishments of the Raccoon.—Its Home and Family.—The " Coon " as a
Pet.—Its Cunning Ways.—Its Extensive Bill of Fare.—Life and Habits of the
Raccoon.—Remarkable Imprint of its Paw.—Season for Trapping the Coon.—
How to Trap the Coon.—Various Modes of Setting the Trap.—Use of the
" Medicines " or Scent Baits."—Other Traps for the Animal.—Directions for Re-
moving the Skin, and Stretching the Pelt.—THE BADGER.—Its Peculiar Mark-
ings.—Use of the Hair.—Nest of the Badger.—Number of Young.—Food of the
Animal.—Its Remarkable Fondness for Honey.—Its Cunning.—Remarkable In-
stincts.—Its Shrewdness.—How to Trap the Badger.—Various Baits.—Use of
" Medicine."—Capture of the Animal by Flooding its Burrow.—How to Skin the
Badger.—Directions for Stretching the Pelt.—THE BEAVER.—Description of the
Animal.—Its Nature and Habits.—The Beaver Village.—The " Lodges," or
Beaver Houses.—Remarkable Construction of the Huts.—The Dam of the Bea-
ver.—Wonderful Skill shown in its Construction.—Nocturnal Habits of the Bea-
ver.—Remarkable Engineering Instincts of the Animal.—How the Beaver Cuts
Timber.—How the Dam is Constructed.—The Formation of " Reefs."—The
Tail of the Beaver as a Means of Transportation.—Subterranean Passage to the
Huts.— How Beavers are Hunted.—Young of the Beaver.—How to Trap the
Beaver.—The Necessary Precautions.—Castoreum or Bark Stone.—Its Great
Value in the Capture of the Beaver.—Various Methods of Setting the Trap.—
How to Apply the Castoreum.—Use of the Sliding Pole.—Food of the Beaver.
—Directions for Skinning the Animal and Stretching the Pelt.—THE MUSK-
RAT.—General Description of the Animal.—Its Beaver-like Huts.—Its Noctur-
nal Habits.—Its Food.—The Flesh of the Musk-rat as an Article of Diet.—De-
scription of the Hut.—Extensive Family of the Musk-Rat.—Its Home.—How
the Musk-Rat swims beneath Unbroken Ice.—How it is Killed by being Driven
Away from its Breath.—Spearing the Musk-Rat.—Construction of the Spear.—
How to Trap the Musk-Rat.—Use of the Sliding Pole.—Various Modes of Setting Trap.—The Spring Pole.—Scent Baits.—Various Devices for Capturing
the Musk-Rat.—The Barrel-Trap.—Remarkable Success of the Trap.—The
Trail.—Skinning the Musk-Rat.—How to Stretch the Pelt.—THE OTTER.—Description of the Animal.—Beauty of its Fur.— How the " Otter Fur " of Fashion
is Prepared.—Food of the Otter.— Its Natural Endowments for Swimming.—Habitation of the Otter.—Its Nest and Young.—The Track or " Seal " of the animal.—How the Otter is Hunted.—Its Fierceness when Attacked.—The Otter as
a Pet.—Fishing for its Master.—The Otter " Slide."—How Utilized by the Trapper.—Playfulness of the Otter.—How the Animal is Trapped.—Various Modes
of Setting Trap.—The Sliding Pole.—The Spring Pole.—Scent Baits.—How
Applied.—Necessary Precautions.—How to Skin the Otter.—Directions for
Stretching the Pelt.—THE MINK.—Its Form and Color.—Value of the Fur.—
Habits of the Animal.—Its Diet.—Its Perpetual Greed.—Ease with which it
may be Trapped.—Habitation of the Mink.—Its Nest and Young.—How to Trap
the Mink.—Various Methods of Setting the Trap.—Baits.—The Sliding Pole.—
"Medicine."—The Runways of the Mink.—How Utilized in Trapping.—The
Trail.—Various Traps Used in the Capture of the Mink.—How to Skin the Animal.—THE PINE MARTEN.—Description of the Animal.—Its Natural Characteristics.—Its Nocturnal Habits.—Its Wonderful Stealth and Activity.—Its " Bill
of Fare."—Its Strange mode of Seizing Prey.—The Marten as a Pet.—Its
Agreeable Odor.—Various Traps Used in the Capture of the Marten.—Baits for
the Marten.—The Steel Trap.—Several Modes of Setting.—Directions for Skinning the Animal.—THE FISHER.—Its Form and Color.—Its Habitation and
Young.—How the Animal is Trapped.—Various Methods.—The Spring Pole.—
Baits for the Fisher.—Principal Devices Used in its Capture.—The Skin.—How

Removed and Stretched.—THE SKUNK,—Its Fetid Stench.—Origin of the Odor.—Its Effect on Man and Beast.—"Premonitory Symptoms" of Attack.— Acrid Qualities of the Secretion.—Its Terrible Effect on the Eyes.—Interesting Adventure with a Skunk.—"Appearances are often Deceitful."—The Skunk as a Pet.—Color of the Animal.—Habits of the Animal.—Its Food.—Its Young.— "Alaska Sable."—How to Trap the Skunk.—Various Traps Used.—The Steel Trap.—Different Modes of Setting.—Baits.—The Dead Fall.—Modification in its Construction.—The Twitch-up.—Its Peculiar Advantages for the Capture of the Skunk.—Chloride of Lime as an Antidote.—Method of Eradicating the Odor from the Clothing.—Directions for Removing and Stretching the Skin.—THE WOLVERINE,—Its Desperate Fierceness and voracity.—Its General Character- istics.—Its Form and Color.—Food of the Wolverine.—Its Trap-Robbing Pro- pensities.—How to Trap the Wolverine.—Baits.—Use of the "Medicine."—The Gun Trap and Dead Fall.—The Steel Trap.—Various Modes of Setting.—Home and Young of the Animal.—How the Skin should be Removed and Stretched.— THE OPOSSUM.—Description of the Animal.—Its Nature and Habits.—Its Home. —Remarkable Mode of Carrying its Young.—Nocturnal Habits of the Animal.— Its Food.—Its Especial Fondness for Persimmons.—Its Remarkable Tenacity as a Climber.—"Playing Possum."—How the Opossum is Hunted.—How Trapped.—Various Devices Used in its Capture.—Scent Baits.—How the Skin is Removed and Stretched.—THE RABBIT.—Wide-spread Distribution of the Various Species.—Their Remarkable Powers of Speed.—Nest of the Rabbit.—Its Prolific Offspring,—Food of the Rabbit.—Its Enemies.—Various Devices Used in Trapping the Animal.—Necessary Precautions in Skinning the Rabbit.—THE WOODCHUCK.—Description of the Animal.—Its Habits.—Its Burrows—Its Food —Toughness of the Skin.—Its Use.—Nest of the Animal.—The Woodchuck as Food.—How the Animal is Trapped.—The Steel Trap.—The Spring Pole.—The Twitch-up.—How the Woodchuck is "Drowned Out."—The Turtle as a Ferret.— Smoking the Burrows.—Directions for Skinning the Animal,—THE GOPHER.— Its Burrows.—Its Food.—Remarkable Cheek Pouches of the Animal.—Their Use.—How to Trap the Animal.—How the Skin is Removed.—THE MOLE.—Its Varied Accomplishments.—Its Remarkable Dwellings.—Complicated Structure of the Habitation.—The Fury and Voracity of the Mole.—Peculiarities of Its Fur. —A Waistcoat of Mole Skins.—Odor of the Mole.—Mole Traps.—Various Species of the Mole.—The Mole of the Cape of Good Hope.—Marvellous Beauty of Its Fur.—SQUIRRELS.—Their General Peculiarities of Form and Habit.—Their Food.—Their Provident Instincts.—"Nutting" in Midwinter.—The Nest of the Squirrel.—Burrowing Squirrels.—The Various American Species.—The Grey Squirrel.—The Chipmuck.—The Chickaree.—The Flying Squirrel, &c.—How Squirrels are Trapped.—Various Traps Used in their Capture.—Removal of Skin.—THE DEER.—Difficulty of Hunting the Animal in Dry Seasons.— Various American Species of the Deer.—How the Deer is Trapped.—Peculiar Construction of the Trap.—Scent Bait for the Deer.—Various Methods of Setting the Trap.—Violence of the Deer when Trapped.—The Clog.—Dead Falls.— Food of the Deer.—Deer "Yards."—Natural Enemies of the Deer.—How the Deer is Hunted.—"Still Hunting."—The Deer's Acute Sense of Smell. —How to Detect the Direction of the Wind.—Natural Habits of the Deer. —"Night Hunting."—Luminosity of the Eyes of the Deer at Night.—Hunting the deer with dogs.—"Deer Licks."—How Salt is used in Hunting the Deer. —Hunting from a Scaffolding.—Peculiar Sight of Deer.—"Salt Licks" used in Night Hunting.—Head Lantern.—How made.—How used.—The fiery Eyes of the Deer.—"Fox Fire" or Phosphorescent wood.—How used by the Hunter.—Seasons for Deer hunting.—How to skin the Deer.—THE MOOSE.— Description of the animal.—Immense size of its Horns.—Moose yards.—Hunted on Snow shoes.—The dangers of Moose Hunting.—Exquisite sense of Smell.—How the Moose is Trapped.—Directions for removing the Skin of the Animal.—ROCKY MOUNTAIN SHEEP.—Description of the Animal.—Its enormous Horns.—Habits of the creature.—Its flesh as Food.—How the Animal is Trapped.—THE BUFFALO.— Its Habits.—Its Food.—Buffalo-grass.—How the Animal is Hunted and Trapped.

Buffalo flesh as Food.—Buffalo skins.—THE PRONG HORN ANTELOPE.—Description of the Animal—Peculiarity of Horn.—How the creature is Hunted and Destroyed by the Indians.—Remarkable sense of Smell of the Animal.—Its Beauty and grace.—Flesh of the Antelope as Food.—How the Animal is Trapped.—Various Traps used in their Capture.—The Dead-fall.—Pit-fall.—How to remove the Hide of the Animal.—SHOOTING AND POISONING.—" Shot furs."—" Poisoned furs."— " Trapped furs."—Their relative Value in the Fur Market.—Effect of grazing shot on fur.—Effect of Poison on Fur.—Remarks on the use of Poison.—Strychnine.— Poisoning Wolves.—Recipe for mixing the Poison.—Poisoning the Bear.—How the Dose is Prepared....... .... PAGES 137-222·

BOOK VII.

CAMPAIGN LIFE IN THE WILDERNESS.

Introductory Remarks.—" Amateur Trapping."—PLAN OF CAMPAIGN.—Selection of Trapping-ground.—Advantages of a Watered District.—Labor of transportation lightened by Boating.—Lakes, Ponds and Streams.—The Adirondacks and Alleghanies.—Remarks on the " Home Shanty."—Selection of Site for building.—Value 'of a good Axe—Remarks on the Bark Shanty.—Its value in case of Storms.— Wise fore-sight—Remarks on the Indian Birch-bark Canoe.—Dug-out and Bateau.— Commencement of Trapping Season.—Advantages of preliminary preparation.— Extensive route of the Professional Trapper.—Sixty pounds of Personal Luggage.—How the traps and provisions are distributed along the Trapping lines.—Use of the " Home Shanty."—" Keeping Shanty."—Necessity of its being Guarded. —Wolves and Bears as thieves.—Steel Traps considered.—Number used in a Professional Campaign.—Number for an Amateur Campaign.—Their Probable Cost.—The average size of Trap.—Dead-falls, Twitchups, &c., considered.—Requisite Tools for a Campaign.—A " House-wife " a valuable necessity.—" Cleanliness next to Godliness."—The Trappers' Light.—Comparative value of Lanterns and Candles.—The Trappers' Personal outfit.—The jack-knife.—The Pocket-Compass.—Necessity of preparing for Emergencies.—Shot guns and Rifles.— Both combined in the same weapon.—Oil for Fire Arms.—Fat of the Grouse Used on Fire Arms.—Fishing tackle.—The Trappers' portable stove.—The Stove versus The Open Fire.—The Trapper's Clothing.—The Material and Color.— Boots.—High-topped Boots.—Short Boots.—Their Relative Qualities.—Waterproof Boot Dressing.—Recipe.—The Trapping Season.—Hints on Trapping-lines. —The " Wheel " plan.—Mode of following the lines.—" Trap Robbers " or " Poachers."—How to guard against them.—Hiding furs.—How to store Traps from Season to Season.—Gnats and Mosquitoes.—The " Smudge."—How made. —FOOD AND COOKING UTENSILS.—" Roughing it."—" A chance Chip for a Frying Pan."—A " happy medium " between two extremes.—Cosy and Comfortable living on a Campaign.—Portable Food.—Combined Nutriment and lightness in weight to be desired.—The Trappers' Culinary Outfit.—Indian meal as Food.— The Trappers' " Staff of Life."—Wheat flour.—Salt Pork.—Seasoning.—Pork Fritters a luxury.—Cooking Utensils.—The " Telescope " drinking cup.—Recipe for making Pork Fritters.—" Chop Sticks " à la " Chinee."—A Flat Chip as a Plate.—Boiled Mush.—Old " Stand by."—Recipe.—Fried Mush.—Indian meal Cakes.—Recipe.—Johnny Cake.—Recipe.—Hoe Cakes.—Recipe.—Fresh fish.— How to Cook fish in a most Delicious manner.—Prof. Blot, and Delmonico, out-done.—The " NE PLUS ULTRA " of delicacies.—All the sweet Juices of the Fish preserved.—Disadvantages of the ordinary method of cooking.—Partridge, Duck, Quail, Cooked deliciously.—Roasting unrivalled!—Hints on Broiling.—An extemporized Spider or Toaster.—Roasting on a spit.—Venison, Bear, and Moose Meat broiled in the best style.—Venison cutlets.—The Camp fire.—Usual mode

of building Fire.—How the Kettle is suspended.—"Luxuries" considered.—The
Knapsack a desirable Acquisition.—Matches.—The Bottle Match-safe.—Water-
proof Matches.—How made.—Lucifer Matches.—Recipe for Waterproof preparation.—The Pocket Sun Glass.—A necessary adjunct to a Trapper's Outfit.—Its
Advantages in cases of emergency.—"Touch wood" or "Punk Tinder," valuable
in lighting fires.—How to light Fires without matches or Sun glass.—How to light
a fire without Matches, Sun Glass, Powder, or Percussion Caps.—A last Resort.—
Matches best in the long run.—The Portable Camp Stove described.—Its accompanying Furniture.—The Combination Camp-knife.—Hints on Provisions.—Pota-
toes as food.—Beans.—"Self raising" Wheat flour.—Light Bread, Biscuit and
Pancakes in Camp.—Various accessories.—Olive Oil for purposes of Frying.—
Pork.—Indian meal.—Crackers.—Wheaten Grits.—Rice and Oatmeal.—Tea and
Coffee.—Soups.—Liebig's Extract of Beef.—Canned Vegetables.—Lemonade.—
Waterproof bags for provisions.—Painted bags.—Caution!—Waterproof prepara-
tion.—Air-tight jars for Butter.—Knapsack or Shoulder Basket.—Venison as food.
—To preserve the overplus of meat.—"Jerked Venison" Recipe and Process.—
Moose and Bear meat and Fish, similarly prepared.—How to protect provisions
from Wolves.—The Moufflon and Prong-horn as food.—"Small game," Squirrels,
Rabbits, and Woodchucks.—"Skunk Meat" as a delicacy.—The Buffalo as food·
—Grouse, the universal Food of Trappers and Hunters.—Various species of
Grouse.—The Sage Cock.—The Ptarmigan.—How they are trapped by the In-
dians in the Hudson'sBay Country.—Waterfowl.—Sea and Inland Ducks.—Various
species of Duck.—Mallard.—Muscovy.—Wigeon.—Merganser.—Canvass Back.
—Teal, &c.—Wild Geese.—Fish as food.—Angling and Spearing.—Salmon
Spearing in the North.—Description of the Salmon Spear used by the Indians.—
Salmon Spearing at night.—Requisites of a good Spearsman.—Fishing through
the Ice.—Cow's udder and Hogs liver as Bait.—Other Baits.—Assafœtida and
Sweet Cicely as fish Baits.—Trout fishing with Tip-up's.—Pickerel fishing in
Winter.—Pickerel Spearing through the Ice.—The Box Hut.—The "Fish Lan-
tern" or Fish Trap.—Fish Attracted by light.—Light as Bait.—How the Fish
Lantern is made and used.—THE TRAPPER'S SHELTER.—Introductory remarks.
—The Perils of a Life in the Wilderness.—A Shelter of some form a Necessity.—
The Log Shanty.—Full directions for building.—Ingenious manner of constructing
roof.—How the Chimney is built.—Spacious interior of the Shanty.—THE BARK
SHANTY.—A Temporary structure.—Full directions for its construction.—Selec-
tion of building site.—TENTS.—Advantages of their use.—Various kinds of Tents.
—The House Tent.—The Fly Tent.—The Shelter Tent.—Directions for making
the Tent.—Tent Cloth.—How to render tents Water and Fire-proof.—Valuable
recipe.—BEDS AND BEDDING.—Perfect rest and comfort to the tired Trapper.
—A portable Spring bed for the woods.—A Hammock bed.—Bed Clothes.—The
Canton Flannel Bag.—Hammocks.—TENT CARPETING.—Spruce and Hemlock
boughs as bedding.—How to cover the ground evenly. The Rubber Blanket.
                                                     pages 225-251.

BOOK VIII.

THE TRAPPER'S MISCELLANY.

A Warning to the Novice.—Winged Cannibals of the Woods.—INSECT OINTMENTS.
—Mosquitoes and Gnats.—Their aversion to the scent of Pennyroyal.—Pennyroyal Ointment·—Recipe.—Mutton tallow Ointment.—Tar and Sweet Oil Liniment.—Recipe.—Its effect on the Complexion.—Invasions of Insects by night.—
Their pertinacity and severity.—The experience of our Adirondack guide.—The
bloodthirsty propensities of the Mosquito admirably depicted.—The "Smudge"
Smoke versus Insect Bites.—"Punkeys" and "Midgets."—Their terrible voracity.—Painful effects of their Bites.—Pennyroyal an effective Antidote.—Depraved

appetite of the mosquito.—A Warning to the Intemperate.—Use and abuse of Alcohol.—A Popular error corrected.—A substitute for Whiskey and Brandy.—Red Pepper Tea.—Its great value as a remedy in Illness.—The Mosquitoes' favorite Victim.—Result of the bite of the insect.—The Mosquito Head-Net.—Directions for making the Net.—Netting attachment for the Hat.—Portable Sun Shade or Hat brim.—Netting attachment for the Hat brim.—BOAT BUILDING.—A Boat of some kind a necessity to the Trapper.—The "Dug-Out" or Log Canoe.—Requisite Tools for its Manufacture.—Selection of the Log.—Directions for making the boat.—Remarkable thinness to which they may be reduced.—Lightness of the boat.—How to gauge the thickness.—How to stop leaks.—THE INDIAN OR BIRCH BARK CANOE.—The Indian as a Canoe-maker.—His remarkable skill.—Perfection of the Indian made Canoe.—Description of the Canoe.—Capacity of the various sizes.—How to construct a Bark Canoe.—Selection of Bark.—How to prevent Leaks.—Material used by the Indians in sewing the Bark.—Advantages of the Birch Bark Canoe.—Basswood, Hemlock, and Spruce Bark Canoes.—A LIGHT HOME-MADE BOAT.—Selection of Boards.—Directions for making the Boat.—Caulking the seams.—Value of Pitch for waterproofing purposes.—How it should be applied.—THE SCOW.—How to construct the ordinary Flat-bottomed Boat.—The Mud-stick.—SNOW SHOES.—A necessity for winter travel.—The "Snow Shoe Race."—The mysteries of a Snow Shoe.—" Taming the Snow Shoe."—How to make the Snow Shoe.—Complicated Net-work.—Two methods of attaching the Net-work.—How the Snow Shoe is worn.—THE TOBOGGAN OR INDIAN SLEDGE.—Its value to the Trapper.—Winter Coasting.—Great sport with the Toboggan.—How to make a Toboggan.—Selection of Boards.—How the Sledge is used.—CURING SKINS.—Importance of Curing Skins properly.—Valuable hints on Skining Animals.—How to dry Skins.—How to dress Skins for Market.—Astringent preparations.—Recipe.—STRETCHERS.—How skins are stretched.—The Board Stretcher.—How it is made and used.—The Wedge Stretcher.—How made and used.—The Bow Stretcher.—The Hoop Stretcher.—TANNING SKINS.—To Tan with the hair on.—Preparation of Skin for Tanning.—Tanning Mixture.—Recipe.—Second Mixture.—Recipe.—Third Mixture and Recipe.—How the Skin is softened and finished.—How TO TAN MINK AND MUSKRAT SKINS.—Preparation of Skin.—Tanning Mixtures.—Various Recipes.—" Fleshing."—The Fleshing-knife.—Substitute for the Fleshing-knife.—How TO TAN THE SKINS OF THE BEAVER, OTTER, RACCOON, AND MARTEN.—Tanning Mixtures.—How to soften the Skin.—Simple Tanned Skin.—Recipe for removing the fur.—How to finish the Skin.—OBSERVATIONS ON THE HISTORY OF FURS AND THE FUR TRADE.—Some bits of History in connection with Furs.—Ancient use of Furs.—Furs a medium of Exchange.—Furs and Fashion.—Extravagance in Fur Costume.—Choice Furs as Badges of Rank.—Their use restricted to Royal Families.—The Early Fur Trade of Europe.—A Tribute paid in Furs.—Early History of the Fur Trade in America.—Origin of the Hudson's Bay Company.—Hostility of the French Canadian Traders.—Establishment of the North West Company.—Competition and War.—Consolidation of the two Companies.—Great sales of the Hudson's Bay Company.—Importance of the Fur Trade.—Cities founded by the enterprise of the Trapper.—St. Paul.—Montreal and Mackinaw.—Fortunes built up on Fur Traffic.—John Jacob Astor.—Mink and Muskrat Skins.—Their extensive use in America.—Estimated value of the annual yield of Raw Furs throughout the World.—Classification of Furs by American Dealers.—" Home " Furs.—" Shipping " Furs.—Table of Sales of Hudson's Bay Company, in 1873.—March Sale.—September Sale.—Price according to Quality.—Estimated average per Skin.—List of American " Shipping " Furs.—List of American " Home " Furs.—MARKET VALUE OF FUR SKINS.—Eccentricities of the Fur Market.—Demand governed by Fashion.—How Fashion runs the Fur Trade.—The Amateur Trapper and the Fur Trade.—Difficulty of a profitable disposal of Furs.—Advice to the Novice.—How to realize on the sale of Furs.—TABLE OF VALUES OF AMERICAN FUR SKINS.—A complete list of American Fur bearing Animals.—Various prices of Skins according to Quality.—USES OF AMERICAN FURS AT HOME AND ABROAD.—The Silver Fox.—Fifty Guineas for a Fur Skin.—Red Fox Fur.—

Its use in Oriental Countries.—Beaver Fur.—Its various uses.—Raccoon Skins, a great Staple for Russia and Germany.—Bear Skins and their various uses.—Lynx, Fisher, and Marten Skins.—The Mink.—Use of its hair for Artists pencils.—Muskrat Skins.—Three millions annually exported to Germany alone.—Their extensive use among the American poorer classes.—Otter Fur.—Sleigh Robes from Wolf Skins.—Rabbit Fur.—Its use in the Manufacture of Hats.—Breeding Rabbits for their Fur.—The Wolverine.—Skunk Fur, dignified by the name of Alaska Sable.—Large shipments to Foreign Countries.—How the Fur of the Badger is used.—Opossum, Puma, and Wild Cat Fur.—Robes for the Fashionable.—Squirrel and Mole Skins. . . . . PAGES 255-286.

ILLUSTRATIONS.

FULL PAGES.

PAGE.

1. Caught at last...........................Frontispiece
2. Traps for Large Game...................................... 15
3. Snares or Noose Traps.................................... 37
4. Traps for Feathered Game................................. 63
5. Miscellaneous Traps....................................... 101
6. Household Traps.. 123
7. Steel Traps, and the art of Trapping..................... 137
8. Almost Persuaded.——to face.............................. 154
9. The Campaign.. 223
10. Trapper's Miscellany.................................... 253

ILLUSTRATIONS IN THE TEXT.

		PAGE.
11.	"Preface"..	3
12.	Initial to Preface...	3
13.	End piece to Preface..	6
14.	"Contents"...	7
15.	"Illustrations"...	xvi
16.	Initial to Book I..	17
17.	Dead fall for large Animals.................................	18
18.	Explanatory drawing of pieces..............................	19
19.	The Gun Trap...	21
20.	The Bow Trap..	23
21.	" " " arrangement of parts............................	24
22.	" " " Section...	25
23.	Foot String Bow Trap......................................	26
24.	The Down fall..	27
25.	The Bear Trap..	30
26.	End piece to Book I...	36
27.	Initial to Book II...	39
28.	Quail Nooses..	40
29.	Hedge Nooses...	42
30.	The Triangle Snare..	42
31.	The Twitch-up...	44
32.	Method of Setting...	45
33.	" " " No. 2..	46
34.	" " " No. 3..	47
35.	" " " No. 4..	47
36.	" " " No. 5..	48
37.	The Poacher's Snare...	49
38.	The Portable Snare..	51
39.	The "Simplest" Snare..	52
40.	Modification No. 2...	53
41.	" " 3...	54
42.	The Quail Snare...	54
43.	The Box Snare...	55
44.	The Double Box Snare.......................................	57
45.	The Old fashioned Springle..................................	59
46.	The Improved Springle......................................	60
47.	The Figure Four Ground Snare..............................	61
48.	The Platform Snare..	62
49.	End piece..	62
50.	Initial to Book III..	65
51.	The Brick Trap..	66
52.	Method of Setting...	67
53.	The Coop Trap..	68
54.	The Bat fowling Net...	71
55.	The Clap Net..	72
56.	The Bird Whistle..	74
57.	The Trap Cage..	76
58.	Diagrams of Cage...	77
59.	The Spring Net Trap...	81

		PAGE.
60.	Section of Spring Net Trap	82
61.	A Simpler Net Trap	83
62.	The Upright Net Trap	86
63.	Second Method "	87
64.	The Box Owl Trap	89
65.	The Box Bird Trap	91
66.	The Pendent Box Bird Trap	92
67.	The Hawk Trap	93
68.	The Wild Duck Net	94
69.	The Hook Trap	95
70.	The Fool's Cap Trap	96
71.	The Limed Twig	97
72.	Humming-bird Trap	99
73.	Initial to Book IV	103
74.	The Common Box Trap	104
75.	Two Modes of Setting	105
76.	Box Trap	106
77.	The Figure Four Trap	107
78.	Parts of "	108
79.	The "Double Ender"	109
80.	The Self-Setting Trap	110
81.	The Dead fall	111
82.	Method No. 2	114
83.	The Garotte	115
84.	Arrangement of " Setting "	116
85.	The Bow Garotte Trap	117
86.	A Fish Trap	120
87.	End Piece " Maternal advice "	121
88.	Initial to Book V	125
89.	The Barrel Trap	126
90.	The Box Dead Fall	129
91.	The Board Flap	130
92.	The Box Pit-fall	132
93.	Diagram of "	133
94.	Cage Trap	134
95.	Initial to Book VI	137
96.	Steel Trap. No. (o) or Rat Trap	138
97.	Steel Trap. No. 1, or Muskrat Trap	141
98.	" " No. 2, or Mink Trap	141
99.	" " No. 2½, or Fox Trap	141
100.	" " No. 3, or Otter Trap	141
101.	" " No. 4, or Beaver Trap	141
102.	" The Great Bear Tamer," Steel Trap	142
103.	Steel Trap No. 5, or Small Bear Trap	143
104.	Steel Trap set in pen	143
105.	The Spring Pole	143
106.	The Sliding pole	145
107.	The Grappling Iron	146
108.	The Wolf	147
109.	The Puma	159
110.	The Canada Lynx	162
		165

PAGE.

111. The Wild Cat... 167
112. The Bear... 170
113. The Raccoon... 174
114. The Badger.. 176
115. The Beaver.. 178
116. The Otter 186
117. The Mink.. 190
118. The Marten.. 192
119. The Skunk... 196
120. The Wolverine 199
121. The Opossum... 201
122. The Squirrel.. 212
123. The Moose... 219
124. Initial to Book VII....................................... 225
125. Portable Drinking Cup..................................... 231
126. The Home Shanty... 243
127. The Shelter tent.. 247
128. The Trapper's Bed... 248
129. End Piece... 251
130. Initial to Book VIII...................................... 255
131. Head Net.. 257
132. Portable Hat-brim... 258
133. Hat-brim with netting attachment 258
134. The Dug-out or Log Canoe.................................. 259
135. The Birch-Bark Canoe 263
136. A Light Home-made Boat.................................... 265
137. Diagram view of Boat——.................................... 266
138. The Snow Shoe... 269
139. The Toboggan or Indian Sledge............................. 270
140. The Board Stretcher....................................... 273
141. The Wedge Stretcher....................................... 274
142. The Bow Stretcher... 275
143. " The End "... 286

BOOK I.

TRAPS FOR LARGE GAME.

OWEVER free our forests may be from the lurking dangers of a tropical jungle, they nevertheless shelter a few large and formidable beasts which are legitimate and deserving subjects of the Trapper's Art. Chief among them are the Puma, or Cougar, Bear, Lynx, Wolf and Wolverine.

Although commonly taken in steel traps, as described respectively in a later portion of this work, these animals are nevertheless often captured by Deadfalls and other devices, which are well known to the professional Trapper, and which serve excellently in cases of emergency, or in the scarcity of steel traps.

THE DEAD-FALL.

There are several varieties of this trap, some of which are described in other parts of this volume. In general construction they all bear a similarity, the methods of setting being slightly changed to suit the various game desired for capture. For large animals, and particularly the Bear, the trap is sprung by the pressure of the animal's foot, while reaching for the bait. Select some favorite haunt of the Bear, and proceed to construct a pen of large stakes. These should consist of young trees, or straight branches, about three inches in diameter, and should be of such a length as to reach a height of four or five feet when set in the ground, this being the required height of the pen. Its width should be about two and a half or three feet; its depth, four feet; and the top should be roofed over with cross pieces of timber, to prevent the bait from be·

ing taken from above. A straight log, about eight inches in diameter, and six feet in length should now be rolled against the opening of the pen, and hemmed in by two upright posts, one on each side, directly on a line with the sides of the enclosure. Another log, or tree trunk, of the same diameter, and about fifteen or twenty feet in length, should next be procured. Having this in readiness, we will now proceed to the construction of the other pieces. In order to understand the arrangement of these, we present a separate drawing of the parts

as they appear when the trap is set. (*a*), An upright post, is supplied at the upper end with a notch, having its flat face on the lower side. This post should be driven into the ground in the left hand back corner of the pen, and should be three feet or more in height. Another post (*b*) of similar dimensions, is provided with a notch at its upper end, the notch being reversed, *i. e.*, having its flat side *uppermost*. This post should be set in the ground, *outside* of the pen, on the right hand side and on a line with the first. A third post (*c*), is provided with a crotch on its upper end. This should be planted outside of the pen on the right hand side, and on a line with the front. The treadle piece consists of a forked branch, about three feet in length, supplied with a square board secured across its ends. At the junction of the forks, an augur hole is bored, into which a stiff stick about three feet in length is inserted. This is shown at (*h*). Two poles, (*d*) and (*e*), should next be procured, each about four feet in length. These complete the number of pieces, and the trap may then be set. Pass the pole (*d*) between

the stakes of the pen, laying one end in the notch in the post (*a*), and holding the other beneath the notch in the upright (*b*). The second pole (*e*) should then be adjusted, one end being placed in the crotch post (*c*), and the other caught beneath the projecting end of the pole (*d*), as is fully illustrated in the engraving. The dead-log should then be rested on the front extremity of the pole last adjusted, thus effecting an equilibrium.

The treadle-piece should now be placed in position over a short stick of wood (*f*), with its platform raised in front, and the upright stick at the back secured beneath the edge of the latch pole (*d*).

The best bait consists of *honey*, for which Bears have a remarkable fondness. It may 'be placed on the ground at the back part of the enclosure, or smeared on a piece of meat hung at the end of the pen. The dead-log should now be weighted by resting heavy timbers against its elevated end, as seen in the main drawing, after which the machine is ready for its deadly work.

A Bear will never hesitate to risk his life where a feast of honey is in view, and the odd arrangement of timbers has no fears for him after that tempting bait has once been discovered. Passing beneath the suspended log, his heavy paw encounters the broad board on the treadle-piece, which immediately sinks with his weight. The upright pole at the back of the treadle is thus raised, forcing the latch-piece from the notch : this in turn sets free the side pole, and the heavy log is released, falling with a crushing weight over the back of hapless Bruin.

There are many other methods of setting the Dead-fall, several of which appear in another section of this book. The above is the one more commonly used for the capture of Bears,

but the others are equally applicable and effective when enlarged to the proper size.

In South America and other countries, where Lions, Tigers,
Leopards, and Jaguars abound, these and other rude extempore
traps are almost the only ones used, and are always very successful. The pit-fall often allures the Bengal Tiger to his destruction, and the Leopard often terminates his career at the
muzzle of a rifle baited as seen in our page illustration. A gun
thus arranged forms a most sure and deadly trap, and one which
may be easily extemporized at a few moments' warning, in cases
of emergency. The Puma of our northern forests, although
by no means so terrible a foe as the Leopard, is still a blood-
thirsty creature, and while he shuns the gaze of man with the
utmost fear, he is nevertheless constantly on the alert to spring
upon him unawares, either in an unguarded moment or during
sleep. A hungry Puma, who excites suspicion by his stealthy
prowling and ominous growl, may easily be led to his destruction
at the muzzle of a gun, baited as we shall now describe.

THE GUN TRAP.

After a Puma has succeeded in capturing his prey, and has
satisfied his appetite by devouring a portion of its carcass, he
leaves the remainder for a second meal, and his early return to
a second banquet is almost a matter of certainty. Where such
a remnant of a bygone feast is found, the capture of the Cougar is an easy matter. Any carcass left in a neighborhood
where Pumas are known to exist is sure to attract them, and
day after day its bulk will be found to decrease until the bones
only remain. By thus "baiting" a certain place and drawing
the Pumas thither, the way is paved for their most certain destruction. The gun-trap is very simply constructed, and may
be put in working order in a very few moments. The weapon
may be a rifle or shot-gun. In the latter case it should be heavily loaded with buck-shot. The stock should be first firmly tied
to some tree, or secured in a stout crotch driven into the
ground, the barrel being similarly supported.

The gun should be about three feet from the ground, and
should be aimed at some near tree to avoid possible accident to
a chance passer-by within its range. The gun should then be
cocked, *but not capped*, due caution being always used, and the
cap adjusted the very last thing after the trap is baited and

set. Where a rifle is used, the cartridge should not be inserted until the last thing.

It is next necessary to cut a small sapling about a foot or two in length. Its diameter should allow it to fit snugly inside the guard in front of the trigger, without springing the hammer. Its other end should now be supported by a very slight crotch, as shown in our illustration. Another sapling should next be procured, its length being sufficient to reach from the muzzle of the gun to the end of the first stick, and having a branch stub or hook on one end. The other extremity should be attached by a string to the tip of the first stick.

Now take a portion of the carcass and draw it firmly over the hook in the long stick. Prop the latter in such a position as that the bait shall hang directly in front of the muzzle. The crotch supporting the bait stick should be firmly implanted in the ground in order to hold the bait from being drawn to either side of the muzzle.

The gun-trap is now set, and its merits may be tested. Before adjusting the cap the pieces should be tried several times to insure their perfect working. A slight pull on the bait from the front will draw the short stick forward. This immediately acts on the trigger and causes the hammer to snap. By a few trials, the sticks can be arranged so as to spring the trigger easily, and where a hair trigger is used, a mere touch on the bait will suffice to discharge the gun. When all is found to work perfectly, the trap should be surrounded by a rude pen of sticks and branches, extending two or three feet beyond the muzzle, in order to insure an approach directly in the aim of the gun. The cap should now be placed on the nipple, after which the deadly device may be left to do its certain work. The remaining portion of the carcass should be removed, and where the locality is likely to be frequented by other hunters or trappers, it is well to put up a "danger" signal to guard against accident. If desired two or three guns may be arranged like the spokes of a wheel, all aiming near the bait. Even with one gun the victim stands but little chance, but where two or three pour their contents into his body, his death is an absolute certainty.

By fastening the gun three feet above ground the load is discharged upward into the mouth of its victim, and thus directly through the brain. Where two or more guns are used, it is advisable to aim at least one in such a direction as will send its charge into the *breast* of the animal.

The Indian Panther is very commonly taken by the gun trap, and even Lions are sometimes secured by the same device, only increased in power by a larger number of guns.

There are several other methods of setting the gun trap. One way consists in attaching a string to the finger piece of the trigger, passing it back through a small staple or screw eye inserted in the under side of the stock for that purpose, and then drawing the string forward and attaching it to the top of the bait stick. This latter is stuck in the ground directly in front of the muzzle and the bait secured to its extremity. When the tempting morsel is grasped, the bait stick is drawn forward and the string pulled, the result of course being the discharge of the gun. By still another method, an elastic is passed through the screw eye in the stock and over the finger piece of the trigger, thus tending continually to draw it back and spring the hammer. To set the gun a short stick is inserted behind the finger piece, thus overcoming the power of the elastic. It should be very delicately adjusted, so that a mere touch will dislodge it. Its length should be about six inches, and to its other end the bait stick should be attached and arranged as first described. Although a rather dangerous trap to be set at random it is nevertheless often utilized and has brought many a dreaded marauder to his doom.

The bear, lynx, and other large animals are sometimes taken by the gun trap, but it is most generally set for the Puma.

THE BOW TRAP.

This device does duty in India and Southern Asia, where it is known as the *tiger trap*.

It is easily constructed as follows : First cut a stout board five inches in width, two and a half feet in length and about two inches in thickness. Shave off one end to a point so that it may be driven into the ground. At the other extremity, in the middle of the board and about two inches from the edge, a hole one half an inch in diameter and three quarters of an inch in height, should be made ; two auger holes, one directly above the other, with the sides flatly trimmed, will answer perfectly. The arrow should next be constructed. This should be made of seasoned oak or ash, two feet in length, perfectly straight, smooth and round, and one third of an inch in diameter. One end should be notched for the bow string and vaned with thin feathers after the manner of ordinary arrows. The other extremity should be armed with a steel barb sharply pointed, and firmly riveted in place. Any blacksmith can forge such a tip; the shape of which is plainly seen in our engraving. The bow should consist of a piece of stout seasoned hickory, oak or ash four feet long, if such a bow is not at hand, a stout sapling may be used. The bow string may consist of cat-gut, or stout Indian twine.

Before setting the trap, it is advisable to attract the game to the spot selected as already alluded to in connection with the gun trap, and particularly so when the Puma is the victim sought. In our illustration we see the trap as it appears when set, and the same precaution of aiming at some tree should be exercised as advised with the gun trap. The bow should first be secured in place directly beneath and one eighth of an inch from the edge of the hole in the board, as seen at (*a*). Two large wire staples may

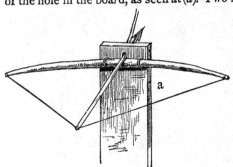

be used for this purpose, being passed over the bow through holes in the board and clinched on the opposite side. The bend of the bow and length of string should now be determined, one end of the latter being attached to the tip of the bow and the other end supplied with a loop. The board should then be driven into the ground to the depth of about eight inches. We will next take up the arrow. Pass the barb through the hole in the board and adjust the notch over the bow-string, draw the arrow back and release the string. If the arrow slide easily and swiftly, through the board, keeping true to its aim, the contrivance is in perfect working order and is ready to be set. This is accomplished by the very simple and ingenious mechanical arrangement, shown at (*b*). On the under side of the arrow just behind the barb, a flat notch one eighth of an inch in depth and two and a half inches in length is cut, with rounded ends, as seen in the illustration. The bait stick should consist of a sapling about three feet in length, the large end being trimmed so as to fit in the hole over the arrow while the notch in the latter rests in the bottom of the aperture as seen in the illustration (*b*).

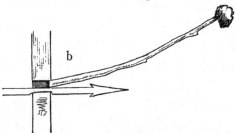

The trap may then be set. Draw back the arrow, until the notch rests in the hole in the board. Insert the bait stick *very lightly* above the arrow as shown at (*b*), propping it in place at the angle seen in the main drawing. The bait for a puma should consist of a portion of some carcass, or if for other animals, any of the baits given in our section on " trapping " may be used. In order to secure the bait firmly to the bait stick, a small hole and a peg at the side of the baited end will effectually prevent its removal and the trap will thus most surely be sprung. The prop which sustains the bait stick need be only a small crotch inserted a little to one side of the trap. The bow should now be surrounded by a wide pen, allowing room for the spring of the ends. The top of the enclosure should also be guarded by a few sticks or branches laid across. Directly in front of the trap and extending from it, a double row of rough stakes three feet high should be constructed, thus insuring an approach in the direct range of the arrow. Without this precaution the bait might be approached from the side, and the arrow pass beneath the head of the animal, whereas on the other hand it is sure to take effect in the neck or breast of its victim. Of course the success of this trap depends entirely upon the strength of the bow. When a large and powerful one is used its effect is almost surely fatal.

Another form of the bow trap, much used in the capture of the tiger, forms the subject of our next illustration ; no bait is here used. The trap is set at the side of the beaten path of the tiger and is sprung by the animal pressing against a string in passing. The bow is large and powerful and is secured to two upright posts about eight inches apart. The string is drawn back and a blunt stick is then inserted between the bow string and the inside centre of the bow, thus holding the latter in a bent position. A stout stick, with a flattened end is next inserted between the end of the blunt stick and the inside of the bow, the remaining part of the stick extending downwards, as our illustration shows. To the lower end of this stick a string is attached and carried across the path in the direct range of the arrow, being secured to a stake on the opposite side. The arrow is generally barbed with a steel or flint point, and wound with thread saturated with a deadly poison. This is now rested on the top of the bow between the upright parts, and its notch caught in the bow-string. Everything is then in readiness. The tiger soon steals along his beaten track. He comes nearer and nearer the trap until at last his breast presses the string. Twang, goes the bow and the arrow is imbedded in the flesh of its victim. He writhes for a few moments, until he is released from his torments by the certain death which follows the course of the poison through his veins.

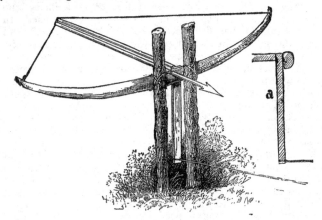

The use of the poison is very dangerous: a mere scratch through the skin is likely to prove fatal, and the trapper is thus likely to prove his own victim. Poisoned arrows are little used by trappers; and the bow trap, when properly constructed, is sufficiently effective without the venom.

THE DOWN-FALL.

This is the famous harpoon trap, so commonly used in Africa for the capture of the hippopotamus. There is no reason why

it may not be successfully employed in our own country for taking large game, or modified on a reduced scale for smaller animals.

The hippopotamus makes his daily rounds in regular beaten pathways; and the trapper, knowing this peculiarity, turns it to advantage. This is a common habit with many animals; and these "runways" are easily detected by the matted leaves and grass and the broken twigs. Over such a beaten track the harpoon-trap is suspended.

The harpoon used by the native African trappers somewhat resembles a double-barbed arrowhead, and has a reflexed prong on the shaft just behind the barbs, — a sort of combination between a spear and a fish-hook. It is a terrible weapon; and, when once launched into the flesh of its victim, its withdrawal is impossible, on account of the reflexed barb. Any sharp steel shaft will answer the purpose of the harpoon; it should be eight or ten inches in length, and filed to a keen point. We will now construct the trap. The first requisite is a straight section of the branch of some tree. This should be about four inches in diameter, and four feet in length. Into one end of this beam the harpoon should be firmly imbedded, allowing the point to project about six inches. This beam should then be weighted with two large stones, attached firmly by a rope, about eighteen inches above the harpoon. At about six inches from the other end of the log a notch should be cut, having its flat side uppermost, as shown plainly in our illustration. The implement is now ready.

Select some favorably situated tree, whose branches extend over the pathway chosen for the trap. By the aid of a rope secured to the log, and thrown over the limb, the weighted beam may be drawn up into the tree. While thus held by a person below, the trapper should climb the tree to complete operations. For this purpose, a smaller branch about three feet in length should be cut. One end should be flattened off on both sides, so as to fit in the notch in the beam; and the part which rests on the limb, as seen in the illustration, should also be flattened to prevent turning. A piece of stout Indian twine should next be fastened to the unwhittled end of the stick, which may then be adjusted in the notch of the harpoon beam, as seen in the engraving. The string may then be thrown down, and grasped by the companion below, who holds it firmly, after which the original rope may be removed. It will be noticed that the weight of the harpoon and accompaniments rests on the short arm of the lever which passes over the limb of the tree, and the tension on the string from the long arm is thus very slight. This precaution is necessary for the perfect working of the trap. To complete the contrivance, a small peg with a rounded notch should be cut, and driven into the ground directly plumb beneath the long end of the lever. It should be inserted into the earth only sufficiently to hold the string without pulling out, and the *side* of the notch should face the path; its height should be about a foot. Into the notch the string should be passed, being afterwards drawn across the path and secured on the opposite side at the same height. The trap is now set; and woe to the unlucky quadruped that dares make too free with that string! A very slight pressure from either side is equally liable to slip the string from the notch, or loosen the peg from the ground; and the result is the same in either case, — down comes the weighted harpoon, carrying death and destruction to its victim.

For large animals, this mode of setting will be found to work perfectly. When constructed on a smaller scale, it may be slightly modified. It will be noticed that, when the string is approached from one side, it is merely slipped out of the notch,— a slight pressure being sufficient to dislodge it,—while the pressure from the opposite direction must be strong enough to lift the peg out of the ground bodily. This is easily done when the peg is lightly inserted ; but, to *insure* success, even with *light* pressure from either side, an additional precaution may be used, if desired. Instead of fastening the end of the string securely to some object on the further side of the path, it is well to provide the end of the cord with a ring or loop, which should be passed over a nail or short peg driven in some tree or branch, or fastened into an upright stake, firmly embedded into the ground. The nail should point in the opposite direction from the notch in the peg, and its angle should incline slightly toward the path. It will thus be seen that an approach from one side forces the string from the notch in the peg, while an opposite pressure slides the ring from the nail.

This mode of setting is especially desirable for small animals, on account of its being more sensitive.

Such a trap may be successfully used for the puma, bear, and the lynx. When constructed for smaller animals, the harpoon may be dispensed with, a large stone being equally effective in its death-dealing qualities

THE BEAR TRAP.

This trap is constructed after the idea of the old-fashioned box or rabbit trap, and has been the means of securing many a hungry bear, or even puma, whose voracity has exceeded its cunning. The lynx and wild-cat are also among its occasional victims ; and inasmuch as its prisoners are taken alive great sport is often realized before the captive is brought under control.

Our illustration gives a very clear idea of the affair. The sides are built of stout young tree-trunks, cut into sections and firmly driven into the ground close together. For a large animal,— a bear, for instance,—the enclosure should be about seven feet deep, two and a half feet wide, and four feet high. The top should be built in with the sides, after the manner of the log cabin, described in page (244.) The two posts at the entrance should be first set up. On the back side of each, near the end, a deep notch should be cut for the reception of the cross piece at the top. This should likewise be notched in a similar manner on both sides of each end, so as to fit singly into the notches in the uprights on the one side, and into the second pair of uprights on the other. These latter should next be inserted firmly into the ground, having been previously notched on both sides of their upper ends, as described for the cross piece. They may either be fixed in place and the cross piece sprung in between them at the top, or the latter may be held in the notches of the first pair, while the second are being inserted. Continue thus until the full length of the sides are reached, when the end may be closed by an upright wall of plain logs, either hammered into the ground, after the manner of the sides, or arranged one above another in notches between the two end uprights. The sliding door is next required. This should be large enough to cover the

opening, and should be made of stout board slabs, firmly secured by cross pieces. It should be made to slide smoothly into grooves cut into perpendicular logs situated on each side of the opening, or may be arranged to slip easily between the flattened side of one log on each side and the front of the pen. Either way works well. In the latter an additional upright or short board should be inserted in the ground at the edges of the sliding door, to prevent the latter from being forced to either side by the efforts of the enclosed captive.

There are two or three ways of setting the trap, depending upon the desired game. For a bear it is arranged as in our illustration. An upright post, two feet in length, should be cut to an edge at one end, and wedged in between the logs at the top of the trap, near the middle.   Across the top of this, a pole seven feet in length, should be rested; one end being attached by a loop, or secured in a notch in the sliding door, and the other supplied with a strong string about four feet in length, with a stick eight inches in length secured to its end.   Through. the centre log, in the back of the pen, and about two feet from the ground, an auger hole should be made.   The bait stick with bait attached should be inserted through this hole from the inside, and the spindle caught on the outside beween its projecting end and a nail driven in the adjoining upright.   This principle is clearly illustrated on page 105 at (*a*), and, if desired, the method (*b*) may be used also.   For a bear, the bait should consist of a piece of meat scented with burnt honey-comb.   The odor of honey will tempt a bear into almost any trap, and even into such close quarters as the above he will enter without the slightest suspicion, when a feast of honey is in view.

For the cougar, or puma, the best bait is a live lamb or a young pig, encaged in a small pen erected at the end of the trap. A fowl is also excellent.   When thus baited, the setting of the trap is varied.   The upright post at the top of the trap is inserted nearer the front, and the cross pole is stouter.   The auger hole is bored in the top of the trap, through the centre of one of the logs, and about twenty inches from the back end of the trap.   The spindle is dispensed with and the end of the string is provided with a large knot, which is lowered through the auger hole, and is prevented from slipping back by the insertion of a stick beneath.   This stick should be about three feet in length, and of such a size at the end as will snugly fit into the auger hole.   It should be inserted delicately, merely enough to hold the knot from slipping back, and so as to be easily released by a slight movement in any direction.

This mode of setting is more fully detailed on page 52.   As the puma steals in upon his prey he dislodges the stick, the lid falls, and he finds himself imprisoned with his intended victim. This trap is much used in India and Asia for the capture of the tiger, and the jaguar of South America is frequently entrapped by the same devices.

THE PIT-FALL.

The tiger is the scourge of India and Southern Asia, and some sections of these countries are so terribly infested with the brutes that the inhabitants are kept in a continual state of terror by their depredations. Many methods are adopted by the natives for the destruction of the terrible creatures, some of which have already been described. The pit-fall is still another device by which this lurking marauder is often captured and destroyed. It sometimes consists of a mere pit covered and baited in the haunts of the tiger, or is constructed in a continuous deep ditch surrounding the habitations of the natives, and thus acting as a secure protection. The pit is about twelve feet deep and ten feet in width, and its outside edge is lined with a hedge five or six feet in height. As the fierce brute steals upon his intended prey, he nears the hedge and at one spring its highest branch is cleared. He reaches the earth only to find himself at the bottom of a deep pit, from which there is no hope of escape, and where he speedily becomes the merciless victim of a shower of deadly arrows and bullets.

Happily we have no tigers in the United States, but the puma and the lynx are both fit subjects for the pit-fall. These animals cannot be said to exist in such numbers as to become a scourge and a stranger to the inhabitants of any neighborhood, and for this reason the "Moat" arrangement of the pit-fall is not required. The simple pit is often used, and when properly constructed and baited is a very *sure* trap. The hole should be about twelve feet in depth and eight feet across, widening at the bottom. Its opening should be covered with sticks, earth and leaves, so arranged as to resemble the surroundings as much as possible, but so lightly adjusted as that they will easily give way at a slight pressure. One edge of the opening should now be closely built up with stakes firmly inserted into the ground, and so constructed as to form a small pen in the middle, in which to secure the bait, generally a live turkey, goose, or other fowl. The other three sides should also be hedged in by a single row of upright stakes three or four feet in height, and a few inches apart in order that the hungry puma may whet his appetite by glimpses between them.

They should be firmly imbedded in the earth directly at the edge of the pit, and as far as possible trimmed of their branches on the inside. There will thus be a small patch of solid ground for the feet of the fowl, which should be tied by the leg in the enclosure. Our trap is now set, and if there is a puma in the neighborhood he will be sure to pay it a call and probably a *visit.*

Spying his game, he uses every effort to reach it through the

crevices between the stakes. The cries of the frightened fowl
arouse and stimulate his appetite, and at last exasperated by
his futile efforts to seize his victim, he springs over the fence of
stakes and is lodged in the depths of the pit.

The puma is very agile of movement, and unless the pit is at
least twelve feet in depth there is danger of his springing out.
Any projecting branch on the inside of the stakes affords a
grasp for his ready paw, and any such branch, if within the
reach of his leap, is sure to effect his escape. For this reason
it is advisable to trim smoothly all the projections and leave no
stub or knot hole by which he could gain the slightest hold.
The construction of a pit-fall is a rather difficult operation on
account of the digging which it necessitates. On this account
it is not so much used as many other traps which are not only
equally effective but much more easily constructed. The following is an example :—

THE LOG COOP TRAP.

This is commonly set for bears, although a deer or a puma
becomes its frequent tenant. As its name implies it consists of
a coop of logs, arranged after the principle of the Coop Trap
described on page 67. The logs should be about eight feet
in length, notched at the ends as described for the Log
Cabin, page (244). Lay two of the logs parallel about seven
feet apart. Across their ends in the notches, lay two others
and continue building up in "cob-house" fashion until the
height of about six feet is reached. The corners may be secured as they are laid by spikes, or they may be united afterward in mass by a rope firmly twisted about them from top to
bottom. Logs should now be laid across the top of the coop
and firmly secured by the spikes or rope knots. There are
several ways of setting the trap. A modification of that described on page 67 works very well, or an arrangement of spindle and
bait stick, as in the Box Trap, page 105, may also be employed. In the latter case, the bait stick is either inserted between
the logs at the back of the coop, or a hole is bored through one
of them for this purpose. For this mode of setting, the coop
should be constructed beneath some tree. It is set by means of
a rope attached to the upper edge of one of its sides, the rope
being thrown over a limb of the tree and the loose end brought
down and secured to the bait stick by a spindle, as described

for the trap on page (195). The limb here acts in place of the
tall end piece of the Box Trap, and by raising the coop up to
such an angle as that it will be nearly poised, the setting may
be made so delicate that a mere touch on the bait stick from
the interior will dislodge the pieces and let fall the enclosure.
The *simplest* mode of setting the trap is that embodied in the
" snare " method on page (52). The rope is here provided
with a knot, which must pass easily between the logs, or
through the hole at the back of the coop, the length of rope
being so arranged as that the coop shall be sufficiently raised
where the knot projects into the interior. The introduction of
the bait stick beneath the knot will thus prevent the latter from
being drawn back, and thus our trap is set. The bait stick in
any case should be about two feet in length ; and with this
leverage but a slight touch will be required to spring the pieces.
In the latter method the limb of the tree is not necessary. A
stout crotched stake driven into the ground about twenty feet,
at the back of the coop, will answer every purpose, and the coop
may be constructed wherever desired. This is a most excellent
trap for large animals. It secures the game alive, and is thus
often productive of most exciting sport. For the bear, the
bait should consist of honey or raw meat. Full directions for
baiting all kinds of American game are given under their respective heads in another part of this book. The Coop Trap may
be constructed of any dimensions, from the small example on
page (67) to the size above described.

There are several other inventions commonly used for the
capture of large animals in various parts of the globe, which
would be of little avail in this country. Such is the African
Corrall, or Hopo, by which whole herds of quaggas, elands, and
buffalo are often destroyed. The trap consists of two hedges
in the form of the letter V, which are very high and thick at
the angle. Instead of the hedges being joined at this point,
they are made to form a lane about two hundred feet in length,
at the extremity of which a giant pit is formed. Trunks of
trees are laid across the margins to prevent the animals from
escaping. The opening of this pit is then covered with light
reeds and small green boughs. The hedges often extend miles
in length and are equally as far apart at these extremities. The
tribe of hunters make a circle, three or four miles around the
country adjacent to the opening, and gradually closing up are
almost sure to enclose a large body of game, which, by shouts
and skilfully hurled javelins, they drive into the narrowing walls

of the Hopo. The affrighted animals rush headlong to the gate presented at the end of the converging hedges and here plunge pell-mell into the pit, which is soon filled with a living mass. Some escape by running over the others; and the natives, wild with excitement, spear the poor animals with mad delight, while others of the brutes are smothered and crushed by the weight of their dead and dying companions. It is a most cruel and inhuman device, and its effects are sometimes appalling.

THE NET TRAP.

The lion and tiger are often taken in a net, which is secured to a frame work and suspended over a tempting bait. When the latter is touched the net falls, and the victim becomes entangled in the meshes and is securely caught. So far as we know, this mode of capture is never tried in this country. For the puma, lynx and wild-cat we fancy it might work admirably. The net should be of stout cord, and should be secured to a heavy square frame work, tilted as in the coop trap, already described. There should be plenty of slack in the net, and the looseness should be drawn flat over the framework in folds. The contrivance may be set by a large figure four trap, page (107), or the device described under the coop trap, page (67).

The use of bird lime, for the capture of a tiger, certainly seems odd; but it is, nevertheless, a common mode of taking the animal, in the countries where this marauder abounds. The viscid, tenacious preparation known as bird lime is described on page (97) and is familiar to most of our readers. For the capture of birds it is unfailing, when once their delicate plumage comes in contact with it. Its effect on the tiger is surprising, and many a hunter has secured his striped foe by its aid. For this purpose, the cans of the preparation are arranged on elevated boards around a bed of leaves, in which the bait is placed. A small platform is so placed that the tiger shall step upon it in reaching for the bait, which, by the aid of strings, tilts the boards and tips off the cans. The lime spills on its victim and over the bed of leaves, and the tiger, in his endeavors to free himself from the sticky substance only succeeds in spreading it, and as he rolls and tumbles on the ground he soon becomes completely smeared and covered with the dry leaves, from which it is impossible for him to extricate himself.

In his frantic rage he writhes upon the ground and becomes

an easy prey to the hunter, who is generally on hand for the fray.

Steel traps are much used for the capture of large game, and are made in sizes especially adapted for the purpose. These are described under the proper head, in another portion of this work ; and the various baits and modes of setting required for the different animals, are clearly set forth under their respective titles of the latter, in the section "Art of Trapping."

SNARES

OR

NOOSE-TRAPS

BOOK II.

SNARES OR NOOSE TRAPS.

 HESE devices, although properly coming under the head of "traps," differ from them in the sense in which they are generally understood. A *snare* naturally implies an *entanglement;* and for this reason the term is applied to those contrivances which secure their victims by the aid of strings or nooses. Inventions of this kind are among the most useful and successful to the professional Trapper, and their varieties are numerous. The "Twitch-up" will be recognized as a familiar example by many of our country readers, who may have seen it during their rambles, cautiously set in the low underbrush, awaiting its prey, or perhaps holding aloft its misguided victim.

Snares are among the most interesting and ingenious of the trap kind, besides being the most sure and efficacious. They possess one advantage over all other traps; they can be made in the woods, and out of the commonest material.

Let the young trapper supply himself with a small, sharp hatchet, and a stout, keen edged jack-knife,—these being the only tools required. He should also provide himself with a coil of fine brass "sucker wire," or a quantity of horse-hair nooses (which will be described further on), a small ball of tough twine and a pocket full of bait, such as apples, corn, oats and the like, of course depending upon the game he intends to trap. With these, his requirements are complete, and he has the material for a score of capital snares, which will do him much excellent service if properly constructed. Perhaps the most common of the noose traps is the ordinary

QUAIL SNARE,

which forms the subject of our first illustration. This consists of a series of nooses fastened to a strong twine or wire. They

may be of any number, and should either consist of fine wire,
horse-hair, or fine fish-line. If of wire, common brass "sucker
wire," to be found in nearly all hardware establishments and
country stores, is the best. Each noose should be about four
inches in diameter. To make it, a small loop should be twisted
on one end of the wire, and the other passed through it, thus
making a slipping loop, which will be found to work very easily.
Fifteen or twenty of these nooses should be made, after which
they should be fastened either to a stout string or wire, at
distances of about four inches from each other, as seen in our
illustration. Each end of the long string supporting the nooses
should then be fastened to a wooden peg. After selecting the
ground, the pegs should be driven into the earth, drawing the

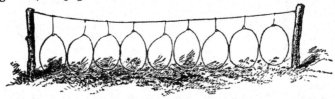

string tightly, as seen in our illustration. The ground around
the nooses should then be sprinkled with corn, oats, and the like,
and the trap is set. As a general thing, it is advisable to set it
in a neighborhood where quails are known to abound; and as
they run all over the ground in search of food, they are sure to
come across the bait strewn for them, and equally as certain to
be caught and entangled in the nooses. The writer has known
as many as six quails to be thus caught at a time, on a string of
only twelve nooses. Partridges and woodcock will occasionally
be found entangled in the snare, and it will oft-times happen
that a rabbit will be secured by the device.

HOOP NOOSES.

This is a variation from the above, the noose being attached
to a barrel hoop and the latter being fastened to two stout posts,
which are firmly driven into the ground. By their scattering
the bait inside the hoop, and adjusting the loops, the contrivance
is complete.

This is a very old and approved method.

In the initial (T) at the head of this section we give also

another suggestion for a noose trap. The cross pieces are tacked to the top of the upright, and a noose suspended from each end,—the bait adjusted as there seen.

We have mentioned horse-hair nooses as being desirable, and they are commonly used; but, as it takes considerable time to make them, and the wire answering the purpose fully as well, we rather recommend the wire in preference. We will give a few simple directions, however, for the making of the horse-hair nooses, in case our readers might desire to use them instead.

Select long, stout hairs from the tail of any horse, (we would recommend that it be a good tempered horse), take one of the hairs and double it in the middle, hold the double between the thumb and fore-finger of the left hand, letting the two ends hang from the under side of the thumb, and keeping the hairs between the thumb and finger, about a third of an inch apart. Now proceed to twist the two hairs toward the end of the finger, letting them twist together as the loop emerges on the upper side of the thumb.

A little practice will overcome what at first seems very difficult. To keep the two hairs between the fingers at the right distance of separation, and at the same time to twist them and draw the loop from between the fingers as they *are* twisted, seems quite a complicated operation ; and so it will be found at first. But when once mastered by practice, the twisting of five nooses a minute will be an easy matter. When the entire length of the hairs are twisted, the ends should be cut off even and then passed through the small loop at the folded end. The noose is then ready to be fastened to the main string of support. Horse-hair nooses are commonly used in nearly all snares as they are always to be had, and possess considerable strength. The fine brass wire is also extensively used, and the writer rather prefers it. It is very strong and slips easily, besides doing away with the trouble of twisting the loops, which to some might be a very difficult and tedious operation. We recommend the wire, and shall allude to it chiefly in the future, although the horse-hair may be substituted whenever desired.

There is another modification of the foregoing quail-traps very commonly utilized by professional trappers of many countries. A low hedge is constructed, often hundreds of feet in length small openings are left here and there, in which the nooses are placed, as in the accompanying engraving. The bait is strewn around on both sides of the hedge, and the grouse or other game, on its discovery, are almost sure to become entangled sooner or later. It is a well-known fact about these birds, that they will always seek to pass *under* an object which comes in their way rather than fly over it; and although the hedge of this trap is only a foot or more in height, the birds will almost invariably run about until they find an opening, in preference to flying over it. It is owing to this peculiarity of habit that they are so easily taken by this method. Our illustration gives only a very short section of hedge; it may be extended to any length. The writer's experience with the hedge nooses has been very satisfactory, although never using a length greater

than ten feet. It is well to set the hedge in the locality where quails or partridges are *known* to run. And in setting, it is always desirable to build the hedge so that it will stretch over some open ground, and connect with two trees or bushes. Cedar boughs are excellent for the purpose, but any close brushwood will answer very well. Strew the ground with corn, oats and the like. A small quantity only is necessary.

There is another noose trap commonly used abroad, and very little known here. It is a *tree* trap, and goes by the name of the "triangle snare." It is not designed for the capture of any *particular* kind of bird, although it often will secure fine and rare specimens. It consists of a sapling of wood, bent and tied in the form of a triangle, as shown in our illustration.

This may be of any size, depending altogether on the bird the young trapper fancies to secure. A noose should be suspended in the triangle from its longest point. This noose should hang as indicated in our illustration, falling low enough to leave a space of an inch or so below it at the bottom of the triangle. The bait, consisting of a piece of an apple, a berry, insect, or piece of

meat, according to the wish of the trapper, should then be suspended in the centre of the noose, after which the contrivance
should be hung in some tree to await events. As they are so
easily made and can be carried with so little trouble, it is an
excellent plan to set out with a dozen or so, hanging them all in
different parts of the woods; as, under circumstances of so many
being set, scarcely a day will pass in which the trapper will not
be rewarded by some one of the snares. The writer once knew
of a case where a hawk was captured by one of these simple
devices. In this case it had been set expressly, and the wire
was extra strong. This trap, we believe, is quite common in
parts of Germany, but, as far as we know, has not been utilized
to any great extent in our country. We recommend it with
great confidence.

For the capture of woodchucks, muskrats and house-rats, the
wire noose may also be adapted to good purpose. Many a
woodchuck has been secured by the aid of this simple invention.
It is only necessary to arrange the loop in the opening of the burrow, securing the wire to a stout stick, firmly driven into the
ground. If properly "set" the animal, on emerging from the
burrow, will become entangled, and by his efforts to disengage
himself will only tighten the loop and thus render escape impossible. For rats, the noose should be attached to a nail, and
the wire similarly arranged over the hole.

The slipping-noose thus simply adapted becomes a most
effective trap, and is always sure to hold its victim when once
within its grasp, as every struggle only tends to draw the noose
tighter. They are quick in their action, and produce death
without much pain, and for this reason are to be commended.

THE "TWITCH-UP."

Our next example of the snare, we imagine, is one which all
our boy-readers will immediately recognize; for it would certainly seem that any country boy who does not know the
"Twitch-up" must be far behind the times, and live in a locality where there are no rabbits, quail, or even boys, besides
himself, to suggest it. This snare is a *universal favorite*
among nearly all country boys, and our illustration will immediately bring it to mind. Its name, "The Twitch-up," conveys
perfectly its method of working. Our illustration represents
the trap as it appears when set. It has many varieties, of which
we will select the best. They may be divided into two classes—
those with upright nooses, and those in which the noose is

spread on the ground, the latter of which are commonly called "ground snares." We will give our attention first to the "upright" style. These are rather entitled to preference on account of the harmless death which they inflict, invariably catching by the neck. Whereas the ground nooses as frequently lift their prey into the air by their feet, and thus prolong their suffering. Twitch-ups are the most successful and sure of any snares, and that, too, without being complicated. The writer, in his younger days, was quite an expert in trapping, and he can

truthfully say that he found more enjoyment and had better success with these than with any other kinds of traps he employed.

They are generally set in thickets or woods where either rabbits or partridges are known to abound. Having arrived at his chosen trapping ground, the young trapper should first select some slender, elastic sapling; that of the hickory is the best, and is generally to be found in open woods—if not, some other kind will answer very well. It should be about five or six feet in length, (trimmed of its branches,) and in diameter need be no larger than an axe-handle or a broom-stick. When this is decided, some spot about five feet distant from the sapling should then be selected. The hatchet and knife will now come into excellent use, in cutting the sticks for the little inclosure shown in our drawing. This should be about eight or ten inches in diameter, and of about the same height. The sticks should be driven into the ground in a circle, leaving an open space of about six inches on one side. A stout switch as large as a man's little finger, and nearly two feet long, should then be cut and nicely sharpened at both ends. This should then be driven into the ground in the form of an arch, at the opening of the inclosure.

We will now ask our readers to turn their attention to the next illustration, in order to understand what is to follow. This picture shows the method of setting the trap.

After the arch is firmly fixed in its place, a short piece of stick should be cut, of a length corresponding to the height of the arch. To the middle of this stick the bait should be at-

tached, being either tied to it or stuck on a plug driven into the stick, the latter being sharpened on one end. Next proceed to cut another stick, of about six inches in length; let this be flattened on one end. The wire noose should then be fastened to the opposite end. The noose in this case should be large enough to fill the opening of the arch. We will now go back to the sapling again. It should be bent down slightly, and a piece of the strong twine should be tied to its tip. Taking hold of the string, proceed to bend down the end of the sapling, in the direction of the inclosure, until it draws with a force strong enough to lift a rabbit if he were tied to the end of it. Thus holding it down with the string against the front of the inclosure, cut off the twine at the place where it crosses the top of the arch, as this will be the required length. It is now necessary to tie the end of this string to the same piece of wood and at the same place to which the noose was tied. When this is done the trap may be set as shown in the cut. The spring sapling should be bent as seen in the first illustration. The piece of wood holding the noose should be passed beneath the top of the arch, as far as it will go, with its long end pointing inside the inclosure. By now supporting the inside end with the bait stick, and carefully adjusting the noose so as to com letely fill the arch, the trap will be set.

In order to reach the bait, the rabbit or b.rd *must* necessarily pass its head through the noose, after which, if the bait be scarcely *touched*, the animal's doom is sealed, and he is lifted into the air, generally suffering almost instant death. It is well known that in the case of a rabbit the neck is broken by a very slight blow, a strong snap of the finger being often sufficient. It is therefore safe to conclude that when thus suddenly caught and lifted by the noose, death must occur almost instantaneously from the same cause.

It is not really necessary to success that the force of the sapling should be strong enough to lift the rabbit from the ground, as a mere strong tightening of the noose would be sufficient to cause strangulation and death. But we recommend the former method as being less painful and more rapid in its effects.

If the young trapper should experience any difficulty in finding saplings of the right size, in the locality where he desires to set his traps, the difficulty may be easily mended by cutting the poles elsewhere, and carrying them to his trapping-ground, this answering the purpose equally well. They should be sharpened nicely on the large end, and firmly stuck into ground. The "Twitch-up" may be used for the capture of all varieties of game, and when set with the noose in the opening of a hollow tree, a stray coon will occasionally be entrapped.

The next figure represents another method of constructing this trap. The picture explains itself. Instead of the arch, two notched sticks are driven into the ground, one on each side of the opening of the pen. The other piece should be of the shape shown in the figure, made either in one piece or in two pieces fastened together. They may all be constructed from twigs in the woods. Let the noose and draw-string now be fastened to the middle of the cross piece, and when set it will appear as in our figure. It will easily be seen that a slight pull on the bait will turn the cross piece from beneath the notches, and allow it to fly into the air.

Method No. 2.

In our next instance the same principle is employed. **The** notched pegs are here driven in the back part of the pen, about

five inches apart, with their notches towards the front. A forked bait stick of the shape shown is then procured. The draw-string should be attached near the end furthest from the fork. By now inserting the ends lightly beneath the notches in the pegs, at the same

Method No. 3.

time letting the bait incline near the ground, the trap will be set on a very slight lift, as the bait will dislodge the pieces. Of course the noose must be arranged in the opening of the pen, as in the previous varieties. The bait stick in both cases should be set cautiously beneath the notches, as shown at (a), so that the slightest turn will cause it to roll out of position.

A fourth method of snaring is shown in our next figure. In this instance the original arch is used, or else some circular opening constructed in the front of the pen. Inside, at the back part of the inclosure, a smaller arch is placed. Two sticks are then to be made similar to those mentioned in our first example of the " Twitch-up." Let the draw-string be tied to the end of one of these sticks; after which it should be passed under the inside arch, being brought out in front of it, and there supported by the bait-stick, as seen in our illustration.

The noose should then be attached to the draw-string above the pen, and afterward brought down and arranged in front of the opening. The trap is then set, and will be found on trial to work admirably.

One of the simplest as well as *surest* of " Twitch-up " traps forms the subject of our next illustration. Like the foregoing varieties it is of course to be surrounded by its pen, and supplied with a circular opening or arch at one side, in which

Method No. 4.

to hang the noose. It is constructed of three twigs. A simple crotch (a) should be firmly inserted in the ground at

Method No. 5.

the back part of the pen ; (*b*) the bait stick, consists of a straight twig, five or six inches in length, and should be attached to the draw-string at about half an inch from the large end ; (*c*) is another forked stick with unequal arms, the long one being driven into the ground near the opening of the pen and a little to one side, letting the remaining arm point directly towards the crotch-stick at the back of the pen. The noose having been attached to the draw-string, the trap may now be set. Lower the bait stick and pass the large end under the crotch at the back of the pen, catching the baited end underneath the tip of the forked stick near the pen's opening. Arrange the noose in front of the entrance, and the thing is done. A mere touch on the bait will suffice to throw the pieces asunder. It is an excellent plan to sharpen the point of the forked stick (*c*) where it comes in contact with the bait stick, in order to make the bearing more slight, and consequently more easily thrown from its balance.

THE POACHER'S SNARE.

Our next example represents one of the oldest and best snares in existence, — simple in construction, and almost infallible in its operations. It is the one in most common use among the poachers of England, hence its name. The pieces are three in number, and may be cut from pine wood, affording easy and profitable employment for the jack-knife during odd hours and rainy days, when time hangs heavily.

The pieces are so simple in form and easy of construction that a sufficient number for fifty traps might be whittled in less than two hours, by any smart boy, who is at all "handy" with his jack-knife.

If a few good broad shingles can be found, the work is even much easier,—mere splitting and notching being then all that is necessary. The bait stick should be about eight inches long, pointed at one end, and supplied with a notch in the other at about half an inch from the tip. The upright stick should be considerably shorter than the bait stick, and have a length of about ten inches, one end being nicely pointed, and the broad side of the other extremity supplied with a notch similar to the bait stick. About four inches from the blunt end, and on the narrow side of the stick, a square notch should be cut, sufficiently large to admit the bait stick loosely. The catch piece now remains. This should be about two and a-half inches in length, half an inch in width, and bevelled off at each end into a flat edge. The shapes of the different pieces, together with their setting, will be readily understood by a look at our illustration.

A hundred of these pieces will make a small bundle, and may be easily carried by the young trapper, together with his other necessaries, as he starts off into the woods. He will thus be supplied with parts for thirty-three traps, all ready to be set, only requiring the stakes for the pens, which may be easily cut in the woods. Having selected a flexible sapling about five feet in length, and having stripped it of its branches, proceed to adjust the pieces. Take one of the upright sticks, and insert it firmly in the ground, with its upper notch facing the sapling, and at about four feet distant from it. Bend down the "springer," and by its force determine the required length for the draw-string attaching one end to the tip of the sapling, and the other near the end of a catch piece, the latter having its bevelled side uppermost. The wire noose should then be attached to the draw-string about six inches above the catch-piece. The pen should now be constructed as previously directed. Its entrance should be on the side *furthest* from the springer, and should be so built as that the peg in the ground shall be at the back part of the enclosure. The pen being finished, the trap may be set.

Insert the bait stick with bait attached into the square notch in the side of the upright peg; or, if desired, it may be adjusted by a pivot or nail through both sticks, as seen in our illustration, always letting the baited end project toward the opening. Draw down the catch piece, and fit its ends into the notches in the back of the upright peg and extremity of the bait-stick. By now pulling the latter slightly, and gently withdrawing the hand, the pieces will hold themselves together, only awaiting a lift at the bait to dislodge them. Adjust the wire loop at the opening of the pen, and you may leave the trap with the utmost confidence in its ability to take care of itself, and any unlucky intruder who tries to steal its property.

Most of the snares which we shall describe are constructed from rough twigs, as these are always to be found in the woods, and with a little practice are easily cut and shaped into the desired forms. If desired, however, many of them may be whittled from pine wood like the foregoing, and the pieces carried in a bundle, ready for immediate use. In either case, whether made from the rough twigs or seasoned wood, it is a good plan to have them already prepared, and thus save time at the trapping ground when time is more valuable.

THE PORTABLE SNARE.

This is simply a modification of the snare just described, but possesses decided advantages over it in many respects. In the first place, it requires little or no protection in the shape of an enclosure. It can be set in trees or in swamps, or in short in *any* place where an upright elastic branch can be found or adjusted. Like the foregoing, it is to be commended for its portability, fifty or sixty of the pieces making but a small parcel, and furnishing material for a score of traps. We call it the "portable snare" partly in order to distinguish it from the one just described, but chiefly because this particular variety is generally called by that name in countries where it is most used.

It is composed of three pieces, all to be cut from a shingle or thin board. Let the first be about eight inches long, and three-quarters of an inch in width. This is for the upright. An oblong mortise should be cut through this piece, one inch in length, and beginning at about an inch from the end of the stick. Three inches from the other end, and on one of the broad sides of the stick, a notch should be made, corresponding in shape to that shown in our illustration. The bait stick should be four or five inches long, one end fitting easily into the mortise, where it should be secured by a wire or smooth nail driven through so as to form a hinge, on which it will work easily. On the upper side of this stick, and two inches distant from the pivot, a notch should be cut, similar to that in the upright. The catch piece should be about two inches in length, and bevelled off to a flat edge at each end. This completes the pieces.

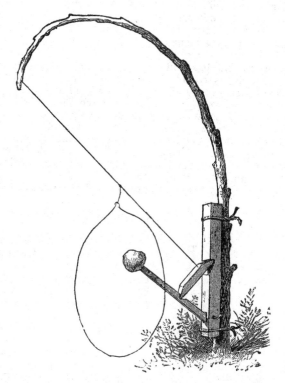

To set the trap, it is only necessary to find some stout sapling, after which the upright stick may be attached to it close to the ground, by the aid of two pieces of stout iron wire, twisted firmly around both. It is well to cut slight grooves at each end of the upright for the reception of the wires, in order to prevent slipping. Tie a strong piece of twine around one end of the catch piece, knotting it on the beveled side. Cut the string about two feet in length, and attach the other end to the tip of the sapling. Adjust the bait stick on its pivot. By now lowering the catch piece, and lodging the knotted end beneath the notch in the upright and the other end in the notch on the bait stick, the pieces will appear as in our drawing. Care should be taken to set the catch pieces as slightly as possible in the notches, in order to insure sensitiveness. At about four inches from the catch piece, the wire noose should be attached and arranged in a circle directly around the bait. By now backing up the trap with a few sticks to prevent the bait from being approached from behind, the thing is complete, and woe to the misguided creature that dares to test its efficacy. By adjusting the drawstring so far as the upper end of the catch piece, the leverage on the bait stick is so slight as to require a mere touch to overcome it; and we may safely say that, when this trap is once baited, it will stay baited, so far as animal intruders are concerned, as we never yet have seen a rabbit or bird skilful enough to remove the tempting morsel before being summarily dealt with by the noose on guard duty.

For portability, however, the following has no equal.

THE "SIMPLEST" SNARE.

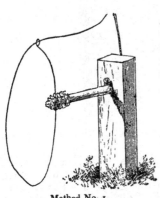

Method No. 1.

This is one of the most ingenious and effective devices used in the art of trapping; and the principle is so simple and universal in its application to traps in general as to become a matter of great value to all who are at all interested in the subject. There is scarcely a trap of any kind which could not be set with the knotted string and bait stick, at the expense of a little thought and ingenuity. The principle is easily understood by a look at our engraving, which probably represents the *simplest* twitch-up it is possible to construct. A stout wooden peg, having a hole the size of a lead pencil near the top, is driven firmly into the ground. The "knot" is made on the end of the raw-string, and passed through the hole in the peg from behind, being secured in place by the insertion of the bait stick in front. The latter should be about four inches long, and should be inserted very lightly,—merely enough to prevent the knot from slipping back. The noose should be fastened to the draw-string six or seven inches from the knot, and arranged in front of the bait at the opening of the pen, which should be constructed as previously directed. The peg should be about six inches long and the hole should be made with a 1-3 inch auger. Dozens of these pegs may be carried without inconvenience, and utilized in the same number of snares, in a very short time. We have already described the so-called "portable snare;" but, for portability, there is no noose-trap to be compared with the above. We give also a few other applications of the same principle.

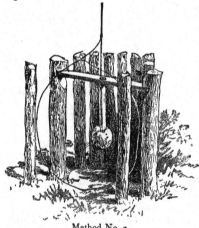

Method No. 2.

In the second example, a horizontal stick is used instead of the peg, the hole being made in its centre. Its ends are caught in notches in opposite sticks at the back part of the pen, and the noose arranged at the opening.

Again, by a third method (see engraving next page), these notched sticks may be driven into the ground first, and a row of twigs continued on them on both sides, thus leaving a passage-way between, as represented in the illustration. A noose may then be set at each opening, with the bait in the middle ; so that, at whichever side it is approached, the result is the same, besides affording a chance of securing two birds at the same time.

THE QUAIL SNARE.

That quails are sociable in their habits, and that they run together in broods in search of their food, is a fact well known to all sportsmen. A most excellent opportunity is thus afforded the hunter to secure several at one shot, and the same advantage may be gained by the trapper by specially arranging for it. For this purpose there is no invention more desirable or effective than the snare we next illustrate; and on account of the companionable habits of the quail, it is just as sure to catch six birds as one. The principle on which the trap works, is the same as in the three foregoing.

Two notched pegs are first driven into the ground, about four inches apart, and the flat stick with the hole in the centre

caught beneath these summits, as just described. It should be firmly secured; several nooses are next to be attached to the drawstring, and the trap set as already directed.

The best bait consists of a "nub" of pop-corn, firmly impaled on the spindle, together with a few loose grains scattered on the

Method No. 3.

ground right beneath it. The nooses should be arranged around the bait so as to touch or overlap each other, and the bait stick introduced into the hole a little more firmly than when set

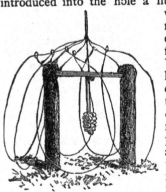

with one noose. The quail on reaching the trap all rush for the corn on the ground, and thus fill nearly if not all the nooses. When the supply here is exhausted, then united attacks are directed towards the "nub" on the bait stick, which soon becomes loosened: the knot is thus released and each noose will probably launch a victim in midair. This invention is original with the author of this work, so far as he knows; and it will be found the simplest as well as most effective quail snare in existence. Pop-corn is mentioned is bait partly on account of its being a favorite food with the quail; but particularly because the *pecking* which it necessitates in order to remove the grains from the cob, is sure to spring the trap. If pop corn cannot be had, common Indian corn will answer very well Oats or buckwheat may also be used, as the ground bait, if desired.

THE BOX SNARE.

This is a most unique device, and will well repay any one

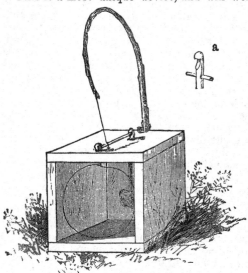

who may desire to test its merits. It may be set for rabbits, coon, or feathered game, of course varying the size of the box accordingly. For ordinary purposes, it should be seven or eight inches square, leaving one end open. Place it in the position shown in the illustration and proceed to bore an auger hole in the top board, one and a half inches from the back edge.

This is for the reception of the bait stick. Directly opposite to this and an inch from the front edge of the board a notched peg should be inserted. A gimlet hole should now be bored on a line between the auger hole and notched peg, and half an inch from the latter. A small stout screw eye should next be inserted at the rear edge of the board, and another one fastened to the back board, two inches from the bottom. With these simple preparations the box is complete. The bait stick should be about five or six inches long and supplied with a notch at the upper end. It should be of such a size as to pass easily into the auger hole, and provided with a peg inserted through it at about an inch and a half from the notched end, as shown in our illustration at (a). The object of this peg is to prevent the bait stick from being drawn entirely through the hole by the force of the pull from above. The catch piece should be only long enough to secure its ends beneath the notches in the peg at the top of the box and the projecting bait stick. It should be bevelled off at the tips as in the instances previously described, and attached to a piece of sucker wire, the point of attachment being at about an inch from the end of the stick. The wire should be about two and a half feet in length, the catch piece being fastened at about six inches from one end. To set this neat little invention it is first necessary to procure a strong and elastic switch about four feet in length, sharpen it slightly at the large end and insert it firmly in the screw eye at the back of the box, securing it in place at the top by strings through the screw eye at that place. By now attaching the short end of the wire to the tip of the sapling, inserting the bait stick from the inside of the box, and securing the catch piece in the notches, the other pieces will be in equilibrium, and the only remaining thing to be done is to pass the long end of the wire through the gimlet hole, and form it into a slipping noose which shall completely fill the opening of the box. In order to reach the bait the animal must pass his head through the noose, and it can be easily seen that the slightest pull on that tempting morsel will release the catch piece and tighten the wire around the neck of the intruder. Where the trap is small and the captured animal is large, it will sometimes happen that the box will be carried a distance of several feet before overpowering its victim; but it is sure to do it in the end if the spring powers of the sapling are strong and it is firmly secured to the box. If desired, the box may be tied to a neighboring stone or tree to prevent any such capers; but it will generally be found unnecessary, and a few minutes' search will always reveal it with its unlucky captive.

We have described the box with its spring attached; but this is not a requisite, as it may be used with growing sapling when required.

The same trap may be constructed of a pasteboard box and whalebone, for the capture of small birds, and used with good success. The size we have mentioned is adaptable for rabbits and animals of the same size, but is really larger than necessary for feathered game.

THE DOUBLE BOX SNARE.

This is another embodiment of the same principle which has already been described, viz.—the knotted string. By many it is considered an improvement on the box snare just mentioned, owing to the possibility of its taking two victims at the same time. It may be set for rabbits, mink, or muskrat, and will be found very efficient.

It consists of a box about eight inches square, one foot in length, and open at both ends. In the centre of the top board

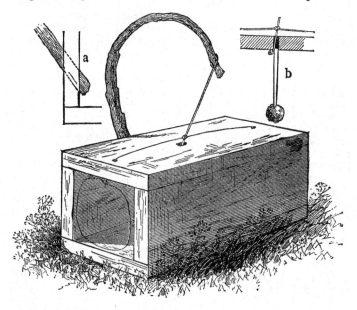

a hole of the diameter of a lead pencil should be bored, and a smaller aperture also made in the middle of each end near the edge as seen in the accompanying engraving. The spring is next required. This should consist of an elastic switch or small pole, three or more feet in length. It should be inserted in a slanting auger hole, made through the middle of one of the side boards near the bottom at the angle shown at (*a*). Should the switch fit loosely it may be easily tightened by a small wedge driven in beside it. The bait stick (*b*) should be about four inches in length, and large enough to fit easily into the hole in the centre of the top board. Next procure a stout bit of cord about eight inches in length. Tie one end to the tip of the switch and provide the other with a large double knot. A second knot should then be made, about an inch and a half above the first.   A piece of sucker wire is the next necessity. Its length should be about five feet, and its centre should be tied over the uppermost knot in the string.   If the bait is now in readiness, the trap may be set.   Bend down the switch until the end knot will pass through the hole in the centre of the board.   When it appears in the inside of the box, it should then be secured by the insertion of the top of the bait stick, as shown at (*b*).   This insertion need be only very slight, a sixteenth of an inch being all that is sufficient to prevent the knot from slipping back.   The spring is thus held in the position seen in the drawing, and the loose ends of the sucker wire should then be passed downward through the small holes and arranged in nooses at both openings of the box.   Our trap is now set, and the unlucky creature which attempts to move that bait from either approach, will bring its career to an untimely end.   The bait stick may be so delicately adjusted as to need only the slightest touch to dislodge it.   Such a fine setting is to be guarded against, however, being as likely to be sprung by a mouse as by a larger animal.   The setting is easily regulated, being entirely dependent upon the slight or firm insertion of the bait stick.   Among all the "modi operandi" in the construction of traps, there is scarcely one more simple than the principle embodied in this variety, and there is none more effective.

The box snare already described may be set by the same method, and indeed the principle may be applied to almost any trap, from the simplest snare described on page (52) to the largest dead-fall.

GROUND SNARES.

THE OLD-FASHIONED SPRINGLE.

This is the variety of snare which has been in very common use for ages, and has always been the one solitary example of a noose trap which our "boys' books" have invariably pounced upon for illustration.   For the capture of small birds it works very nicely; and as without it our list of traps would be incomplete, we will give an illustration of it as it appears when

set and ready for its work. In constructing the affair it is first
necessary to cut a flexible twig of willow or bramble about
eighteen inches in length, and form it into a loop as seen at (a),
securing the tips by a few circuits of string, and allowing the
larger end to project an inch or more beyond the other. This
loop, which is called the "spreader," should now be laid down
flat; and on the upper side of the large end and about an inch
from its tip, a notch should be cut as our illustration shows.
The spring should next be procured, and should consist of
a pliant, elastic switch, about four feet in length. A piece of
fish line about two feet long, should now be fastened to the tip
of the switch, and the loose end of the cord attached to a catch
piece of the shape shown at (b). This catch may be about an
inch and a half long, and should be whittled off to an edge on
one end, the string being attached at about its centre. A slipping noose, made from strong horse hair, or piece of fine

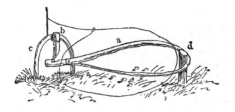

wire about two feet long, should now be fastened to the string
about two inches above the catch. Having the switch thus
prepared, it is ready to be inserted in the ground at the place
selected for the trap. When this is done, another small flexible twig about a foot in length should cut, and being sharpened at both ends, should be inserted in the ground in the form
of an arch (c), at about three feet distant from the spring,
and having its broad side toward it. Insert the notch of the
spreader exactly under the top of the arc, and note the spot
where the curved end of the former touches the ground. At
this point a peg (d) should be driven leaving a projecting portion of about two inches. The pieces are now ready to be

adjusted. Pass the curved end of the spreader over the peg, bringing the notched end beneath the arc with the notch uppermost. Draw down the catch piece, and pass it beneath the arc from the opposite side letting the bevelled end catch in the notch in the spreader, the other end resting against the upper part of the arc. Arrange the slipping noose over the spreader as our drawing indicates, bringing it *inside* the peg, as there shown, as otherwise it would catch upon it when the snare is sprung. Strew the bait, consisting of berries, bird-seed, or the like, *inside* the spreader, and all is ready. Presently a little bird is seen to settle on the ground in the neighborhood of the trap; he spies the bait and hopping towards it, gradually makes bold enough to alight upon the spreader, which by his weight immediately falls, the catch is released, the switch flies up, and the unlucky bird dangles in the air by the legs. If the trapper is near he can easily release the struggling creature before it is at all injured, otherwise it will flutter itself into a speedy death.

THE IMPROVED SPRINGLE.

The accompanying cut illustrates an improvement on the last mentioned trap, whereby it can be used for the capture of larger game, and with most excellent success. In place of the "spreader" a crotched stick is used, the crotch of which catches around the peg, the other end being supplied with a notch as  in the case of the spreader. On the upper side of this stick a small pasteboard platform is tacked, over which and beneath which the bait is thrown. Instead of the arc, a stout crotch stick is substituted. The noose should be at least ten inches in diameter and constructed of sucker wire. It should be arranged on the ground around the bait and inside of the peg. When the snare is set, the crotched end of the bait stick will thus rest near the earth, the notched end only being lifted in order to reach the catch piece. It is well to insert a few small sticks inside the edge of the noose in order to keep it in correct position. If properly set, the quail or partridge in approaching the trap will have to step *inside* the noose in order to reach the bait, and while thus regaling itself with a choice meal of oats, berries, or other delicacies, will be sure to press upon the bait stick either by pecking, or treading upon it, and will thus set the catch piece free, only to find itself secured by a grasp from which he will never escape alive. This is a very effectual snare ; but on account of its securing its victim by the legs and thus torturing them to death, it is to be deprecated. We would recommend in preference, those varieties already described as being fully as successful, and far less cruel. They effect almost instant death, either by broken necks or strangulation, and are in this regard among the most humane traps on record.

THE FIGURE FOUR GROUND SNARE.

For simplicity in construction there are few snare traps which can compare with this variety, although it is somewhat similar to those last mentioned, and like them, catches by the feet. The trap consists of three pieces. A catch piece about three inches long, a bait stick of about six inches, and a stout crotch of the proportionate size shown in our illustration, a glance at which will make the setting too clear to need description. Be

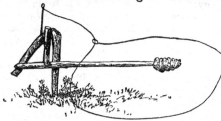

careful that the bait stick is set *fine* and rests *just beneath* the *tip* of the catch-piece so that a mere touch on the bait will release it. Arrange the noose as in the instance last de-scribed, and bait either as therein directed or with an apple or nubbin of corn, as our accompanying cut indicates. Always remembering that the noose should be sufficiently large to require the birds to step *inside* of it in order to reach the bait.

THE PLATFORM SNARE.

This odd invention will be found to work capitally as a game trap, and the only extra requisite necessary consists of a slab or light board about seven inches wide, and a foot in length. Having selected the spot for the trap, proceed to cut a stiff

switch abou. five feet in length, and having sharpened the larger end to a nice point, insert it firmly into the ground in a

slanting direction
as our drawing il-
lustrates. Next
bend down the
tip of the sapling,
and resting one
end of the board
on the ground,
catch the tip of
the switch against
the other end, as
our illustration al-
so shows. A little
experimenting will soon determine the right place for the board,
after which two pegs should be driven in the ground at its edge
to hold it against the pressure on the opposite end. This being
done fasten a wire noose to the tip of the switch, after which
the pen is the only thing required. This should be built of
simple little twigs arranged around three sides of the board,
leaving the front end open. To set the snare, lower the switch
and raising the board slightly at the back end, catch the tip of
the springer behind it, afterwards arranging the noose over the
platform, and scattering the bait inside. If the trap has been
constructed properly and set "fine" it will take but a very
slight weight on the platform to lower it from its bearing, the
weight of an ordinary bird being sufficient, and the springer
thus released will fly forward either catching its victim by the
neck or legs, as the case may be. It may sometimes be found
necessary to cut a slight notch in the end of the springer to
receive the board, but in every case it should be tried several
times in order to be sure that it works sensitively.

TRAPS

FOR FEATHERED GAME

BOOK III.

TRAPS FOR FEATHERED GAME.

MONG the following will be found the various net and cage traps commonly used in the capture of winged game, besides several other unique devices in the shape of box traps, etc., many of which are original with the author of this work and appear in the present volume for the first time in book form. Commonest among bird-catching machines, is the well known invention of

THE SIEVE TRAP.

This device certainly possesses one great advantage :—*it is not complicated.* Any one possessed of a sieve and a piece of string can get up the trap at two minutes' notice, and provided he has patience, and can wait for his little bird, he is almost sure to be rewarded for his pains,—if he wait long enough. This of course depends upon circumstances : when the birds are plenty and are not shy, it is a common thing to secure three or four at once in a very few minutes, while at other times an hour's patient waiting is unrewarded.

The trap consists only of a sieve tilted up on edge and thus propped in position by a slender stick. To this stick a string or thread is attached and the same carried to some near place of concealment, when the trapper may retire out of sight and watch for his "little bird." The ground beneath the sieve is strewn with bread crumbs, seed or other bait, and while the unsuspecting birds are enjoying their repast, the string is pulled and they are made prisoners. The sieve may be arranged with a spindle as described for the coop trap, page (68), and may thus be left to take care of itself. Where the birds are plenty and easily captured, the former method answers the purpose perfectly, but when tedious waiting is likely to ensue the self-acting trap is better.

THE BRICK TRAP.

This is a very old invention, and has always been one of the three or four stereotyped specimens of traps selected for publication in all Boys' Books. It is probably well known to most of our readers.

Take four bricks, and arrange them on the ground, as seen in our engraving, letting them rest on their *narrow* sides. If properly arranged, they should have a space between them, nearly as large as the broad surface of the brick. A small, forked twig of the shape shown in the separate drawing (*b*) having a small piece cut away from each side of the end, should then be procured. Next cut a slender stick, about four inches in length, bluntly

pointed at each end. A small plug with a flat top should now be driven into the ground, inside the trap, about three inches from either of the end bricks and projecting about two inches from the ground. The trap is then ready to be set. Lay the flat end of the forked twig over the top of the plug, with the forks pointing forward, or toward the end of the enclosure nearest the plug. The pointed stick should then be adjusted, placing one end on the flat end of the fork, over the plug, and the other beneath the fifth brick, which should be rested upon it. The drawing (*b*) clearly shows the arrangement of the pieces. The bait, consisting of berries, bird-seed, or other similar substances, should then be scattered on the ground on the inside of the inclosure. When the bird flies to the trap he will generally alight on the forked twig, which by his weight tilts to one side and dislodges the pieces, thus letting fall the sustained brick.

It is not intended to kill the bird, and when rightly constructed will capture it alive. Care is necessary in setting the topmost brick in such a position that it will fall aright, and completely

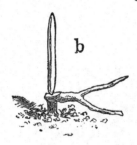

cover the open space. This is a very simple and effectual little contrivance, and can be made with a *box* instead of bricks, if desired. A piece of board may also be substituted for the top brick, and the enclosure beneath made larger by spreading the bricks further apart, thus making a more roomy dungeon for the captive bird.

THE COOP TRAP.

This is another excellent device for the capture of birds and large feathered game, and is used to a considerable extent by trappers throughout the country. Like the brick trap, it secures its victims without harm and furnishes the additional advantage of good ventilation for the encaged unfortunate. Any ordinary coop may be used in the construction of this trap, although the homely one we illustrate is most commonly employed on account of its simplicity and easy manufacture. It also does away with the troublesome necessity of carrying a coop to the trapping ground, as it can be made in a very few minutes with common rough hewn twigs by the clever use of the jack knife. The only remaining requisites consist of a few yards of very stout Indian twine, several small squares of brown pasteboard, a dozen tacks and a number of pieces of board five inches square, each one having a hole through its centre, as our engraving (*b*) indicates. Having these, the young trapper starts out with material sufficient for several coops, and if he is smart will find no difficulty in making and setting a dozen traps in a forenoon.

In constructing the coop, the first thing to be done is to cut four stout twigs about an inch in thickness and fifteen inches in length and tie them together at the corners, letting the knot come on the inside as our illustration (*a*) explains and leaving a loose

length of about two feet of string from each corner. This forms the base of the coop. Next collect from a number of twigs of about the same thickness, and from them select two more corresponding in length to the bottom pieces. Having placed the base of the coop on the ground, and collected the strings inside proceed to lay the two selected sticks across the ends of the uppermost two of the square, and directly above the lower two. Another pair of twigs exactly similar in size should then be cut and laid across the ends of the last two, and directly above the second set of the bottom portion, thus forming two squares of equal size, one directly over the other. The next pair of sticks should be a trifle shorter than the previous ones and should be placed a little inside the square. Let the next two be of the same size as the last and also rest a little inside of those beneath them, thus forming the commencement of the conical shape which our engraving presents. By thus continuing alternate layers of the two sticks cob-house fashion, each layer being closer than the one previous, the pyramid will be easily and quickly formed. After ten or a dozen sets have been laid in place, the arm should be introduced into the opening at the top, and the four cords drawn out, letting each one lay along its inside corner of the pyramid. Taking the strings loosely in the left hand and having the twigs in readiness, proceed to build up the sides until the opening at the top is reduced to only four or five inches across. The square board will now come into play. Pass the ends of the cords through the hole in its centre and rest the edge of the board on the top pair of sticks, taking care that it is the tip of the grain of the wood instead of its side, as otherwise it would be likely to crack from the pressure that is about to be brought upon it. Have ready a stout peg of hard wood, and laying it over the hole in the board, and between the strings, proceed to tie the latter as tightly as possible over it. By now turning the peg, the cords will be twisted and tightened and the various pieces of the coops will be drawn together with great firmness, in which state they may be secured by the aid of a tack driven in the top board against the end of the peg as shown at (*b*). Thus we have a neat and serviceable coop, which will last for many seasons. To *set* the affair it is necessary to cut three sticks of the shapes shown in our illustration. The prop piece is a slender forked twig about ten inches in length from the tip to the base of the crotch. The spindle is another hooked twig of the same length: the bait piece is quite similar to the latter, only an inch shorter and supplied with a square notch at the tip. It is also slightly whittled off on the upper side to receive the square of pasteboard or tin, which is to hold the bait and which may be easily fastened in place by a tack. All of these twigs may be easily found in any thicket by a little practice in searching. In setting the trap, it is only necessary to raise up one side of the coop to the height of the prop stick, insert the short arm of the spindle through the fork and beneath the edge of the coop. While holding it thus in position, hook the crotch of the bait stick around the lower piece at the back of the coop, and pushing the end of the spindle inside the coop, catch it in the notch of the bait stick where it will hold, and the trap is ready to be baited. The bait may consist of oats, wheat, "nannie berries" or the like, and should be strewn both on the platform and over the ground directly *beneath* and around it. If properly set, a mere peck at the corn will be sufficient to dislodge the pieces and the coop will fall over its captive. It is not an uncommon thing to find two or even three quail encaged in a trap of this kind at one fall, and after the first momentary fright is over, they seem to resign themselves to their fate and take to their confinement as naturally as if they had been brought up to it.

The method of setting the coop trap above described is a great improvement on the old style of setting, and is an improvement original with the author of this work. In the old method a semi-circular hoop of rattan is used in place of the bait stick above. The ends of the rattan are fastened to one of the lower back pieces of the coop, and the hoop is just large enough to fit inside the opening of the coop. This rattan rests just above the ground, and the spindle catches against its inside edge in place of the notch in the bait stick already described, the bait being scattered inside the hoop. When the bird approaches, it steps upon the rattan, and thus pressing it downward releases the spindle and the coop falls; but experience has shown the author that it does not always secure its intruders, but as often falls upon their backs and sends them off limping to regain their lost senses. By the author's improvement it will be seen that the whole body of the bird *must* be *beneath* the coop before the bait sticks can be reached and that when properly set it is absolutely certain to secure its victim. The author can recommend it as infallible, and he feels certain that any one giving both methods a fair trial will discard the old method as worthless in comparison.

THE BAT FOWLING NET.

With English bird-catchers this contrivance is in common use, but so far as we know it has not been utilized to any great extent in this country. It is chiefly used at night by the aid of a lantern, and large numbers of sparrows and other birds are often secured.

Our illustration gives a very clear idea of the net, which may be constructed as follows: Procure two light flexible poles, about eight feet in length; to the tip of each a cord should be attached, and the same secured to the middle of the pole, having drawn down the tip to the bend, shown in our engraving. The two bent ends should now be attached together by a hinge of leather. A piece of mosquito netting is next in order, and it should be of such a size as to cover the upper bent halves of the poles, as seen in the illustration—the bottom edge being turned up into a bag, about ten inches in depth. The contrivance is now complete, and is used as follows: Three persons are generally required, and a dark night is chosen. Hay stacks, evergreens, and thick bushes offer a favorite shelter to numerous small birds, and it is here that they are sought by the bird-hunters. A breezy night is preferable, as the birds perch low, and are not so easily startled by unusual sounds.

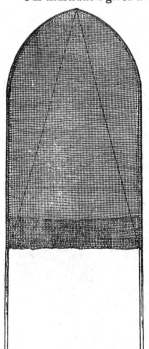

Great caution, however, is used in the approach. One party holds the light, which is generally a *dark* lantern, another takes the net, and the third arms himself with a switch with which to beat the bushes. The net is first held upright about a foot from the bush, and the light thrown upon the back of it. The bush is then moderately beaten, and the birds affrighted and bewildered fly against the net, which is instantly closed. The bird is thus captured, and when a full roost can be discovered a large number may be taken in a single night. The lantern should be closed while not in actual use, and everything should be done as quietly as possible. The dark lantern in itself is useful without the net. The light often so bewilders the bird that it flies directly in the face of the lantern and flutters to the ground, where it may be easily taken with the hand.

THE CLAP NET.

In Asia, Africa, South America and Europe, this trap is a
common resource for the capture of wild birds of various kinds.
It may be called a "decoy" trap, from the fact that "call birds"
are generally used in connection with it. They are placed at
distances around the trap, and attract the wild birds to the
spot by their cries. These birds are especially trained for
the purpose, but almost any tamed bird that chirps will
attract its mates from the near neighborhood, and answer the
purpose very well. Sometimes the "decoys" are entirely
dispensed with, and the "bird whistle" used in their stead.
This will be described hereafter, and inasmuch as the training
of a "decoy" would be a rather difficult matter, we rather
recommend the use of the bird whistle. The skill and absolute
perfection of mimicry which is often attained by bird fanciers,
with the use of this little whistle, is something surprising.

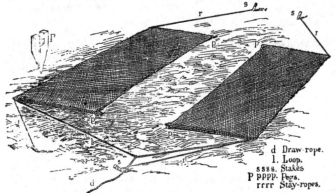

d Draw·rope.
l. Loop.
s s s s. Stakes
P pppp. Pegs.
rrrr Stay-ropes.

No matter what the species of bird—whether crow, bobolink,
thrush or sparrow, the song or call is so exactly imitated as to
deceive the most experienced naturalist, and even various birds
themselves. Of course this requires practice, but even a tyro
may soon learn to use the whistle to good advantage.

The clap net commonly used, is a large contrivance—so large
that several hundred pigeons are often caught at once. It
is "sprung" by the bird-hunter, who lies in ambush watching
for the game. The net is generally constructed as follows, and
may be made smaller if desired:—

Procure two pieces of strong thread netting, each about fifteen feet in length, and five feet in width. Four wooden rods one inch in thickness and five feet in length are next required. These may be constructed of pine, ash, or any other light wood, and one should be securely whipped to each end of the netting.

Now by the aid of a gimlet or a red-hot iron, the size of a slate pencil, bore a hole through one end of every piece one inch from the tip, taking care that the ends selected lay on the same side of the net. The other extremities of the four poles should be supplied, each with a large screw eye. Four pegs are next in order—one of which is shown separate at (*P*). It should be about eight inches in length, and three inches in width, and an inch in thickness, and sharpened to a point at one end. The other end should be supplied with a notch two inches in depth and of such a width as will easily secure the perforated end of one of the poles already described. By the use of the gimlet or a red-hot nail, a hole should now be bored through the side of every peg across the centre of the notch for the reception of a wire pin or smooth nail.

The nets may now be rolled up on the poles, and the trapper may thus easily carry them to his selected trapping ground. This should be smooth and free from stones and irregularities. Unroll the nets and spread them flatly on the ground, as seen in the illustration. Let the perforated ends of the poles be innermost, and allow a space of six feet between the inner edges of the nets. Draw the net flatly on the ground, and drive one of the notched pegs at each of the inside corners, securing the poles into the slots by the aid of the wire pins or nails. Next cut four stakes eight or ten inches long. The places for these may be seen by a look at our engraving. Each one should be inserted *five feet* distant from the notched peg, and *exactly* on a line with the *inside* edge of the net—one for each corner. They should slant from the net in every case. To each one of these stakes a stay-rope should be secured, and the other end passed through the screw eye of the nearest pole, drawing the string tightly, so as to stretch the net perfectly square. Next, take a piece of cord, about twenty feet in length, and fasten it across the ends of the net into the screw eyes in the poles. This is the loop to which the draw-string is attached, and either end of the net may be chosen for this purpose. To this loop, and a *little one side of the middle*, the draw-string should be fastened. If secured exactly in the middle of the loop, the two nets will *strike* when the draw-rope is pulled, whereas when adjusted a little to one side, the nearest net will move a trifle faster than the other, and they will overlap neatly and without striking—completely covering the ground between them. When the trap is spread the draw-rope should extend to some near shelter where the bird-catcher may secrete himself from view. Spreading the bait on the ground between the nets, and arranging his call birds at the proper distances, he awaits his opportunity of springing his nets. At the proper minute, when the ground is dotted with his game, he pulls the draw-string, and the birds are secured.

Immense numbers of wild fowl are often captured in this way.

The "bird whistle," already alluded to, is often used with good effect, it being only sufficient to attract the birds to such a proximity to the net as will enable them to spy the bait, after which their capture is easily effected.

THE BIRD WHISTLE.

This instrument, also known as the prairie whistle, is clearly shown in our illustration. It is constructed as follows: First, procure a piece of morocco or thin leather. From it cut a circular piece one inch and a quarter in diameter. Through the centre of this disc, cut a round hole, one-third of an inch in diameter. A semi-circular piece of tin is next required. It should be of the shape of an arc, as seen in our illustration; its width  across the ends being about three-quarters of an inch, and its entire length being pierced with a row of fine holes. Next procure a piece of thin sheet India rubber or gold beater's skin. Cut a strip about an inch in length by half an inch in width, and lay one of its long edges directly across the opening in the leather disc. Fold the leather in half (over the rubber), and draw the latter tightly. Next lay on the arc of tin in the position shown in the illustration, and by the aid of a fine needle and thread sew it through the holes, including both leather and rubber in the stitches. When this is done, the whistle is complete. If the gold beater's skin is not attainable, a good substitute may be found in the thin outer membrane of the leaf of a tough onion or leak, the pulp being scraped away.

To use the whistle, place it against the roof of the mouth, tin side up, and with the edge of the rubber towards the front. When once wet, it will adhere to the roof of the mouth, and by skilful blowing, it can be made to send forth a most surprising variety of sounds. The quack of the duck and the song of the thrush may be made to follow each other in a single breath, and the squeal of a pig or the neigh of a horse are equally within its scope. In short, there is scarcely any animal, whether bird or quadruped, the cry of which may not be easily imitated by a skilful use of the prairie whistle, or, indeed, as it might with propriety be called, the "menagerie whistle."

THE WILD GOOSE TRAP.

In our northern cold regions, where the wild geese and ptarmigan flock in immense numbers, this trap is commonly utilized. It consists merely of a large net fifty feet in length, and fifteen in width, arranged on a framework, and propped in a slanting position by two poles, after the manner of the sieve trap. It is generally set on the ice; and the trapper, after attaching his strings to the props, and sprinkling his bait at the foot of the net, retires to a distance to await his chances. Tame geese are often used as decoys, and sometimes the bird whistle already described is used for the same purpose. For the capture of the ptarmigan, the bait consists of a heap of gravel. It is hard to imagine a less tempting allurement, but, as the food of the birds during the winter is sapless and hard, it becomes necessary for them to swallow a considerable amount of gravel to promote digestion. The great depth of the snow renders this commodity very scarce during the winter season; and the Indians, taking advantage of this fact, succeed in capturing immense numbers of the game in nets by the use of that simple allurement. The gravel is packed on the surface of a pile of snow, placed under the centre of the net, and the draw-string is carried to some neighboring shrubbery or place of concealment, where the trapper can always get at it without being seen by the birds under the net.

When everything is thus prepared, the hunters start out into the adjacent woods and willows, and drive their game toward the nets. This is generally an easy matter, and, no sooner do the birds come in sight of the heap of gravel, than they fly towards it *en masse*, and the ground beneath the net is soon covered with the hungry game. The hunter then goes to the end of the line, and, with a sudden pull, hauls down the stakes : the net falls over the birds, and they are prisoners.

Hundreds of ptarmigan are often thus caught by a single sweep of the net. The trap is simply arranged, and may be constructed on a reduced scale for smaller birds, if desired.

THE TRAP CAGE.

Among bird-catchers generally, this is the favorite and most universal trap; and, where a *decoy* bird is used, it is particularly successful. The cage is arranged in two compart-

ments, one above the other, — the lower one being occupied
by the call-birds. The making of the cage requires considerable ingenuity and much patience ; and, for the benefit of those
who may desire to exercise that patient ingenuity, we will subjoin a few hints, which may help them along in their efforts.
For an ordinary cage, the height should be about one foot,
the broad sides the same, and the top and other two sides
eight inches. First cut four corner uprights. These should
be three-quarters of an inch square, and one foot in length.
Next cut a bottom board of pine, twelve inches by eight
inches, and one inch in thickness. From each of its corners,
cut a small cube of the wood, exactly three-quarters of an inch

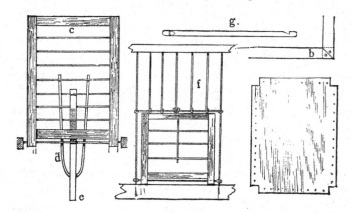

square, thus leaving four notches, which will exactly receive
the ends of the uprights, as seen at (*a*). Before adjusting
these pieces, the four sides of the boards should be pierced
with small holes, as is also shown in the diagram (*a*). These
may be punched with a brad-awl, and should be about half
an inch apart, and three-eighths of an inch from the edge of
the board. Each one of the uprights may then be secured
in place by two long brads, one being hammered each way
into each side of the notch. Next proceed to cut four more
of the square sticks. Two of these should be one foot in
length, and the remaining two eight inches. The corners of
these should now be neatly bevelled off, so as to fit after the
manner of a picture-frame. They should then be attached to

the upper ends of the uprights by a brad through the corner of each, as seen at (*b*), the dotted lines indicating the end of the upright beneath. These sticks should likewise be pierced with holes to correspond with those in the bottom board, and running up and down in the direction of the wires.

The middle tier of braces are next required. Two of these should be ten and a half inches in length, and the other two six and a-half, and the ends should be perfectly smooth. These should now be punched with holes corresponding with those above, after which they may be inserted between the uprights as seen in the engraving, and secured by a brad at each end.

The trap door is shown separate at (*c*). The side sticks should be eight inches in length, and one-half an inch square, and the top and bottom sticks five inches in length. They should be set in *between* the side sticks, and the lower one should be secured about half an inch above the lower ends of the uprights, as seen in the illustration. The holes should be made in the side pieces, and the wire run across from side to side, as shown. Annealed iron, or copper wire is best for this purpose. The door should now be pivoted or hinged at the top of the cage, between the long sides, in such a position as that the top end shall rest on one of the narrow upper edges of the cage. A stiff wire should be used for the hinge, being passed through the top pieces of the cage into the lower ends of the door pieces. The cage may now be wired throughout. This is an easy matter, if the holes are properly made. About thirty yards of the wire will be required: iron wire is generally used. It should be about the size of a hair-pin, and should work easily. Commence by passing it from the under side of the bottom board through one of the holes next to the corner. Pass the wire upward, through the centre braces, again upward through the top piece and across to the opposite broad side and corresponding hole. From this point it should pass downwards, through centre brace, and again through the bottom. Draw the wire tightly and passing it upward through the hole next to it, bring it over the top of the cage and around again to the bottom edge from which it started. Continue thus until the hinge of the door is reached; after which the wire should be passed up and down on the same side and thus carried around the small end of the cage until it finally meets at the door hinge on the opposite side. The two halves of the cage should now be separated by a grating of wire, as seen in the main illustration. This may be accomplished either by passing the wire from side to side, around the base of each upright wire, or an additional horizontal row of holes below the others may be punched for the purpose. The door through which the call-bird is introduced should next be made in the bottom section. There are two ways of doing this : one method consists in sawing a hole three inches square in the bottom board of the cage ; and a cover consisting of a piece of tin is made to slide beneath the heads of four tacks, two of which are placed on each side of the opening. This form of door is perhaps the simplest of the two. The other is shown separate at (f), together with its mode of attachment.

It consists of two side pieces of wood, about a third of an inch square, and three inches in length, and two shorter ones, two inches in length. These are arranged into a square framework by a board in each corner. Four holes are to be pierced in each side piece, at equal distances. Commencing at the top, the door should then be wired as directed for the cage. The lowest hole on each side should be left open for a separate piece of wire. The cage should now receive attention. The broad side is generally selected for the door. Find the seven centre wires and connect them across the middle by another horizontal bit of wire. This may be easily done with a pair of pincers, by compressing a loop at each end of the wire around the two which run perpendicularly at its ends. When this is performed the five intermediate wires should be cut off about a quarter of an inch below the horizontal wire, and the projecting tips looped back over the cross piece, and made fast by the pincers. The lower parts of the upright wires may now be cut off close to the board. We will now take up the door. Pass a piece of wire through the holes at the bottom, clap the door over the opening, and loop the ends of the projecting wire loosely around the upright wires at each side. This will allow the door to slide easily up and down. Another wire should now be interlaced downwards through the centre of the door, and bent into a ring at the top. Let the door rest on the bottom of the cage, and, while in this position, adjust the ring at the top around the central wire directly behind it. The door is then complete, and, if properly made, will look neat and work easily.

The "trap" at the top of the cage is next in order. To complete this it is first necessary to interweave a *stiff* wire loop, as seen at (d). The loop should extend on the *inside* of the lower piece of the door and about two inches below it. The

spring power consists of a piece of stiff hoop-skirt wire, inter-
woven between the wires of the top of the cage, and those of
the door, while the latter is shut. · The force of this will be
sufficient to bring down the door with a snap; and for further
security a catch, such as is described in page (88), may be added
if desired.

The spindle is next required. This is shown at (*g*), and
consists of a small perch of wood seven inches in length, and
notched at each end. In setting the trap, the door should be
raised as seen in the main illustration. One of the notches in
the spindle should now be caught beneath the loop and the
other around one of the central wires in the end of the cage.
The bait, consisting of a berry, bird-seed, or what-not, may be
either fastened to the spindle or placed beneath on the wires.
The call-bird having been introduced, the trap may now be left
to itself. If the call-bird is well trained it will not be many
minutes before the birds of the neighborhood will be attracted
to the spot by its cries. Ere long one less cautious than the
rest will be seen to perch upon the top of the cage. He soon
discovers the bait, and alighting upon the perch, throws it
asunder, and in an instant the trap door closes over its captive.
The cage is sometimes constructed double, having two compart-
ments beneath for call-birds, and two traps above, in general
resembling two of the single traps placed side by side. The
decoy bird is not an absolute necessity to the success of the
trap. Many birds are caught simply by the bait alone. The
trap cage, when constructed on a larger scale, is often successfully employed in the capture of the owl. In this case it is
baited with a live mouse or bird, and set during the evening in
a conspicuous place. A trap working on this principle, being
especially adapted to the capture of the owl, will be noticed
hereafter.

THE SPRING NET TRAP.

Although slightly complicated in construction, our next illustration presents one of the prettiest bird traps on record, and
may be made in the following manner, and by frequently refer-
ring to the picture, our explanation will be easily understood.

The first step is to make or procure a low flat box, about
fifteen inches long, by ten inches in width, with a depth of
about two inches. Next fasten an interior box, of the same

height, leaving a space of about three-quarters of an inch between them all round. A platform should now be made. Let
it be of such a size that it will just fit in the interior box, with a
very slight space all around its edge. It should then be pivoted in the upper part of this box by two small slender pins, one
being driven through into its edge, at the centre of each end.
Let it be sensitively poised. The next thing to be done, is to
arrange the spindle and catch. The latter should consist of a
tack or small bit of wood fastened on the middle of the platform,
about an inch from one end, as seen both in the main illustration and in the diagram at (*b*).

The spindle should consist of a flat piece of wood, secured
with a leather hinge to the edge of the outside box, directly op-

posite the catch. Let it be long enough to reach and barely
hold itself beneath the catch. When thus in its position, two
small plugs should next be driven into the edge of the inner
box, one on each side of the spindle, thus holding it in place.
A glance at our illustration makes this clear. The netting and
"hoop" are next in order. The hoop should consist of an iron
wire of the diameter of common telegraph wire.

For a box of the size we have given, a length of about twenty-
eight inches will be found to answer. Before making the hoop,
however, its hinges should be ready for it. Two screw eyes,
or staples of bent wire should be driven into the bottom of the
box between the two walls, one in the exact middle of each
side. The iron wire should now be bent so as to fit round and
settle into the space between the boxes, letting each end rest

over the screws in the bottom. It will be found that there will be
enough surplus wire on each end to form into a loop with the pincers. These loops should be passed through the screws or rings
already inserted, and then pinched together; the hinge will thus
be made, and will appear as at (c). If properly done, they should
allow the hoop to pass freely from one end of the box to the other,
and settle easily between the partitions. If this hinge should
prove too complicated for our young readers, they may resort
to another method, which, although not so durable, will answer
very well. In this case the wire will only need to reach to the
exact middle of the long sides. No surplus being necessary, a
length of twenty-six inches will be exactly right. On each end
a short loop of tough Indian twine should be tied. By now
fastening these loops to the bottom of the box with tacks, in
the place of screws, it will form a hinge which will answer the
purpose of the more complicated one.

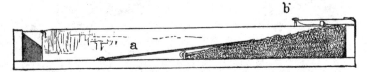

The netting should consist of common mosquito gauze, or, if
this cannot be had, any thin cloth may be substituted. It should
be sewed fast to the iron wire, from hinge to hinge, and then,
with the hoops resting in its groove, the netting should be
drawn over the platform, and tacked to the bottom of the
groove, on its remaining half. It should rest loosely over the
platform to allow plenty of space for the bird.

But one more addition, and the trap is finished. We have
mentioned the use of elastics in other varieties: they are of
equal use here, and should be attached to the hoop as seen at
(a) in the section drawing, the remaining ends being fastened to
the bottom of the groove, as there indicated. These elastics
should be placed on both sides, and stretched to such a tension
as will draw the hoop quickly from one side to the other.

It will now be easy to set the trap. Draw the hoop back to
the opposite end, tucking the netting into the groove; lower
the spindle over it, resting it between the two little plugs, and
securing its end beneath the catch on the platform. If the bait,

consisting of bread-crumbs, berries, insects, or the like, be now sprinkled on the platform, the trap is ready for its feathered victim. It will easily be seen that the slightest weight on *either* side of this poised platform will throw the catch from the end of the spindle, and release the hoop and the platform in an instant is covered by the net, capturing whatever unlucky little bird may have chanced to jump upon it. This is a very pretty little trap, and will well repay the trouble of making it.

A SIMPLER NET TRAP.

Much ingenuity has been displayed in the construction of bird traps of various kinds, but often the ingenuity has been misplaced, and the result has been so complicated as to mar its usefulness for practical purposes. The examples of net traps presented in this volume are so simple that the merest tyro can readily understand them. What can be more so than the present example, and yet it is as sure in its effect, and *surer* than those other varieties of more complicated construction. One necessary element in a trap of any kind is, that the bearings are

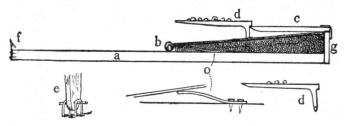

slight and that they spring easily. To obtain this requisite it is necessary to overcome friction as much as possible, using only a small number of pieces, and having as few joints and hinges only as are absolutely necessary. The present variety possesses advantages on this account. It is constructed somewhat on the principle of the ordinary steel trap, and also resembles in other respects the one we have just described, although much simpler. We give only a section drawing, as this will be sufficient. The long side of a flat board of about eight by sixteen inches is shown at (*a*); (*b*) indicates the loops of a bent wire, to which the netting is attached, as in the trap just described, the loops being fastened to the board as in the other variety; (g) consists of a small bit of wood an inch or so in length and half an inch in width. It should be tacked on to the middle of the one end of the board and project about a half inch above the surface. To the top of this the spindle (c) should be attached by a leather or staple hinge. The spindle should be of light pine, five inches in length and a quarter of an inch square, bevelled; on the under side of one end (d) is the catch or bait piece, and should be whittled out of a shingle or pine stick of the shape shown, the width being about a half an inch or less. One side should be supplied with a slight notch for the reception of the spindle, and the other should project out two or three inches, being covered on the top with a little platform of pasteboard, tin, or thin wood either glued or tacked in place. To attach this piece to the main board, two small wire staples may be used, one being inserted into the bottom end of the piece and the other being hooked through it, and afterward tacked to the bottom of the trap, thus forming a loop hinge. Another method is to make a hole through the lower tip of the bait piece by the aid of a red-hot wire, as seen at (d), afterwards inserting a pin and overlapping its ends with two staples driven into the bottom board, as shown at (e). In our last mentioned net trap the spring power consisted of rubber elastic, and the same may be used in this case, if desired, but by way of variety we here introduce another form of spring which may be successfully employed in the construction of traps of various kinds. It is shown at (o) and consists merely of a piece of tempered hoop iron, so bent as to act with an upward pressure. It should be about three inches long by half an inch wide. About three-quarters of an inch should be allowed for the two screws by which it is to be attached to the board. The rest should be bent upward and thus tempered by first heating almost to redness, and then cooling in cold water.

One of these springs should be fastened to the board on each side, directly under the wire and quite near the hinge, in the position shown in the main drawing. Now draw back the net, lower the spindle and catch its extremity in the notch of the bait piece, and the trap is set as in our illustration. Sprinkle the bait on the platform, and lay the machine on the ground where birds are known to frequent; and it is only a matter of a few hours or perhaps minutes, before it will prove its efficacy. In order to prevent the bird from raising the wire and thereby escaping, it is well to fasten a little tin catch (f) at the end of the board. This will spring over the wire and hold it in its place.

THE UPRIGHT NET TRAP.

The following is another novelty in the way of a bird-trap, somewhat similar to the one we have just described, in its manner of working.

Procure two pieces of board about a foot square. Nail one to the edge of the other, as represented in our engraving. A stout wire is the next requisite. It should be about thirty inches long, and bent either into a curve or into two corners, making three equal sides. Each end of the wire should then be bent into a very small loop for the hinge. On to this wire the netting should then be secured as in the two previous examples, after which the ends of the wire may be tied with string or hinged on wire staples into the angle of the two boards, as seen in our illustration. Allow the wire now to lie flat on the bottom board, and then proceed to tack the netting around the edges of the upright board. Two elastics should next be fastened to the wire on each side, securing their loose ends to the bottom of the trap. They should be tightly drawn so as to bring the wire down with a snap. The spindle of this trap should be about eight or nine inches long, square and slender,—the lower end being flattened, and the upper end secured to the top edge of the upright board by a hinge of leather or string. An excellent hinge may be made with a piece of leather an inch and a half long, by half an inch in width, one half of the length being tied around the end of the spindle, and the other tacked on to the upper edge of the board.

The platform is given by itself at (a) in the same picture. It may be made of very thin wood—cigar box wood, for instance, or even thick pasteboard. It consists of three pieces. The piece which is hinged into the angle of the boards should be about three inches in length ; the platform piece ought not to be more than four inches square, and the upright piece only long enough to reach the tip of the spindle when the platform is raised, as shown in our engraving. The hinge piece should be cut to an edge on that end where the leather is fastened, the opposite end being bevelled off in order that the platform may rest and be tacked or glued firmly upon it. The diagram (a) will make this all very clear.

When the platform is all made and fastened in its place, the trap may be set. Draw the hoop back as far as possible, and lower the spindle over its edge, catching it behind the upright stick on the platform. If the trap is properly constructed, the pressure of the spindle on the platform will suffice to hold it up as seen in our illustration. The upright stick on the back of the platform should never be more than an inch and a half from the back of the trap. If need be, a slight notch may be made in the end of the spindle and a small tack driven into the back of the upright stick to correspond to it. By thus fitting the notch under the head of the tack, it will be sure to hold the platform in the

right position. But it should be carefully tested before setting, to see that it springs easily.

When thus set sprinkle the bait on the platform, scattering a little also on the bottom of the trap and on the ground directly around it. The little birds will soon spy the tempting morsels, and alighting on the trap are misled, and the slightest peck or pressure on the platform where the bait is most bounteously spread brings down the wire and net with a *snap*, and the little creature is secured without harm.

Our next illustration shows another method of constructing the platform. It should be about three or four inches square, and on the middle of one of its edges the upright catch piece should be fastened. This piece, as will be seen in our engraving, should be cut spreading at the bottom so as to admit of being secured to the platform by two brads, the tip being cut to a point. The total length of this piece should not be over two and a half inches. When tacked in place, a third brad should be inserted between the other two and exactly in the centre of the side of the platform. This latter brad is to act as the pivot, or hinge, and should project about a quarter of an inch, as seen at (*a*). On the opposite edge of the platform another larger brad should be driven, having its end filed to a blunt point, as in (*b*). If the filing would be too tedious, a plug of hard wood of the required shape would answer every purpose. The upright props which support the platform should be

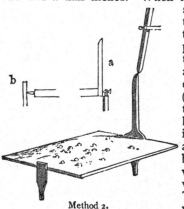

Method 2.

cut of thin wood. Let one be an inch and a half long and half an inch wide, the other being an inch in length. Each should have one end whittled to a point, which will admit of its being inserted in a gimlet hole in the bottom of the trap. These gimlet holes should be made at least half an inch in depth. Make the first at about an inch or so from the back of the trap. Into this insert the shorter pieces, broadside front. Lay the pivot brad of the platform on the top of this piece and insert over it a small wire staple, as seen at (*a*). Elevate the platform evenly and determine the spot for the other gimlet hole, which should be directly beneath the point of the filed brad. Be sure that it is in the middle of the board, so that the platform may set squarely, and be perfectly parallel with the sides. Insert the remaining prop in its place, and the platform is complete. The overhanging spindle now requires a little attention. This should be whittled off on each side, bringing it to a point at the tip. On each side of the spindle a long plug should then be driven into the back piece, as our illustration shows. These should be far enough apart to allow the spindle to pass easily between them. The *setting* of the trap is plainly shown in our engraving. The spindle being lowered between the plugs is caught finely on the tip of the catch-piece. The blunt point at the opposite end of the platform should have a slight hollow made for it in the prop against which it presses. If the platform be now strewn with bait, the little machine is ready. It is certainly very simple and will be found very effective.

THE BOX OWL TRAP.

The use of a box trap for the capture of an owl is certainly an odd idea, but we nevertheless illustrate a contrivance which has been successfully used for that purpose.

The box in this case should be of the proportions shown in our engraving, and well ventilated with holes, as indicated. (This ventilation is, by-the-way, a good feature to introduce in *all* traps.) Having made or selected a suitable box—say, fourteen or more inches wide, provided with a cover, working on a hinge—proceed to fasten on the outside of the lid a loop of stiff wire, bent in the shape shown at (*e*). This may be fastened to the cover by means of small staples, or even tacks, and should project over the edge about two inches. When this is done, the lid should be raised to the angle shown in our illustration, and the spot where the end of the wire loop touches the back of the box should be marked and a slit cut through the wood at this place, large enough for the angle of the loop to pass through. Two elastics should now be fastened to the inside of the box, being secured to the bottom at the side, and the other to the edge of the cover, as seen in the illustration. They should be sufficiently strong to draw down the cover quickly. The perch, or spindle, should consist of a light stick of wood, as shown at (*b*,) one end provided with a slight notch, and the other fastened to the inside of the front of the box by a string or leather hinge, (*c*,) keeping the notch on the *upper* side of the stick. It will be now seen that by opening the cover, until the loop enters through the groove, and by then hooking the notch in the spindle *under* the loop as seen at (*a*) the trap will be set, and if properly done it will be found that a very slight weight on the spindle will set it free from the loop and let the cover down with swiftness.

To secure the cover in place a small tin catch should now be applied to the front edge of the box, as shown in the illustration. A piece of tin two inches in length by a half an inch in breadth will answer for this purpose. One end should be bent down half an inch at a pretty sharp angle, and the other attached by two tacks, to the edge of the box, in the position shown in the cut. This precaution will effectually prevent the escape of whatever bird, large or small, the trap may chance to secure. It is a necessary feature of the trap, as without it the elastics might be torn asunder and the lid thereby easily raised.

This trap may be baited in a variety of ways. As it is particularly designed for a *bird* trap, it is well to sprinkle the bottom of the box with berries, bird-seed, small insects, such as

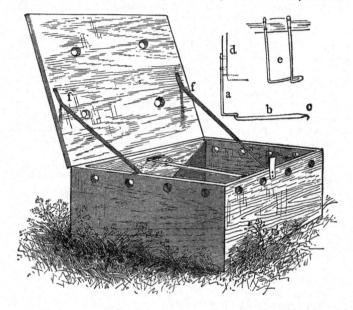

crickets, grasshoppers, etc. These latter are very apt to jump out, and it may be well to fasten one or two of them to the bottom with a pin through the body, just behind the head.

There are many kinds of birds which live almost exclusively on insects; and as this bait is of rather a lively kind, there is scarcely any other method to retain them in their position. A bird on approaching this trap will almost irresistibly alight on the perch, and if not at *first*, it is generally sure to do so before long. If desired, a pasteboard platform may be fastened on the top of the perch with small tacks, and the bait scattered upon it. This will act in the same manner, and might, perhaps, be a trifle more certain. We will leave it to our readers to experiment upon.

We have given this variety the name of "owl-trap," because it may be used with success in this direction. When set for this purpose, it should be baited with a live mouse, small rat or bird, either fastened to the bottom of the trap, if a bird, or set in with the trap inclosing it, if a mouse. A small bird is the preferable bait, as it may be easily fastened to the bottom of the box by a string, and as a general thing is more sure to attract the attention of the owl by its chirping.

The trap should be set in an open, conspicuous spot, in the neighborhood where the owls in the night are heard to "hoot." The chances are that the box will contain an owl on the following morning.

This bird is a very interesting and beautiful creature, and if our young reader could only catch one, and find rats and mice enough to keep it well fed, he would not only greatly diminish the number of rats in his neighborhood, but he would realize a great deal of enjoyment in watching and studying the habits of the bird.

Should it be difficult to supply the above mentioned food, raw meat will answer equally well. The bird should either be kept in a cage or inclosure and in the latter case, its wings will require to be clipped.

THE BOX BIRD TRAP.

Here we have another invention somewhat resembling the foregoing. Our engraving represents the arrangement of the parts as the trap appears when set.

The box may be of almost any shape. A large sized cigar box has been used with excellent success, and for small birds is just the thing. The cover of the box in any case should work on a hinge of some sort. The trap is easily made. The first thing to be done is to cut an upright slot, about two inches in length, through the centre of the backboard, commencing at the upper edge. To the inside centre edge of the cover a small square strap, about four inches in length, should then be secured. It should be so adjusted as that one-half shall project toward the inside of the box, as seen in the illustration, and at the same time pass easily through the slot beneath where the cover is closed. The lid should now be supplied with elastics as described in the foregoing. Next in order comes the bait stick. Its shape is clearly shown in our illustration, and it may be either cut in one piece or consist of two parts joined together

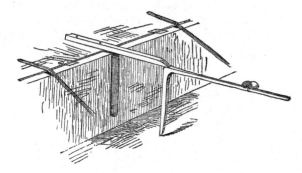

at the angle. To the long arm the bait should be attached and the upright portion should be just long enough to suspend the cover in a position on a line with the top of the box. The trap may now be set, as seen in our illustration, and should be supplied with the necessary tin catch, described in the foregoing.

THE PENDENT BOX TRAP.

This invention is original with the author of this work, and when properly made and set will prove an excellent device for the capture of small birds.

The general appearance of the trap, as set, is clearly shown in our illustration. A thin wooden box is the first requisite, it should be about a foot square and six inches in depth, and supplied with a close fitting cover, working on hinges. The sides should then be perforated with a few auger holes for purposes of ventilation.

Two elastics are next in order, and they should be attached to the cover and box, one on each side, as shown at (a.) They should be drawn to a strong tension, so as to hold the cover firmly against the box.

The mechanism of the trap centres in the bait stick, which differs in construction from any other described in this book.

It should be made about the size of a lead pencil, and eleven inches or so in length, depending of course upon the size of the box.

It should then be divided in two pieces by a perfectly flat cut, the longer part being six inches in length. This piece should be attached to the back board of the box by a small string and a tack, as shown at (*c*), its end being bluntly pointed. Its attachment should be about five inches above the bottom board, and in the exact centre of the width of the back.

Near the flat end of the other piece the bait consisting of a berry or other fruit, should be secured, and the further extremity of the stick should then be rounded to a blunt point. The trap is now easily set. Raise the lid and lift the long stick to the position given in the illustration. Adjust the flat end of the bait stick against that of the former, and allow the

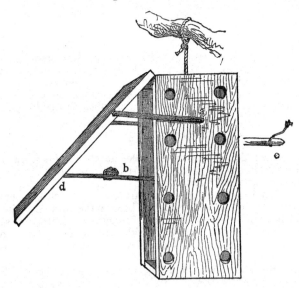

pressure of the lid to bear against the blunt point of the short stick at (*d*), as shown in the illustration, a straight dent being made in the cover to receive it, as also in the back of the box for the other piece. If properly constructed, this pressure will be sufficient to hold the sticks end to end, as our engraving

represents, and the trap is thus set. The slightest weight on
the false perch thus made will throw the parts asunder, and the
cover closes with a snap.

The greatest difficulties in constructing the trap will be
found in the bearings of the bait sticks (*b*), the ends of which
must be perfectly flat and join snugly, in order to hold themselves together. The box may now be suspended in a tree by
the aid of a string at the top. The first bird that makes bold
enough to alight on the perch is a sure captive, and is secured
without harm. If desired, the elastic may be attached to the
inside of the cover, extending to the back of the box, as seen
in the initial at the head of this chapter. If the elastic in
any event shows tendencies toward relaxing, the tin catch described on page 88 should be adjusted to the lower edge of
the box to insure capture.

THE HAWK TRAP.

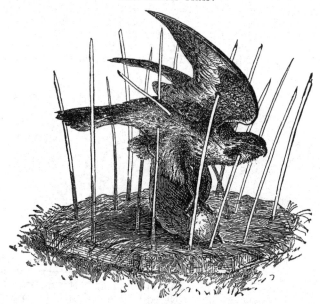

Our illustration represents a hawk in a sad plight. The
memory of a recent feast has attracted it to the scene of many of

its depredations: but the ingenious farmer has at last outwitted his feathered foe and brought its sanguinary exploits to a timely end. This trap is a "Yankee" invention and has been used with great success in many instances where the hawk has become a scourge to the poultry yard. The contrivance is clearly shown in an illustration, consisting merely of a piece of plank two feet square, set with stiff perpendicular pointed wires.

This affair was set on the ground in a conspicuous place, the board covered with grass, and the nice fat Poland hen which was tied to the centre proved a morsel too tempting for the hawk to resist. Hence the "fell swoop" and the fatal consequences depicted in our illustration. The owl has also been successfully captured by the same device.

THE WILD DUCK NET.

Following will be found two examples of traps in very common use for the capture of wild ducks, and in the region of Chesapeake bay, immense numbers of the game are annually taken by their aid. The first is the well known net trap, so extensively used in nearly all countries, both for the capture of

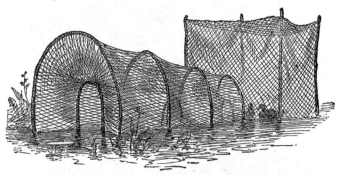

various kinds of fish as well as winged game. Our illustration gives a very clear idea of the construction of the net, and an elaborate description is almost superfluous. It consists of a graduated series of hoops covered by a net work. From each a converging net extends backward ending in a smaller hoop which is held in position by cords extending therefrom to the next larger hoop. The depth of these converging nets should extend backward about three or four feet from the large hoop, and the distance between these latter should be about five feet. The length of the net should be about twenty feet, terminating in a "pound" or netted enclosure, as seen in the illustration. The trap may be set on shore or in the water as seen. "Decoy" birds are generally used, being enclosed in the pound.

When set on land the bait consisting of corn or other grain should be spread about the entrance and through the length of the net.

It is remarkable that a duck which so easily finds its way within the netted enclosure, should be powerless to make its escape, but such seems to be the fact, and even a single hoop with its reflex net, has been known to secure a number of the game.

THE HOOK TRAP

Our second example is one which we are almost tempted to exclude on account of its cruelty, but as our volume is especially devoted to traps of all kinds and as this is a variety in very common use, we feel bound to give it a passing notice. Our illustration fully conveys its painful mode of capture, and a beach at low water is generally the scene of the slaughter. A long stout cord is first stretched across the sand and secured to a peg at each end. To this shorter lines are attached at intervals, each one being supplied with a fish hook baited with a piece of the tender rootstock of a certain water reed, of which the ducks are very fond. The main cord and lines are then imbedded in the sand, the various baits only appearing on the surface, and the success of the device is equal to its cruelty.

THE "FOOL'S CAP" TRAP.

Of all oddities of the trap kind, there is, perhaps, no one more novel and comical than the "Fools's Cap" crow-trap, which forms the subject of our present illustration. Crows are by

no means easy of capture in any form of trap, and they are generally as coy and as shrewd in their approach to a trap as they are bold in their familiarity and disrespect for the sombre scarecrows in the corn field. But this simple device will often mislead the smartest and shrewdest crow, and make a perfect *fool* of him, for it is hard to imagine a more ridiculous sight than is furnished by the strange antics and evolutions of a crow thus embarrassed with his head imbedded in a cap which he finds impossible to remove, and which he in vain endeavors to shake off by all sorts of gymnastic performance. The secret of the little contrivance is easily told. The cap consists of a little cone of stiff paper, about three or four inches in diameter at the opening. This is imbedded in the ground, up to its edge, and a few grains of corn are dropped into it. The inside edge of the opening is then smeared with *bird-lime*, a substance of which we shall speak hereafter.

The crow, on endeavoring to reach the corn, sinks his bill so deep in the cone as to bring the gummy substance in contact with the feathers of his head and neck, to which it adheres in spite of all possible efforts on the part of the bird to throw it off.

The cones may be made of a brownish-colored paper if they are to be placed in the earth, but of white paper when inserted in the snow. It is an excellent plan to insert a few of these cones in the fresh corn hills at planting season, as the crows are always on the watch at this time, and will be sure to partake of the tempting morsels, not dreaming of the result. The writer has often heard of this ingenious device, and has read of its being successfully employed in many instances, but he has never yet had an opportunity of testing it himself. He will leave it for his readers to experiment upon for themselves.

BIRD LIME.

This substance so called to which we have above alluded, and which is sold in our bird marts under that name, is a viscid, sticky preparation, closely resembling a very thick and gummy varnish. It is astonishingly " sticky," and the slightest quantity

between the fingers will hold them together with remarkable tenacity. What its effect must be on the feathers of a bird can easily be imagined.

This preparation is put up in boxes of different sizes, and may be had from any of the taxidermists or bird-fanciers in any of our large towns or cities. Should a *home made* article be required, an excellent substitute may be prepared from the inner bark of the "slippery elm." This should be gathered in the spring or early summer, cut into very small pieces or scraped into threads, and boiled in water sufficient to cover them until the pieces are soft and easily mashed. By this time the water will be pretty much boiled down, and the whole mass should then be poured into a mortar and beaten up, adding at the same time a few grains of wheat. When done, the paste thus made may be put into an earthen vessel and kept. When required to be used, it should be melted or softened over the fire, adding goose grease or linseed oil, instead of water. When of the proper consistency it may be spread upon sticks or twigs prepared for it, and which should afterwards be placed in the locality selected for the capture of the birds.

An excellent bird-lime may be made also from plain linseed-oil, by boiling it down until it becomes thick and gummy. Thick varnish either plain or mixed with oil, but always free from alcohol, also answers the purpose very well. The limed twigs may be either set in trees or placed on poles and stuck in the ground.

If any of our readers chance to become possessed of an owl, they may look forward to grand success with their limed twigs. It is a well known fact in natural history that the *owl* is the universal enemy of nearly all our smaller birds. And when, as often happens, a swarm of various birds are seen flying frantically from limb to limb, seeming to centre on a particular tree, and filling the air with their loud chirping, it may be safely concluded that some sleepy owl has been surprised in his day-dozing, and is being severely pecked and punished for his nightly depredations.

Profiting from this fact, the bird catcher often utilizes the owl with great success. Fastening the bird in the crotch of some tree, he adjusts the limed twigs on all sides, even covering the neighboring branches with the gummy substance. No sooner is the owl spied by *one* bird than the cry is set up, and a *score* of foes are soon at hand, ready for battle. One by one they alight on the beguiling twigs, and one by one find themselves held fast. The more they flutter the more powerless they become, and the more securely are they held. In this way many valuable and rare birds are often captured.

THE HUMMING BIRD TRAP.

One of the most ingenious uses to which bird lime is said to have been applied with success, is in the capture of humming-birds. The lime in this instance is made simply by chewing a few grains of wheat in the mouth until a gum is formed. It is said that by spreading this on the inside opening of the long white lily or trumpet-creeper blossom, the capture of a humming-bird is almost certain, and he will never be able to leave the flower after once fairly having entered the opening. There can be no doubt but that this is perfectly practicable, and we recommend it to our readers.

The object in making the bird-lime from wheat consists in the fact that this is more easily removed from the feathers than the other kinds.

We would not wish our readers to infer from this that a humming-bird might be captured or kept alive, for of all birds, they are the most fragile and delicate, and would die of *fright*, if from nothing else. They are chiefly used for ornamental purposes, and may be caught in a variety of ways. A few silk nooses hung about the flowers where the birds are seen to frequent, will sometimes succeed in ensnaring their tiny forms.

The blow-gun is often used with good success, and the concussion from a gun loaded simply with powder, and aimed in the direction of the bird, will often stun it so that it will fall to the ground. If a strong stream of water be forced upon the little creature, as it is fluttering from flower to flower, the result is the same, as the feathers become so wet that it cannot fly.

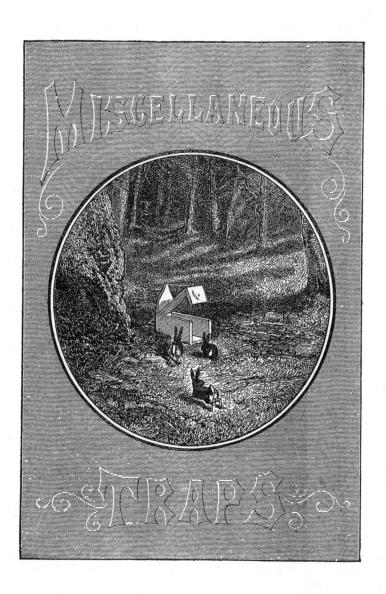

MISCELLANEOUS

TRAPS

BOOK IV.

MISCELLANEOUS TRAPS.

THE COMMON BOX TRAP.

 HE following chapter includes a variety of traps which have not been covered by any of the previous titles. Several novelties are contained in the list, and also a number of well known inventions.

There is probably no more familiar example of the trap kind than that of the common wooden box-trap, better known, perhaps, by our country boys as the rabbit-trap. A glance at our illustration, will readily bring it to mind, and easily explain its working to those not particularly acquainted with it. These traps may be made of any size, but, being usually employed in catching rabbits, require to be made quite large. They should be made of hard seasoned wood—oak or chestnut is the best—and of slabs about an inch in thickness. The pieces may be of the following dimensions: let the bottom board be 20+7 in.; side board, 20+9in.; lid board 19+7 in., and the end piece of lid 7 in. square.

The tall end piece should be about 16 inches high by 7 broad. Let this be sharpened on the upper end, as seen in the engraving, and furnished with a slight groove on the summit, for the reception of the cord. Now to put the pieces together.

Nail the two sides to the edge of the bottom board, and fit in between them the high end piece, securing that also, with nails through the bottom and side boards. Next nail the lid board on to the small, square end piece, and fit the lid thus made neatly into its place.

To make the hinge for the lid, two small holes should be bored through the sides of the trap, about four inches from the tall end, and half an inch from the upper edge of each board. Let small nails now be driven through these holes into the edge of the lid, and it will be found to work freely upon them.

The principal part of the trap is now made, but what remains to be done is of great importance. The "spindle" is a necessary feature in nearly all traps, and the box-trap is useless without it. In this case it should consist merely of a round stick of about the thickness of a lead pencil, and we will say, 7 or 8 in. in length. One end should be pointed and the other should have a small notch cut in it, as seen in the separate drawing of the stick. The spindle being ready, we must

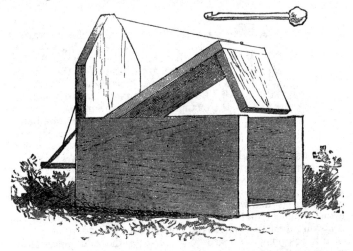

have some place to put it. Another hole should be bored through the middle of the high end piece, and about 4 in. from the bottom. This hole should be large enough to allow the spindle to pass easily through it. If our directions have been carefully followed, the result will now show a complete, closefitting trap.

In setting the trap there are two methods commonly employed, as shown at *a* and *b*. The string, in either case, must be fastened to the end of the lid.

In the first instance (*a*) the lid is raised and made fast by the brace, holding itself beneath the tip of the projecting spindle, and a nail or plug driven into the wood by the side of the hole.

Of course, when the spindle is drawn or moved from the inside the brace will be let loose and the lid will drop.

In the other method (*b*) the spindle is longer, and projects several inches on the outside of the hole. The brace is also longer, and catches itself in the notch on the end of the spindle, and another slight notch in the board, a few inches above the hole.

When the bait is touched from the inside, the brace easily flies out and the lid falls, securing its victim. Either way is sure to succeed, but if there is any preference it is for the former (*a*). It is a wise plan to have a few holes through the trap in different places, to allow for ventilation, and it may be found necessary to line the cracks with tin, as sometimes the

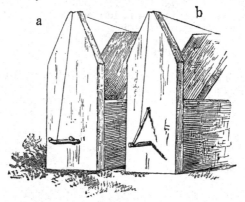

enclosed creature might otherwise gnaw through and make its escape. If there is danger of the lid not closing tightly when sprung, a stone may be fastened upon it to insure that result.

This trap is usually set for rabbits, and these dimensions are especially calculated with that idea. Rabbits abound in all our woods and thickets, and may be attracted by various baits. An apple is most generally used. The box-trap may be made of smaller dimensions, and set in trees for squirrels with very good success.

There is still another well known form of this trap represented in the tail piece at the end of this section. The box is first constructed of the shape already given, only having the lid piece nailed firmly in the top of the box. The tall end piece is also done away with. The whole thing thus representing a simple oblong box with one end open. Two slender cleats should be nailed on each side of this opening, on the interior of the box, to form a groove into which a square end board may easily slide up and down, the top board being slightly sawn away to receive it. An upright stick should then be erected on the top centre of the box, in the tip of which a straight stick should be pivoted, working easily therein, like the arms of a balance. To one end of this balance, the end board should be adjusted by two screw eyes, and to the other the string with spindle attached. By now lowering the spindle to its place, the further end of the balance will be raised and with it the end board, and on the release of the spindle the board will fall. This plan is quite commonly adopted but we rather prefer the former. But as each has its advantages we present them both.

ANOTHER BOX TRAP.

This works after the manner of the ordinary wire rat-trap ; our illustration explains itself.

The box should be of the shape there shown, with one of its end pieces arranged on hinges so as to fall freely. An elastic

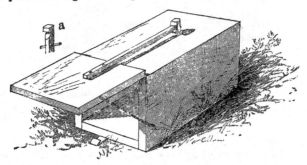

should be fastened from the inside of this end to the inner surface of the top of the box, to insure its closing. If desired, an elastic may be adjusted at the side as shown in the cut and a catch piece of stout tin should be attached to the bottom of the trap to secure the lid when it falls. A small hole should then be bored in the top, near the further end of the trap, and

the spindle, having a notch on its upper end, passed through the
hole thus made. The top of the spindle is shown at (*a*). It
should be held in its place by a small plug or pin through it,
below the surface of the box. A slender stick, long enough to
reach and catch beneath the notch in the spindle should now be
fastened to the lid and the trap is complete. It may be baited with
cheese, bread, and the like, and if set for squirrels, an apple
answers every purpose.

When constructed on a larger and heavier scale it may be used
for the capture of rabbits and animals of a similar size, but for
this purpose the previous variety is preferable

THE FIGURE FOUR TRAP.

One of the most useful as well as the most ancient inventions
in the way of traps is the common *Figure Four Trap*, which
forms the subject of our next illustration. It is a very ingenious
contrivance, and the mechanism, consists merely of three sticks.
It possesses great advantages in the fact that it may be used in a

variety of ways, and a number of the machines may be carried
by the young trapper with very little inconvenience. Our illustration shows the trap already set, only awaiting for a slight
touch at the bait to bring the heavy stone to the ground. A box
may be substituted for the stone, and the animal may thus be

captured alive.   The three sticks are represented separate at
a. b. and *c.*   Of course, there is no regular size for them, as this
would greatly depend upon the purpose for which they are
designed to be used.   If for rabbits, the following proportions
will answer very well.   The sticks should all be square, and
about half an inch in thickness.   The bait-stick, (*a*) should be
about nine or ten inches in length, one end being pointed and
the other furnished with a notch, as indicated.   The upright
stick, (*b*) should be a little shorter, one end being whittled to a
rather sharp edge.   At about three or four inches from the
other end, and on the side next to that whittled, a square notch
should be cut.   This should be about a third of an inch in depth
and half an inch in width, being so cut as exactly to receive the
bait-stick without holding it fast.   The remaining stick (*c*) should
have a length of about seven or eight inches, one end being
whittled, as in the last, to an edge, and the other end furnished
with a notch on the same side of the stick.

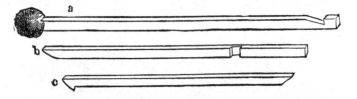

When these are finished, the trap may be set in the following
manner: Place the upright stick, (*b*) with its pointed end uppermost.   Rest the notch of the slanting stick, (*c*) on the summit of
the upright stick, placing the stone upon its end, and holding
the stick in position with the hand.   By now hooking the notch
in the bait-stick on the sharpened edge of the slanting stick and
fitting it into the square notch in the upright, it may easily be
made to catch and hold itself in position.   The bait should
always project beneath the stone.   In case a box is used instead
of a stone, the trap may be set either inside of it or beneath its
edge.   Where the ground is very soft, it would be well to rest the
upright stick on a chip or small flat stone, as otherwise it is apt
to sink into the earth by degrees and spring by itself.

When properly made, it is a very sure and sensitive trap, and
the bait, generally an apple, or "nub" of corn is seldom more
than touched when the stone falls.

THE "DOUBLE ENDER."

This is what we used to call it in New England and it was a great favorite among the boys who were fond of rabbit catching. It was constructed of four boards two feet in length by nine inches in breath secured with nails at their edges, so as to form a long square box. Each end was supplied with a heavy lid working on two hinges. To each of these lids a light strip of wood was fastened, the length of each being sufficient to reach nearly to the middle of the top of the box, as seen in the illustration. At this point a small auger hole was then made downward through the board. A couple of inches of string was next tied to the tip of each stick and supplied with a large knot at the end. The trap was then set on the simple principle of which there are so many examples throughout the pages of this work. The

knots were lowered through the auger hole and the insertion of the bait stick inside the box held them in place. The edge of the bottom board on each end of the trap should be supplied with a tin catch such as is described on page 88 in order to hold the lid in place after it has fallen. No matter from which end the bait is approached it is no sooner touched than both ends fall and "*bunny*" is prisoner. Like many other of our four-footed game, the rabbit manifests a peculiar liking for salt and may be regularly attracted to a given spot by its aid. A salted cotton string is sometimes extended several yards from the trap for the purpose of leading them to it, but this seems a needless precaution, as the rabbit is seldom behind hand in discerning a tempting bait when it is within his reach.

THE SELF SETTING TRAP.

One of the oldest known principles ever embodied in the form
of a trap is that which forms the subject of the accompanying
illustration.   It is very simple in construction, sure in its action ;
and as its name implies, resets itself after each intruder has been
captured.

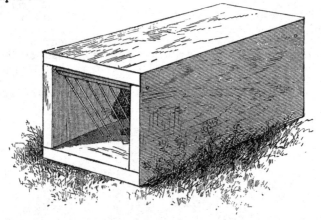

It is well adapted for Rabbits and Coons and when made on a
small scale, may be successfully employed in taking rats and mice.
It is also extensively used in the capture of the Mink and
Muskrat, being set beneath the water, near the haunts of the
animals and weighted by a large stone.   Of course the size of
the box will be governed by the dimensions of the game for
which it is to be set.   Its general proportions should resemble
those of the illustration, both ends being open.   A small gate,
consisting of a square piece of wood supplied with a few stiff
wires is then pivoted inside each opening, so as to work freely
and fall easily when raised.   The bait is fastened inside at the
centre of the box.   The animal, in quest of the bait, finds an easy
entrance, as the wires lift at a slight pressure, but the exit after
the gate has closed is so difficult that escape is almost beyond
the question.
   The wires should be so stiff as to preclude the possibility of
them being bent by struggles of the imprisoned creature in his

efforts to escape, and to insure further strength it is advisable to connect the lower ends of the wires by a cross piece of finer wire, twisted about each.

The simultaneous capture of two rabbits in a trap of this kind is a common occurrence.

THE DEAD-FALL.

In strolling through the woods and on the banks of streams in the country, it is not an uncommon thing to stumble against a contrivance resembling in general appearance our next illustration. Throughout New England, the "dead-fall," as this is called, has always been a most popular favorite among trappers, young and old; and there is really no better rough and ready trap for large game. To entrap a fox by any device is no easy matter; but the writer remembers one

case where Reynard was outwitted, and the heavy log of the "dead-fall" put a speedy end to his existence. The trap was set in a locality where the fox had made himself a nuisance by repeated nocturnal invasions among the poultry, and the bait was cleverly calculated to decoy him. A live duck was tied within the pen, and the morsel proved too tempting for him to resist. Thrusting his head beneath the suspended log, in order to reach his prey, he thus threw down the slender framework of support; and the log, falling across his neck, put him to death.

Our illustration gives a very correct idea of the general construction of the "dead-fall," although differing slightly in its mode of setting from that usually employed.

A pen of rough sticks is first constructed, having an open front. A log about seven or eight feet in length, and five or six inches in diameter, should then be procured. An ordinary fence rail will answer the purpose very well, although the log is preferable. Its large end should be laid across the front of the pen, and two stout sticks driven into the ground outside of it, leaving room for it to rise and fall easily between them and the pen, a second shorter log being placed on the ground beneath it, as described for the bear-trap, page (17). A look at our illustration fully explains the *setting* of the parts. A forked twig, about a foot in length, answers for the bait-stick. The lower end should be pointed, and the fork, with its bait, should incline toward the ground, when set. The upper end should be supplied with a notch, square side down, and directly above the branch which holds the bait. Another straight stick, about fourteen inches in length, should then be cut. Make it quite flat on each end. A small thin stone, chip of wood, or the like, is the only remaining article required. Now proceed to raise the log, as shown in the drawing, place one end of the straight stick beneath it, resting its tip on the flat top of the upright stick on the outside of the log. The baitstick should now be placed in position inside the inclosure, resting the pointed end on the chip, and securing the notch above, as seen in the illustration, beneath the tip of the flat stick. When this is done, the trap is set, but, there are a few little hints in regard to setting it finely, — that is, surely, — which will be necessary. It is very important to avoid bringing too much of the weight of the log on the flat stick, as this would of course bear heavily on the bait-stick, and render considerable force necessary to spring the trap. The leverage at the point where the log rests on the flat stick should be very slight, and the log should be so placed that the upright shall sustain nearly all the weight. By this method, very little pressure is brought to bear on the bait-stick, and a very slight twitch will throw it out of poise. The fork of the bait-stick should point to the side of the inclosure, as, in this case, when the bait is seized by the unlucky intruder, the very turning of the fork forces the notch from beneath the horizontal stick, and throws the parts asunder.

If the trap is set for muskrats, minks, skunks, or animals of similar size, the weight of the log will generally be found sufficient to effect their death ; but, if desired, a heavy stone may be rested against it, or the raised end weighted with other logs (see p. 18), to make sure. When set for a coon or fox, this precaution is necessary. To guard against the cunning which some animals possess, it is frequently necessary to cover the top of the pen with cross-sticks, as there are numerous cases on record where the intended victims have climbed over the side of the inclosure, and taken the bait from the inside, thus keeping clear of the suspended log, and springing the trap without harm to themselves. A few sticks or branches laid across the top of the inclosure will prevent any such capers; and the crafty animals will either have to take the bait at the risk of their lives, or leave it alone.

For trapping the muskrat, the bait may consist of carrots, turnips, apples, and the like. For the mink, a bird's head, or the head of a fowl, is the customary bait; and the skunk may usually be taken with sweet apples, meats, or some portion of a dead fowl.

In the case of the fox, which we have mentioned, the setting of the trap was somewhat varied; and in case our readers might desire to try a similar experiment, we will devote a few lines to a description of it. In this instance, the flat stick which supported the log was not more than eight inches in length; and instead of the bait-stick, a slight framework of slender branches was substituted. This frame or lattice-work was just large enough to fill the opening of the pen, and its upper end supported the flat stick. The duck was fastened to the back part of the pen, which was also closed over the top. The quacking of the fowl attracted the fox; and as he thrust his head through the lattice to reach his prey, the frame was thrown out of balance and Reynard paid the price of his greed and folly.

There is another mode of adjusting the pieces of the dead-fall, commonly employed by professional trappers, whereby the trap is sprung by the foot of the animal in quest of the bait. This construction is shown correctly in the accompanying cut, which gives the front view, the pen being made as before. The stout crotch represented at (a) is rested on the summit of a strong peg, driven into the ground beneath the *outside edge* of the suspended log; (b) is the treacherous stick which seals the doom of any animal that dares rest his foot upon it. This piece should be long enough to stretch across and overlap the guard-pegs at each side of the opening. To set the trap, rest the short crotch of (a) on the top of the peg, and lower the log upon it, keeping the leverage slight, as directed in our last example, letting much of the weight come on the top of the peg. The long arm of the crotch should be pressed inward from the front, and one end of the stick (*b*) should then be caught between its extreme tip, and the upright peg about ten inches above the ground. By now fastening the bait to a peg

at the back part of the pen, the affair is in working order, and will be found perfectly reliable. The ground log (*d*) being rested in place as seen in the illustration. To make assurance doubly sure, it is well to cut a slight notch in the upright stick at (*c*) for the reception of the foot-piece (*b*). By this precaution the stick, when lowered, is bound to sink at the right end, thus ensuring success.

The Figure-Four Trap, already described in another part of this book, is also well adapted to the dead-fall, and is much used. It should be made of stout pieces and erected at the opening of the pen, with the bait pointing toward the interior, the heavy log being poised on its summit.

THE GARROTE.

There is another variety of trap, somewhat resembling the dead-fall, but which seizes its prey in a little different manner.

This trap, which we will call the *Garrote*, is trutly represented by our illustration. A pen is first constructed, similar to that of the dead-fall. At the opening of the pen, two arches are fastened in the ground. They should be about an inch apart. A stout forked stick should then be cut, and firmly fixed in the earth at the side of the arches, and about three feet distant.

Our main illustration gives the general appearance of the trap, but we also subjoin an additional cut, showing the "setting" or arrangement of the pieces. They are three in number, and consist: First, of a notched peg, which is driven into the ground at the back part of the pen, and a little to one side. Second, of a forked twig, the branch of which should point

downward with the bait attached to its end. The third stick being the little hooked piece catching beneath the arches. The first of these is too simple to need description. The second should be about eight inches long; a notch should be cut in each end. The upper one being on the side from which the branch projects, and the other on the *opposite* side of the stick, and at the other end, as is made plain by our illustration. The third stick may consist merely of a hooked crotch of some twig, as this is always to be found. Indeed, nearly *all* the parts of this trap may be found in any woods; and, with the exception of a jack-knife, bait, and string, the trapper need not trouble himself to carry any materials whatever. When the three pieces are thus made the trap only awaits the "Garrote." This should be made from a stiff pole, about six feet in length, having a heavy stone tied to its large end, and a loop of the shape of the letter U, or a slipping noose, made of stout cord or wire, fastened at the smaller end. To arrange the pieces for their destructive work, the pole should be bent down so that the loop shall fall between the arches. The "crotch stick" should then be hooked beneath the front of the arch, letting its arm point inward. After this the bait stick should be placed in its position, with the bait pointing downward, letting one end catch beneath the notch in the ground-peg, and the other over the tip of the crotch stick. This done, and the trap is set.

Like the dead-fall, the bait stick should point toward the side of the pen, as the turning involved in pulling it toward the front is positively *sure* to slip it loose from its catches. Be careful to see that the loop is nicely arranged between the arches, and that the top of the pen is covered with a few twigs. If these direc-

tions are carefully follow- ed, and if the young trapper has selected a good trap- ping ground, it will not be a matter of many days be- fore he will discover the upper portion of the arches occupied by some rabbit, muskrat, or other unlucky creature, either standing on its hind legs, or lift- ed clean off the ground. Coons are frequently se- cured by this trap, al- though, as a general thing, they don't show much enthusiasm over traps of any kind, and seem to prefer to get their food elsewhere, rather than take it off the end of a bait stick.

THE BOW TRAP.

This most excellent and unique machine is an invention of the author's, and possesses great advantages, both on account of its durability and of the speedy death which it inflicts.

Procure a board about two feet in length, by five or six in width, and commencing at about nine inches from one end, cut a hole four or more inches square. This may readily be done with a narrow saw, by first boring a series of gimlet holes in which to insert it. There will now be nine inches of board on one side of the hole and eleven on the other. The shorter end constituting the top of the trap. On the upper edge of the hole a row of stout tin teeth should be firmly tacked, as seen in the illustration. On the other side of the cavity, and three inches from it a small auger hole (the size of a lead pencil), should be bored. After which it should be sand-papered and polished on the interior, by rubbing with some smooth, hard tool, inserted inside. A round plug of wood should next be prepared. Let it be about half an inch in length, being afterwards bevelled nearly the whole length of one side, as shown at (*b*), leaving a

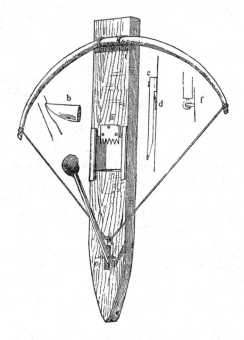

little over an eight of an inch of the wood unwhittled. This little piece of wood is the most important part, of the trap, and should be made very carefully. The remaining end of the board below the auger hole should now be whittled off to a point, in order that it may be driven into the ground. The next requisites consist of two pieces of wood, which are seen at the sides of the square hole, in our illustration, and also seen at (*c*), side view. These pieces should be about six inches in length and about an inch square. A thin piece being cut off from one side of each, to the distance of four inches, and ending in a square notch. The other end should be rounded off, as is also there plainly indicated. Before adjusting the pieces in place, two tin catches should be fastened to the board, one on each side of the hole. This catch is shown at (*d*), and consists merely of a piece of tin, half an inch in width, and three-quarters of an inch in length, tacked to the wood, and having its end raised, as indicated. Its object is to hold the bow-string from being pulled down after once passing it. The upper edge of these catch-pieces should be about an inch and a half from the top of the hole, and, if desired, two or three of them may be arranged one above the other, so that wherever the string may stop against the neck of the inmate it will be sure to hold. The catches being in place, proceed to adjust the pieces of wood, letting the notch be on a line with the top of the pole, or a little above it. Each piece should be fastened with two screws to make secure.

We will now give our attention to the bait stick. This should be about six inches in length, and square, as our illustration shows. There are two ways of attaching the bait stick to the board, both shown at (*e*) and (*f*). The former consists merely of a screw eye inserted into the end of the stick, afterwards hinged to the board by a wire staple. The point for the hinge, in this case, should be about an inch below the auger hole. In the other method (*f*), the bait stick should be a half inch longer, and the spot for the hinge a quarter inch lower. At about a quarter of an inch from the square end of the bait stick a small hole should be made by the use of a hot wire. An oblong mortice should next be cut in the board, so as to receive this end of the stick easily. A stout bit of wire should then be inserted in the little hole in the stick, and laying this across the centre of the mortice, it should be thus secured by two staples, as the drawing shows. This forms a very neat and simple hinge. To determine the place for the catch, insert the flat end of the little plug fairly into the auger-hole above the hinge. Draw up the bait stick, and at the point where it comes in contact with the point of the plug, cut a square notch, as shown in (*b*). Everything now awaits the bow. This should be of hickory or other stout wood; it is well to have it seasoned, although a stout sapling will answer the purpose very well. It should be fastened to the top of the board by two heavy staples, or nails driven on each side of it. The string should be *heavy* Indian twine. Our illustration shows the trap, as it appears when ready for business. The plug is inserted, as already described, with the bevelled face downward, and square end in the hole. Draw down the bow-string and pass it beneath the plug, at the same time catching the tip of the latter in the notch of the bait stick. If properly constructed the string will thus rest on the slight uncut portion of the under side of the peg, and the trap is thus set. If the bait is pushed when approached, the notch is forced off from the plug, and the string flies up with a *twang!* securing the neck of its victim, and pro ucing almost instant death. If the bait is *pulled*, the bait stick thus forces the plug into the hole in the board, and thus slides the cord on to the bevel, which immediately releases it, and the bow is sprung. So that no matter whether the bait is pushed or drawn towards the front, the trap is equally sure to spring.

In setting this curious machine, it is only necessary to insert it into the ground, and surround the bait with a slight pen, in order that it may not be approached from behind. By now laying a stone or a pile of sticks in front of the affair, so that the bait may be more readily reached, the thing is ready. Care is required in setting to arrange the pieces delicately. The plug should be *very slightly* inserted into the auger hole, and the notch in the bait stick should be as small as possible, and hold. All this is made clear in our illustration (*b*).

By observing these little niceties the trap becomes very sure and sensitive.

Bait with small apple, nub of corn, or the like.

THE MOLE TRAP.

If there is any one subject upon which the ingenuity of the farmers has been taxed, it is on the invention of a mole trap which would effectually clear their premises of these blind burrowing vermin. Many patented devices of this character are on the market, and many odd pictured ideas on the subject have gone the rounds of the illustrated press, but they all sink into insignificance when tested beside the trap we here present. It has no equal among mole traps, and it can be made with the utmost ease and without cost. The principle on which it works is the same as the Fish Trap on page 120.

Construct a hollow wooden tube about five inches in diameter, and eight inches in length. A section of a small tree, neatly excavated with a large auger is just the thing. Through the centre of one of the sides a small hole the size of a lead pencil should be bored, this being the upper side. About half an inch distant from each end a smaller hole should be made for the passage of the noose. The spring should consist either of a stout steel rod, whalebone or stiff sapling, a foot or more in length, inserted downward through holes in the side of the tube after the manner of the Fish Trap already alluded to. No bait is required. A simple stick the size of the central hole at one end, and an inch in width at the other being suffi-cient. The trap is set as described in the other instances, and as the introduction of the spindle-stick is sometimes attended with difficulty owing to its position inside the trap, the bottom of the latter is sometimes cut away for two or three inches to facilitate the operation. The trap is then to be imbedded within the burrow of the mole. Find a fresh tunnel and carefully remove the sod above it. Insert the trap and replace the turf. The first mole that starts on his rounds through that burrow is a sure prisoner, no matter from which side he may approach.

Immense numbers of these troublesome vermin have been taken in a single season by a dozen such traps, and they possess great advantages over all other mole traps on account of their simplicity and unfailing success.

A FISH TRAP.

Our list of traps would be incomplete without a Fish Trap, and although we have mentioned some contrivances in this line

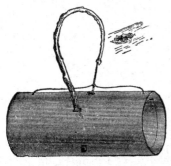

under our article on "Fishing" we here present one which is both new and novel.

Its mode of construction is exactly similar to the Double Box Snare, page (57). A sec-tion of stove-pipe one foot in length should first be obtained. Through the iron at a point equidistant from the ends, a hole should be made with some smooth, sharp pointed instru-ment, the latter being forced *outward* from the *inside* of the pipe, thus causing the ragged edge of the hole to appear on the outside, as seen in our illustration. The diameter of the aper-

ture should be about that of a lead pencil. Considering this as
the *upper side* of the pipe, proceed to pierce two more holes
downward through the side of the circumference, for the ad-
mission of a stout stick or steel rod. This is fully explained
in our illustration. The further arrangement of bait stick and
nooses is exactly identical with that described on page (57). It
may be set for suckers, pickerel, and fish of like size, the bait
stick being inserted with sufficient firmness to withstand the attacks of smaller fish. The bait should be firmly tied to the stick,
or the latter supplied with two hooks at the end on which it
should be firmly impaled. To set the trap, select a locality
abounding in fish. Place a stone inside the bottom of the pipe,
insert the bait stick and arrange the nooses.

By now quietly grasping the curve of the switch the trap
may be easily lowered to the bottom. The bait soon attracts
a multitude of small fishes; these in turn attract the pickerel to
the spot, and before many minutes the trap is sprung and may
be raised from the water with its prisoner. This odd device is
an invention of the author's, and it is as successful as it is
unique

Maternal Advice.

BOOK V.

HOUSEHOLD TRAPS.

OR the most effectual domestic trap on record see our page title to this section. There are several others also which have done good service in many households, and for the sake of pestered housekeepers generally, we devote a corner of our volume for their especial benefit.

Foremost in the list of domestic pests the rat stands pre-eminent, and his proverbial shrewdness and cunning render his capture often a very difficult, if not an impossible task. We subjoin, however, a few hints and suggestions of practical value, together with some perfected ideas in the shape of traps, by which the average rat may be easily outwitted and led to his destruction.

First on the list is

THE BARREL TRAP.

This most ingenious device possesses great advantages in its capabilities of securing an almost unlimited number of the vermin in quick succession. It also takes care of itself, requires no re-baiting or setting after once put in working order, and is sure death to its prisoners.

A water-tight barrel is the first thing required. Into this pour water to the depth of a foot. Next dampen a piece of very thick paper, and stretch it over the top of the barrel, tying it securely below the upper hoops. When the paper dries it will become thoroughly flat and tightened. Its surface should then be strewn with bits of cheese, etc., and the barrel so placed

that the rats may jump upon it from some neighboring surface. As soon as the bait is gone, a fresh supply should be
spread on the paper and the same operation repeated for
several days, until the rats get accustomed to visit the place for
their regular rations, fearlessly and without suspicion. This is
"half the battle," and the capture of the greedy victims of misplaced confidence is now an easy matter. The bait should
again be spread as before and a few pieces of the cheese should
be attached to the paper with gum. It is a good plan to smear

parts of the paper with gum arabic, sprinkling the bait upon it.
When dry, cut a cross in the middle of the paper, as seen in the
illustration, and leave the barrel to take care of itself and the
rats. The first one comes along, spies the tempting morsels,
and with his accustomed confidence, jumps upon the paper.
He suddenly finds himself in the water at the bottom of the
barrel, and the paper above has closed and is ready to practice
its deception on the next comer. There is not long to wait. A
second victim soon tumbles in to keep company with the first.
A third and a fourth soon follow, and a dozen or more are

sometimes thus entrapped in a very short space of time. It is a most excellent and simple trap, and if properly managed, will most effectually curtail the number of rats in any pestered neighborhood.

By some, it is considered an improvement to place in the bottom of the barrel a large stone, which shall project above the water sufficiently to offer a foothold for one rat. The first victim, of course, takes possession of this retreat and on the precipitate arrival of the second a contest ensues for its occupancy. The hubbub which follows is said to attract all the rats in the neighborhood to the spot, and many are thus captured.

We can hardly recommend the addition of the stone as being an improvement. The rat is a most notoriously shrewd and cunning animal, and the despairing cries of his comrades must rather tend to excite his caution and suspicion. By the first method the drowning is soon accomplished and the rat utters no sound whereby to attract and warn his fellows. This contrivance has been thoroughly tested and has proved its efficacy in many households by completely ridding the premises of the vermin.

Another excellent form of Barrel Trap is that embodying the principle described in page (131). A circular platform should be first constructed and hinged in the opening of the barrel. This may be done by driving a couple of small nails through the sides of the barrel into a couple of staples inserted near the opposite edges of the platform. The latter should be delicately weighted, as described on the above mentioned page, and previously to setting, should be baited in a stationary position for several days to gain the confidence of the rats. The bait should at last be secured to the platform with gum, and the bottom of the barrel of course filled with water, as already described. This trap possesses the same advantages as the foregoing. It is *self-setting*, and unfailing in its action.

Another method consists in half-filling the barrel with oats, and allowing the rats to enjoy their repast there for several days. When thus attracted to the spot, remove the oats, and pour the same bulk of water into the barrel, sprinkling the surface thickly with the grain. The delusion is almost perfect, as will be effectually proven when the first rat visits the spot for his accustomed free lunch. Down he goes with a splash, is soon drowned, and sinks to the bottom. The next shares the same fate, and several more are likely to be added to the list of misguided victims.

Many of the devices described throughout this work may be adapted for domestic use to good purpose. The box-trap page 103, box-snare, page 55, figure-four, page 107, are all suitable for the capture of the rat; also, the examples given on pages 106, 109, 110, and 129.

The steel-trap is often used, but should always be concealed from view. It is a good plan to set it in a pan covered with meal, and placed in the haunts of the rats. The trap may also be set at the mouth of the rats' hole, and covered with a piece of dark-colored cloth or paper. The runways between boxes, boards, and the like offer excellent situations for the trap, which should be covered, as before directed.

Without one precaution, however, the trap may be set in vain. Much of the so-called shrewdness of the rat is nothing more than an instinctive caution, through the acute sense of smell which the animal possesses; and a trap which has secured one victim will seldom extend its list, unless all traces of its first occupant are thoroughly eradicated. This may be accomplished by smoking the trap over burning paper, hens' feathers or chips, taking care to avoid a heat so extreme as to affect the temper of the steel springs. All rat-traps should be treated the same way, in order to insure success, and the position and localities of setting should be frequently changed.

THE BOX DEAD-FALL.

This trap is an old invention, simplified by the author, and for the capture of rats and mice will prove very effectual. It consists of a box, constructed of four slabs of 3-4 inch boarding, and open at both ends. The two side boards should be 10 x 18 inches; top and bottom boards, 6 x 18 inches. For the centre of the latter, a square piece should be removed by the aid of the saw. The width of this piece should be four inches, and the length eight inches. Before nailing the boards together, the holes thus left in the bottom board should be supplied with a treadle platform, working on central side pivots. The board for this treadle should be much thinner and lighter than the rest of the trap, and should fit loosely in place, its surface being slightly below the level of the bottom board. This is shown in the interior of the trap. The pivots should be inserted in the exact centre of the sides, through holes made in the edge of the bottom board. These holes may be bored with a gimlet or burned with a red-hot wire. The pivots may consist of stout brass or iron wire ; and the end of one should be flattened with the hammer, as seen at (*a*). This pivot should project an inch from the wood, and should be *firmly* inserted in the treadle-piece. The platform being thus arranged, proceed to fasten the boards together, as shown in the illustration, the top and bottom boards overlapping the others. We will now give our attention to the stick shown at (*b*). This should be whittled

from a piece of hard wood, its length being three inches, and its upper end pointed as seen. The lower end should be pierced with a crevice, which should then be forced over the flattened extremity of the point (*a*) as shown at (*c*), pointed end uppermost. The weight (*a*) is next in order. This should consist of a heavy oak plank two inches in thickness, and of such other dimensions as will allow it to fit loosely in the box, and fall from top to bottom therein without catching between the sides. A stout staple should be driven in the centre of its upper face, and from this a stout string should be passed upward through a hole in the centre of the box. We are now ready for the spindle (*e*). This should be about three inches in length, and bluntly pointed

at each end, a notch being made to secure it at a point five
inches above the pivot (c). To set the trap, raise the weight, as
seen in the illustration ; draw down the string to the point (e),
and attach it to the spindle one-half an inch from its upper
end, which should then be inserted in the notch, the lower end
being caught against the extremity of the pivot stick.   The
parts are now adjusted, and even in the present state the trap
is almost sure to spring at the slighest touch on the treadle-
piece.   An additional precaution is advisable, however.   Two
small wooden pegs (f) should be driven, one on each side of the
spindle, thus preventing any side-movement of the latter.   It
will now be readily seen that the slightest weight on either end
of the treadle-piece within the trap must tilt it to one side,
thus throwing the pivot-piece from its bearing on the spindle ; and the latter being released, lets fall the weight with
crushing effect upon the back of its hapless victim.

The trap is very effective, and is easily constructed.   The
bait should be rested in the centre of the treadle platform.
Built on a larger scale, this device may be successfully adapted
to the capture of the mink, martien, and many other varieties of
game.

THE BOARD-FLAP.

For the capture of mice this is both a simple and effective contrivance, and it may be enlarged so as to be of good service for larger animals. Procure two boards, one foot square and one inch thick, and secure them together by two hinges, as in the illustration. Assuming one as the upper board, proceed to bore a gimlet hole three inches from the hinges. This is for the reception of the bait stick, and should be cut away on the inside, as seen in the section (*a*), thus allowing a free play for the stick. Directly beneath this aperture, and in the lower board, a large auger hole should be made. A stout bit of iron wire, ten inches in length, is now required. This should be inserted perpendicularly in the further end of the lower slab, being bent into a curve which shall slide easily through a gimlet hole in the edge of the upper board. This portion is very important, and should be carefully constructed. The bait stick should be not more than three inches in length, supplied with a notch in its upper end, and secured in the aperture in the board by the aid of a pivot and staples, as is clearly shown in our drawing. The spindle is next in order. It should consist of a light piece of pine eight and a half inches in length, and brought to an edge at each end. A tack should now be driven at the further edge of the upper board on a line with the aperture through which the wire passes. Our illustration represents the trap as it appears when set. The upper band is raised to the full limit of the wire. One end of the spindle is now adjusted beneath the head of the tack, and the other in the notch in the bait stick. The wire thus supports the suspended board by sustaining the spindle, which is held in equilibrium. A slight touch on the bait stick soon destroys this equilibrium: a flap ensues, and a dead mouse is the result. The object of the auger hole in the lower board consists in affording a receptacle for the bait when the boards come together, as otherwise it would defeat its object, by offering an obstruction to the fall of the board, and thus allow its little mouse to escape.

It is, therefore, an essential part of the trap, and should be carefully tested before being finally set.

THE BOX PIT-FALL.

We now come to a variety of trap which differs in its construction from any previously described. It secures its victims alive, and without harm, and, when well made, is very successful. It may be set for squirrels, chipmunks, rats, mice, and the like, and on a large scale for muskrats and mink.

The trap is very easily made, and is represented in section in our illustration, showing the height and interior of the box. For ordinary purposes the box should be about twelve or fourteen inches square, with a depth of about eighteen inches. A platform consisting of a piece of tin should then be procured. This should be just large enough to fit nicely to the outline of the interior of the box without catching. On two opposite sides

of this piece of tin, and at the middle of each of those sides, a small strip of the same material should be wired, or soldered in the form of a loop, as shown in the separate diagram at (*b*). These loops should be only large enough to admit the end of a shingle-nail. A scratch should now be made across the tin from loop to loop, and on the centre of this scratch another and larger strip of tin should be fastened in a similar manner, as shown in our diagram, at (*a*), this being for the balance weight. The latter may consist of a small stone, piece of lead, or the like, and should be suspended by means of a wire bent around it, and secured in a hole in the tin by a bend or knot in the other extremity. Further explanations are almost superfluous, as our main illustration fully explains itself.

After the weight is attached, the platform should be secured in its place, about five inches from the top of the box. To accomplish this and form the hinges, two shingle-nails should be driven through the side of the box into the tin loops prepared for them. To do this nicely requires some considerable accuracy and care, and it should be so done that the platform will swing with perfect freedom and ease, the weight below bringing it to a horizontal poise after a few vibrations. Care should be taken that the weight is not too heavy, as, in such a case, the

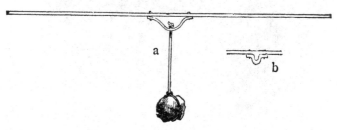

platform will not be sensitive on its balance, and, consequently, would not work so quickly and surely. The weight should be *just heavy enough* to restore the platform to its perfect poise, and no more. This can be easily regulated by experiment. The bait should then be strewn on both sides of the platform, when the trap is set, and the luckless animal, jumping after the bait, feels his footing give way, and suddenly finds himself in the bottom of a dark box, from which it is impossible for him to escape except by gnawing his way out. To prevent this, the interior of the box may be lined with tin.

By *fastening* the bait—a small lump or piece—on each side of the tin, the trap will continually reset itself, and, in this way, two or three individuals may be taken, one after the other. Muskrats are frequently caught in this trap, it being generally buried in the ground so that its top is on a level with the surface. In this case it is necessary to arrange the platform lower down in the box, and the latter should be of much larger dimensions than the one we have described.

For ordinary purposes the box should either be set in the ground or placed near some neighboring object which will afford easy access to it. No less than a dozen rats have been caught in a trap of this kind in a single night.

CAGE TRAP.

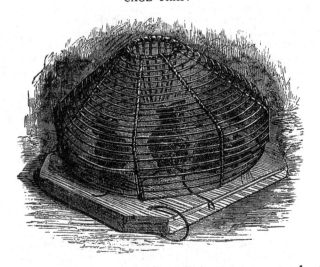

The common cage trap is well known to most of our readers, and for the capture of rats and mice, it is one of the most efficacious devices in existence. The construction of one of these traps is quite a difficult operation, and we would hesitate before advising our inventive reader to exercise his patience and ingenuity in the manufacture of an article which can be bought for such a small price, and which, after all, is only a mouse trap. If it were a device for the capture of the *mink* or *otter*, it might then be well worth the trouble, and would be likely to repay the time and labor expended upon it. We imagine that few would care to exercise their skill over a trap of such complicated structure, while our pages are filled with other simpler and equally effective examples.

For the benefit, however, of such as are of an inventive turn of mind, we subjoin an illustration of the trap to serve as a guide. The principle upon which it works is very simple. The bait is strewn inside the cage, and the rats or mice find their only access to it through the hole at the top. The wires here converge at the bottom, and are pointed at the ends. The passage downwards is an easy matter, but to *escape* through the same opening is impossible, as the pointed ends of the wires effectually prevent the ascent. It is a notable fact, however, that the efforts to escape through this opening are very seldom made. The mode of entering seems to be absolutely forgotten by the captive animals, and they rush frantically about the cage, prying between all the wires in their wild endeavors, never seeming to notice the central opening by which they entered. This is easily explained by the fact that the open grating admits the light from all sides, and the enclosed victims are thus attracted to no one spot in particular, and naturally rush to the extreme edges of the trap, in the hope of finding an exit.

If a thick cloth be placed over the cage, leaving the opening at the top uncovered, the confined creatures are soon attracted by the light, and lose no time in rushing towards it, where their endeavors to ascend are effectually checked by the pointed wires. Profiting by this experiment, the author once improvised a simple trap on the same principle, which proved very effectual. We will call it

THE JAR TRAP.

In place of the wire cage, a glass preserve-jar was substituted. A few bits of cheese were then dropped inside, and the top of a funnel inserted into the opening above. This completed the trap, and it was set on the floor near the flour barrel. On the following morning the jar was occupied by a little mouse, and each successive night for a week added one to the list of victims. A stiff piece of tin, bent into the required shape, may be substituted for the funnel top, or even a very heavy piece of pasteboard might answer.

BOWL TRAPS.

Very effective extempore traps may be set up in a few minutes by the use of a few bowls. There are two methods commonly employed. One consists of the bowl and a knife-blade. An ordinary tableknife is used and a piece of cheese is firmly forced on to the end of the blade, the bowl is then balanced on the edge, allowing the bait to project about an inch and a half beneath the bowl. The odor of cheese will attract a mouse almost anywhere, and he soon finds his way to the tempting morsel in this case. A very slight nibble is sufficient to tilt the blade and the bowl falls over its prisoner.

In the second method a thimble is used in place of the knife. The cheese is forced into its interior, and the open end of the thimble inserted far beneath the bowl, allowing about half its length to project outward.

The mouse is thus obliged to pass under the bowl in order to reach the bait, and in his efforts to grasp the morsel, the thimble is dislodged and the captive secured beneath the vessel. Where a small thimble is used, it becomes necessary to place a bit of pasteboard or flat chip beneath it, in order to raise it sufficiently to afford an easy passage for the mouse. Both of these devices are said to work excellently.

FLY PAPER.

A sheet of common paper, smeared with a mixture composed of molasses one part, and bird-lime six parts (see page 97), will be found to attract large numbers of flies and hold them prisoners upon its surface.

Spruce gum, warmed on the fire, and mixed with a little linseed oil, is also excellent. For a genuine fly trap, the following stands unrivalled.

FLY TRAP.

Take a tumbler, and half-fill it with strong soap suds. Cut a circle of stiff paper which will exactly fit into the top of the glass. In the centre of the paper cut a hole half an inch in diameter, or, better still, a slice of bread may be placed on the glass. Smear one side of the disc with molasses, and insert it in the tumbler with this side downward. Swarms of flies soon surround it, and one by one find their way downward through the hole. Once below the paper, and their doom is sealed. For a short time the molasses absorbs their attention, and they, in turn, absorb the molasses.

In their efforts to escape, they one by one precipitate themselves in the soap suds below, where they speedily perish. The tumbler is soon half-filled with the dead insects, and where a number of the traps are set in a single room, the apartment is soon ridden of the pests.

STEEL TRAPS,

AND THE

ART OF TRAPPING.

BOOK VI.

STEEL TRAPS AND THE ART OF TRAPPING.

ASSING from our full and extended illustrated list of extempore, or "rough and ready" examples of the trap kind, we will now turn our attention to the consideration of that well-known implement, the trade *steel* trap. Although the foregoing varieties often serve to good purpose, the Steel Trap is the principal device used by professional trappers, and possesses great advantages over all other traps. It is portable, sets easily and quickly, either on land or beneath the water; can be concealed with ease; secures its victims without injury to their fur, and by the application of the spring or sliding pole (hereafter described) will most effectually prevent the captive from making his escape by self-amputation, besides placing him beyond the reach of destruction by other animals.

The author has known trappers who have plied their vocation largely by the aid of the various hand made traps, described in the earlier pages of this book, and with good success. But in the regular *business* of systematic trapping, their extensive use is not common. The experience of modern trappers generally, warrants the assertion that for practical utility, from every point of view, the steel trap stands unrivalled.

These traps are made of all sizes, from that suitable for the capture of the house rat, to the immense and wieldy machine adapted to the grizzly, and known as the "bear tamer."

They may be bought at almost any hardware shop, although a large portion of the traps ordinarily sold are defective. They should be selected with care, and the springs always tested before purchase. Besides the temper of the spring, there are also other necessary qualities in a steel trap, which we subjoin in order that the amateur may know how to judge and select his weapons judiciously.

REQUISITES OF A GOOD STEEL TRAP.

1. *The jaws should not be too thin nor sharp cornered.* In the cheaper class of steel traps the jaws approach to the thinness of sheet-iron, and the result is that the thin edges often sever the leg of their would-be captive in a single stroke. At other times the leg is so deeply cut as to easily enable the animal to gnaw or twist it off. This is the common mode of escape, with many animals.

2. *The pan should not be too large.* This is a very common fault with many steel traps and often defeats its very object. Where the pan is small, the foot of the animal in pressing it, will be directly in the centre of the snap of the jaw, and he is thus firmly secured far up on the leg. On the other hand, a large pan nearly filling the space between the jaws as the trap is set, may be sprung by a touch on its extreme edge, and the animal's toe is thus likely to get slightly pinched, if indeed the paw is not thrown off altogether by the forcible snap of the jaw.

3. *The springs should be strong, scientifically tempered, and proportioned.* The strength of a perfectly tempered spring will always remain the same, whether in winter or summer, never losing its elasticity. The best of tempering, however, is useless in a spring badly formed or clumsily tapered.

4. The jaws should be so curved as to give the bow of the spring a proper sweep to work upon. The jaws should lie *flat* when open, and should always work easily on their hinges.

5. Every trap should be furnished with a strong chain with ring and swivel attached, and in every case the swivel should turn easily.

The celebrated "Newhouse Trap" embodies all the above requisites, and has deservedly won a reputation for excellence second to no other in this or any other country.

They are made in eight sizes, as follows:

This is the smallest size and is known as the RAT TRAP. It has a single spring, and the jaws spread three and a half inches when set.

No. 0.

This size is called the MUSKRAT TRAP, and the jaws spread four inches. It is especially designed for the capture of the mink, marten, and animals of similar size.

No 1.

This is known in the trade as the MINK TRAP, and the jaws spread nearly five inches. It is adapted for the fox, raccoon, or fisher.

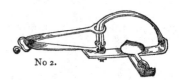

No 2.

This size is called the FOX TRAP. The spread of the jaws is the same as in the foregoing, but the trap is provided with two springs, and consequently has double the power. It is strong enough for the otter, and is generally used for the capture of the fox and fisher.

No 2½.

No. 3 goes by the name of the OTTER TRAP. The jaws spread five and a half inches, and the powerful double springs do excellent service in the capture of the beaver, fox, badger, opossum, wild cat, and animals of like size.

No 3.

Commonly called the BEAVER TRAP. Jaws spread six and a half inches. This size is especially adapted to the wolf, lynx or wolverine. It may also be set for deer, and extra sets of jaws are made expressly for this purpose, being easily inserted in the place of the ordinary jaws, when desired

No 4.

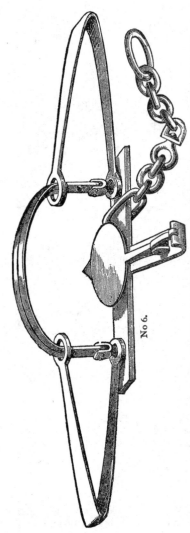

No 6.

This is known as the "GREAT BEAR TAMER," and is a most formidable weapon. The jaws spread sixteen inches, and the weight of the machine is forty-two pounds. It is extensively used in the capture of the moose and grizzly bear, and is the largest and most powerful steel trap made in this or any other country. The springs possess most tremendous power, and require to be set by a lever, as the weight of an ordinary man has not the slightest effect upon them. This lever may be easily applied, as follows: Have at hand four stout straps, supplied with buckles. These should always be carried by the trapper, where the larger double-spring traps are used. To adjust the lever, cut four heavy sticks about three feet long. Take two of them and secure their ends together, side by side, with one of the straps. Now insert the spring of the trap between them, near the strap. Bear down heavily on the other extremity of the lever, and the spring will be found to yield easily, after which the remaining ends of the levers should be secured by a second strap. The other spring should now be treated in the same way, after which the jaws should be spread and the pan adjusted. The removal of the straps and levers is now an easy matter, after which the trap is set. The stoutest spring is easily made to yield by such treatment.

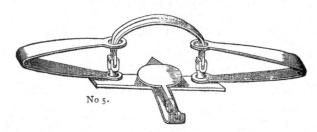

No 5.

The SMALL BEAR TRAP. The jaws of this size spread nearly a foot, and the weight of the trap is seventeen pounds. It is used in the capture of the black bear, puma, and animals of similar size.

All of the foregoing are supplied with swivels and chains.

HINTS ON BAITING THE STEEL TRAP.

There is a very common and erroneous idea current among amateur sportsmen and others in regard to the baiting of the steel trap ; viz., that the pan of the trap is intended for the *bait.*

This was the old custom in the traps of bygone times, but no modern trap is intended to be so misused, and would indeed often defeat its object in such a case, wherein it will be easily seen. The object of the professional trapper is, the acquisition of furs; and a prime fur skin should be without break or bruise, from nose to tail. A trap set as above described, would of course catch its victim by the head or neck, and the fur would be more or less injured at the very spot where it should be particularly free from blemish.

The true object of the steel trap is, that it shall take the animal by the *leg*, thus injuring the skin only in a part where it is totally valueless.

We give, then, this imperative rule—*Never bait a steel trap on the pan.*

The pan is intended for the *foot* of the game, and in order to insure capture by this means, the bait should be so placed as that the attention of the animal will be *drawn away* from the trap; the latter being in such a position as will cause the victim to *step in it* when reaching for the tempting allurement.

There are several ways of doing this, one of which we here illustrate.

A pen of stakes, in the shape of the letter V, is first constructed. The trap is then set in the angle, and the bait attached to the end stake directly over it. Another method is shown in the picture on our title-page to this section, the bait being suspended on a stick above the trap. There are various other methods on the same principle, which will be described hereafter, under the titles of the various game.

THE SPRING POLE.

This is nearly always used in connection with the steel trap, in the capture of the smaller land animals. It not only lifts the creature into the air, and thus prevents its becoming a prey to other animals, but it also guards against the escape of the victim by the amputation of its own leg. This is a very common mode of release with many kinds of game—notably the mink, marten, and muskrat; and for the successful trapping of these, as well as many other animals, the spring and sliding pole are absolute necessities. It is a simple contrivance, consisting merely of a pole inserted in the ground near the trap. The pole is then bent down, and the trap chain secured to its end. A small, notched peg is next driven into the ground and the top of the pole caught in it, and thus held in a bent position. When the animal is caught, its struggles release the pole, and the latter, flying up with a jerk, lifts the trap and its occupant high in the air, out of the reach of marauders, and beyond the power of escape by self-amputation. Even in the capture of large game the spring pole often serves to good purpose. The struggles of a heavy animal are often so

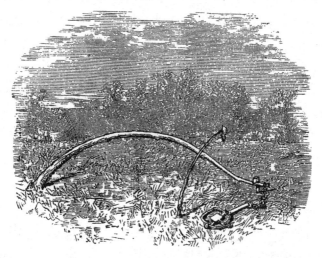

violent as to break a stout trap or chain; and the force of the spring pole, although not sufficient to raise the animal from its feet, often succeeds in easing the strain, and often thus saves a trap from being broken to pieces. The power of the pole must of course be proportionate to the weight of the desired game.

THE SLIDING POLE.

The first impulse with almost every aquatic animal when caught in a trap, is to plunge headlong into deep water. With the smaller animals, such as the mink and muskrat, this is all that is desired by the trapper, as the weight of the trap with the chain is sufficient to drown its victim. But with larger animals, the beaver and otter for instance, an additional precaution, in the shape of the "sliding pole," is necessary. This consists of a pole about ten feet long, smoothly trimmed of its branches, excepting at the tip, where a few stubs should be left. Insert this end obliquely into the bed of the stream, where the water is deep, and secure the large end to the bank by means of a hooked stick, as seen in our illustration. The ring of the chain should be large enough to slide easily down the entire length of the pole. When the trap is set, the ring should be slipped on the

large end of the pole, and held in place by resting a stick against it. The animal, when caught, plunges off into deep water, and guided by the pole, is led to the bottom of the river. The ring slides down to the bed of the stream, and there holds its victim until drowned.

THE CLOG.

A trap which is set for heavy game should never be secured to a stake. Many of the larger and more powerful animals when caught in a trap thus secured, are apt either to pull or twist their legs off, or break both trap and chain to pieces. To guard against this, the chain should be weighted with a pole or small log, of a size proportionate to the dimensions of the game, its weight being merely sufficient to offer a serious incumbrance to the animal, without positively checking its movements. This impediment is called the "clog," and is usually attached to the ring of the trap chain by its larger end, the ring being slipped over the latter, and secured in place by a wedge. A look at our frontispiece will give a clear idea of both clog and attachment.

THE GRAPPLING IRON.

This answers the same purpose as the above, and is often used instead. It is manufactured in connection with the larger

steel traps, and is attached to the chain by a swivel joint. - Its general shape is shown in an engraving, and it offers a serious resistance to the victim, who endeavors to run away with it.

THE SEASON FOR TRAPPING.

The business of trapping for profit must be confined to the season between the first of October and the beginning of May, as furs of all kinds are worthless when taken during the other months of the year. The reason of this is obvious. A "*prime fur*" must be "*thick*" and "*full*," and as all our fur-bearing animals shed their heavy winter coats as warm weather approaches, it necessarily follows that the capture at this season would be unprofitable. As the autumn approaches the new growth appears, and the fur becomes thick and glossy. By the middle of October most furs are in their prime, but the heart of winter is the best time for general trapping. The furs of the mink, muskrat, fisher, marten and beaver are not in their perfect prime until this season. And *all* other furs are *sure* to be in good condition at this time.

THE ART OF TRAPPING.

From time immemorial, and in every nation of the world, the art of trapping has been more or less practised. By some as a means of supplying their wants in the shape of daily food, and by others for the purpose of merchandise or profit.

To be a clever and succesful trapper, much more is required than is generally supposed. The mere fact of a person's being able to set a trap cleverly and judiciously forms but a small part of his proficiency; and unless he enters deeper into the subject and learns something of the nature and habits of the animals he intends to catch, his traps will be set in vain, or at best meet with but indifferent success. The study of natural history here becomes a matter of necessity as well as pleasure and profit. And unless the trapper thoroughly acquaints himself with the habits of his various game, the sagacity and cunning of his intended victim will often outwit his most shrewd endeavors, much to his chagrin. The sense of smell, so largely developed in many animals, becomes one of the trappers most serious obstacles, and seems at times to amount almost to positive *reason*, so perfectly do the creatures baffle the most ingenious attempts of man in his efforts to capture them. A little insight into the ways of these artful animals, however, and a little experience with their odd tricks soon enables one to cope with them successfully and overcome their whims. For the benefit of the amateur who has not had the opportunity of studying for himself, the peculiarities of the various game, the author appends a comprehensive chapter on "Practical Natural History," in which will be found full accounts of the peculiar habits and leading characteristics of all the various animals commonly sought by the trapper, together with detailed directions for trapping each variety, supplemented with a faithful portrait of the animal in nearly every instance. A careful reading of the above mentioned chapter will do much towards acquainting the novice with the ways of the sly creatures, which he hopes to victimize, and will thus prepare him to contend with them successfully.

In the art of trapping the bait is often entirely dispensed with, the traps being set and carefully concealed in the *runways* of the various animals. These by-paths are easily detected by an experienced trapper, and are indicated either by footprints or other evidences of the animal, together with the matted leaves and broken twigs and grasses.

Natural channels, such as hollow logs or crevices between rocks or fallen trees, offer excellent situations for steel traps, and a good trapper is always on the *qui vive* for such chance advantages, thus often saving much of the time and labor which would otherwise be spent in the building of artificial enclosures, etc.

The most effective baits used in the art of trapping are those which are used to attract the animal through its sense of smell, as distinct from that of its mere appetite for food. These baits are known in the profession as "medicine," or scent baits and possess the most remarkable power of attracting the various animals from great distances, and leading them almost irresistibly to any desired spot. Such is the barkstone or castoreum, of such value in the capture of the beaver, and the oil of anise, so commonly used for the trapping of animals in general. These various substances will presently be considered under their proper heading.

Many detailed and specific directions on the subject of trapping will be found in the long chapter following; and, in closing our preliminary remarks, we would add just one more word of general caution, which the young trapper should always bear in mind.

In all cases avoid handling the trap with the bare hand. Many an amateur has set and *reset* his traps in vain, and retired from the field of trapping in disgust, from the mere want of observing this rule. Animals of keen scent are quick in detecting the slightest odors, and that left by the touch of a human hand often suffices to drive the creature away from a trap which, under other circumstances, would have been its certain destruction. To be sure the various scent baits already alluded to, will in a measure overcome human traces, but not always effectually, and in order to insure success no precautions so simple should be neglected. A pair of clean buckskin gloves are valuable requisites to the trapper, and should always be "on hand" when setting or transporting traps.

"MEDICINES," OR SCENT BAITS.

These form one of the most important requisites of the trapper's art. A trap baited simply with the food of the required animal, may and often will be successful, but with the addition of the trapper's "medicine" judicially applied, success is almost a certainty. These scent baits are of various kinds, some being almost universal in their usefulness, while others are attractive only to some particular species of animal. We give a few of the recipes of the most valued preparations used by trappers throughout the land. The application and use of each is fully described in its proper place hereafter.

CASTOREUM.

This substance, commonly known as "*Barkstone,*" by trappers and fur dealers, is obtained from the beaver, and is a remarkable aid in the capture of that animal. It is an acrid secretion of a powerful musky odor, found in two glands beneath the root of the tail of the beaver. These glands are about two inches in length. They are cut out and the contents are squeezed into a small bottle. When fresh the substance is of a yellowish-red color, changing to a light-brown when dried. Both male and female animals yield the castoreum, but that of the male is generally considered the best. Castoreum is a commercial drug, and in many beaver countries it is quite an article of·trade. There are other sacs lying directly behind the castor glands which contain a strong oil of rancid smell. This should not be confounded with the castoreum.

CASTOREUM COMPOSITION.

The Barkstone is used both pure and in combination with other substances, the following prescription being much used : Into the contents of about ten of the castor bags, mix two ground nutmegs, thirty or forty cloves, also powdered, one drop essence of peppermint, and about two thimblefuls of ground cinnamon. Into this stir as much whisky as will give the whole the consistency of paste, after which the preparation should be bottled and kept carefully corked. At the expiration of a few days the odor increases ten-fold in power and is ready for use. A bottle, if thus prepared, will retain its strength for nearly a half year, provided it is kept closely corked. A few drops of either the pure castoreum or the combination spread upon the bait or in the neighborhood of the trap, as described under the chatpter on the Beaver, will entice that animal from a great distance.

MUSK.

This substance is a secretion obtained from several different animals, notably the otter and muskrat. The glands which contain it are located similarly to the castor glands of the beaver, and the musk should be discharged into a vial, as previously described. The musk of the female muskrat is said to be the most powerful, and is chiefly used by trappers in the capture of that animal, the otter being chiefly attracted by its own musk.

ASSAFŒTIDA.

This foul smelling production seems to have a specially attractive fragrance to many animals, and for general use is much esteemed by trappers. It is a vegetable drug from Persia and the East Indies, and is imported in the form of concrete juice, of a brown color.

OIL OF RHODIUM.

This is a vegetable oil obtained from a species of rose, and is quite costly. Its power of attracting animals is surprising, and it is in very common use among trappers.

FISH OIL.

This is especially useful in the capture of the majority of the fur tribe, and particularly the water animals.

The oil may be bought ready for use, or prepared with little trouble. The common method consists in cutting up fish of any kind, especially eels, into small bits, putting them in a bottle, and setting the latter in the full exposure to the sun. It should thus be left for about two weeks, at the end of which time a rancid oil will have formed. A few drops of this oil will entice many animals from surprising distances, often drawing their attention to a bait which otherwise they might never have scented.

OIL OF SKUNK.

This, the *ne plus ultra*, or quintessence of diabolical stench, yields the tempting savor which irrisistibly attracts many animals to their final doom. It is contained in a pouch beneath the insertion of the tail of the animal, and is spread abroad by the creature with lavish extravagance when circumstances demand, or we might say when occasion permits. It may be taken from the animal and bottled as already described in other instances, chloride of lime being used to eradicate the stench from the hands.

OIL OF AMBER.

This substance is frequently referred to in the following pages, and is a vegetable product of the amber gum of commerce. The Oil of Ambergris is also sometimes used by trappers, and is likewise known as Amber Oil. The two are thus often confounded, although the former is supposed to be most generally used.

OIL OF ANISE.

This is strongly recommended by many trappers as a most excellent "universal medicine." It is a vegetable product, and is obtainable at any drug store.

SWEET FENNEL.

This plant is commonly cultivated all over the United States, and the seeds are often powdered and used as a scent bait. The Oil of Fennel is preferable, however, and may be had at almost any drug store.

CUMMIN.

This is another plant, somewhat resembling the former, and, like it, cultivated for its seeds. It has an aromatic taste, and its strong pungent odor renders it of great value to the trapper. The seeds may be powdered and thus used, or the oil of the plant may be easily procured. The latter is preferable.

FENUGREEK.

Like the two foregoing this plant is valuable for its seeds, which are used for medicinal purposes. The oil or bruised seeds may be used.

LAVENDER.

This is another aromatic plant, the oil of which, either pure or diluted with alchohol, is much used in the trapper's art.

COMPOUND.

For ordinary use, a mixture of Assafoetida, Musk, Oil of Anise, and Fish Oil, together with a few drops of the Oil of Rhodium, is especially recommended by our most skilled trappers. This preparation contains the various substances which are known to attract the different fur bearing animals, and its use often insures success where any one of the simple substances would be ineffectual.

THE TRAIL.

The object of the "trail" consists in offering a leading scent which, when followed, will bring the animal to the various traps, and when properly made will be the means of drawing large numbers of game from all quarters and from great distances, whereas without it the traps might remain undiscovered.

Trails are sometimes made to connect a line of traps, as when set along the banks of streams for mink, etc., at other times, as in trapping the fox, for instance, they should extend from the trap on all sides, like the spokes of a wheel from the hub, thus covering considerable area, and rendering success more certain than it would be without this precaution.

The combination " medicine " just described is excellent for the purposes of a trail for minks, otter, muskrat, and many other animals.

Soak a piece of meat, or piece of wood in the preparation, and drag it along the ground between the traps. A dead fish smeared with the fluid will also answer the same purpose. The soles of the boots may also be smeared with the "medicine" and the trail thus accomplished. Trails of various kinds are considered under their respective and appropriate heads in the chapters on animals, all of which will be found useful and effective.

HOW TO TRAP.

In the following pages will be found full and ample directions for the trapping of all our leading game, together with detailed descriptions of peculiar habits of each species. The various articles contain careful descriptions, whereby the species may be readily recognized, and, in nearly every case, are accompanied by faithful illustrations. We add also valuable directions for the best manner of removing the skin of each animal, this being a matter of considerable importance, as affecting their pecuniary value.

THE FOX.

Foremost in the list of animals noted for their sly craft, and the hero of a host of fables and well-authenticated stories, in which artful cunning gains the advantage over human intelligence, Reynard, the fox, reigns supreme. There is scarcely a professional trapper in the land who has not, in his day, been hoodwinked by the wily strategy of this sly creature, whose extreme cunning renders him the most difficult of all animals to trap. The fox belongs to the Dog family, and there are six varieties inhabiting the United States. The red species is the most common and is too well-known to need a description here. The Cross Fox considerably resembles the above, only being much darker in color, the red hair being thickly speckled with black. This species varies considerably in color in different individuals, often much resembling the red variety, and again approaching nearer in color to the Black or Silver Fox. This variation, together with the name of the animal, has given rise among trappers to the wide-spread belief of the animal being a cross between the two species which it so nearly resembles. It seems to be a permanent variety, however, the term cross being applied, we believe, on account of a dark marking on the back, between the shoulders of the animal, suggestive of that title. The Silver or Black Fox is the most beautiful and most rare of the genus, and yields the most valuable fur produced in this country. Its color is black, with the exception of the tip of the tail, which is white. The Prairie Fox is the largest of the species. It inhabits the Western Prairies, and in color resembles the common red variety, only being a trifle yellower.

The Kit, or Swift Fox, is smaller than the Red, and abounds in the Western States.

The Gray Fox is a Southern variety, and is very beautiful. It is less daring and cunning than the Common Fox, and seldom approaches a farm-yard, where it is in close proximity to a dwelling.

The general habits and characteristics of all the foxes are similar. For natural cunning they take the lead of all other animals. They are all built for speed, and their senses of smell and hearing are acutely developed. Their food consists of wild fowl of all kinds, rabbits, squirrels, birds and their eggs, together with many kinds of ripe fruits, "sour grapes" not included. They live in burrows, often usurped, or crevices between rocks ; and their young, from three to nine in number, are brought forth in March.

We are strongly tempted to narrate a few remarkable instances of the animal's cunning, but we forbear for want of space. Our reader must take it for granted that when he attempts to trap a fox, he will be likely to find more than his match in the superior craftiness of that animal. If the trap is overturned and the bait gone, or if repeatedly sprung and found empty, he must not be surprised or discouraged, for he is experiencing only what all other trappers have experienced before him. There are instances on record where this knowing creature has sprung the trap by dropping a stick upon the pan, afterwards removing the suspended bait to enjoy it at his leisure. His movements are as lithe and subtile as those of a snake, and when " cornered " there is no telling what caper that cunning instinct and subtlety of body will not lead him to perform. When pursued by hounds he has been known to lead them a long chase at full speed up to the crest of a hill : here he leaps a shrub, swiftly as an arrow, and landing on the ground on the opposite declivity quickly returns beneath the brushwood and crouches down closely upon the ground. Presently the hounds come along in full cry, and blazing scent they dart over the shrub in full pursuit, dash down the hillside, never stopping until at the bottom of the hill they find they are off the trail. As soon as the hounds are passed, sly Reynard cautiously takes to his legs : creeping adroitly back over the brow of the hill, he runs for a considerable distance on his back trail, and at last, after taking a series of long jumps therefrom returns to his covert at leisure. Page after page might be filled to the glory of this creature's cunning, but enough has been said to give the young trapper an insight into the character of the animal he hopes to victimize, and prepare him for a trial of skill which, without this knowledge, would be a most one-sided affair.

We would not advise our young amateur to calculate very confidently on securing a fox at the first attempt, but we can truthfully vouch that if the creature can be *caught at all*, it can be done by following the directions we now give.

One of the most essential things in the trapping of this, as well as nearly all animals, is that the trap should be *perfectly clean and free from rust*. The steel trap No. 2, page 141 is the best for animals of the size of the Fox. The trap should be washed in weak lye, being afterwards well greased and finally smoked over burning hen's feathers.

All this and even more precaution is necessary. No matter how strongly scented the trap may be, with the smoke, or other substances, a mere touch of the bare hand will leave a *human scent* which the fox perceives as soon as the other, and this is enough to deaden his enthusiasm over the most tempting bait.

On this account, it is necessary always to handle the trap with buckskin gloves, never allowing the bare hand to come in contact with it, on any account, after once prepared for setting.

Before arranging the trap for its work, it is necessary to construct what is called a "bed."   There are several methods of doing this ; but from all we can learn from the most experienced trappers, the following is the most successful. The bed should be made on flat ground, using any of the following substances : Buckwheat chaff, which is the best, oat, wheat, or hay chaff, or in lieu of these, moss or wood ashes. Let the bed be three feet in diameter, and an inch and a half in depth. To insure success it is the best plan to bait the bed itself for several days with scraps of beef or cheese strewn upon, and near it.   If the fox once visits the place, discovers the tempting morsels and enjoys a good meal unmolested, he will be sure to revisit the spot so long as he finds a "free lunch " awaiting him. When he is found to come regularly and take the bait, he is as good as caught, provided our instructions are carefully followed. Take the trap, previously prepared as already described, chain it securely to a small log of wood about two feet long. Dig a hole in the earth in the centre of the bed, large enough to receive the trap, with its log, and chain. Set the traps, supporting the pan by pushing some of the chaff beneath it. Now lay a piece of paper over the pan and sprinkle the chaff over it evenly and smoothly, until every trace of the trap and its appendages is obliterated. Endeavor to make the bed look as it has previously done, and bait it with the same materials. Avoid treading much about the bed and step in the same tracks as far as possible. Touch nothing with the naked hands.   Cover up all the footprints as much as possible, and leave the trap to take care of itself and any intruder. If our directions have been accurately followed, and due care has been exercised on the part of the young trapper, there is every probability that the next morning will reward him with his fox. But if a day or two elapse without success, it is well to resort to the "scent baits" described on page 149. Take the trap out of the bed, and with a feather smear it with melted beeswax, or rub it with a little Oil of Rhodium, Assafœtida, or Musk. Oil of Amber, and Lavender water are also used for the same purpose by many professional trappers. These are not always necessary but are often used as a last resort, and will most always insure success.

Another method of baiting is shown in our page illustration opposite, and consists in suspending the bait by a stick in such a position that the fox will be obliged to step upon the trap in order to reach it. The bed should be baited in this way several times before the trap is set. This method is very commonly employed.

Another still, is to bury the dead body of a rabbit or bird in loose earth, covering the whole with chaff. Sprinkle a few drops of Musk, or Oil of Amber over the bed. After the fox has taken the bait, the place should be rebaited and the trap inserted in the mound and covered with the chaff, being scented as before.

Some trappers employ the following method with good results : The trap is set, in a spring or at the edge of a small shallow brook and attached by a chain to a stake in the bank, the chain being under water. There should be only about an inch and a half of water over the trap, and its distance from the shore should be about a foot and a half, or even less. In order to induce the fox to place his foot in the trap it is necessary to cut a sod of grass, just the size of the inside of the jaws of the trap, and place it over the pan, so that it will project above the water and offer a tempting foot rest for the animal while he reaches for the bait which rests in the water just beyond. To accomplish this device without springing the trap by the weight of the sod, it is necessary to brace up the pan from beneath with a small perpendicular stick, sufficiently to neutralize the pressure from above. The bait may be a dead rabbit or bird thrown on the water outside of the trap and about a foot from it, being secured by a string and peg. If the fox spies the bait he will be almost sure to step upon the sod to reach it, and thus get caught.

If none of these methods are successful, the young trapper may at least content himself with the idea that the particular fox he is after is an *old fellow* and is "not to be caught with chaff" or any thing else,—for if these devices will not secure him *nothing* will. If he is a young and comparatively unsophisticated specimen, he will fall an easy victim to any of the foregoing stratagems.

Athough steel traps are generally used in the capture of foxes, A cleverly constructed and baited dead-fall such as is described on page 113. will often do capital service in that direction. By arranging and baiting the trap as therein described, even a fox is *likely to become* its prey.

To skin the fox the pelt should be first ripped down each hind leg to the vent. The skin being cut loose around this point, the bone of the tail should next be removed. This may be done by holding a split stick tightly over the bone after which the latter may be easily pulled out of the skin.

The hide should then be drawn back, and carefully removed, working with caution around the legs, and particularly so about the eyes, ears, and lips when these points are reached. The skin should be stretched as described on page 273.

THE WOLF.

The United States are blessed with several species of this animal. The Grey Wolf, which is the largest, and the smaller, Prairie Wolf or Coyote, being the most commonly known. There are also the White Wolf, Black Wolf and the Texan or Red Wolf. In outward form they all bear a considerable resemblance to each other, and their habits are generally similar in the different varieties.

Wolves are fierce and dangerous animals, and are very powerful of limb and fleet of foot. They are extremely cowardly in character, and will seldom attack man or animal except when by their greater numbers they would be sure of victory. Wolves are found in almost every quarter of the globe. Mountain and plain, field, jungle and prairie are alike infested with them, and they hunt in united bands, feeding upon almost any animal which by their combined attacks they can overpower.

Their inroads upon herds and sheep folds are sometimes horrifying, and a single wolf has been known to kill as many as forty sheep in a single night, seemingly from mere blood-thirsty desire.

In the early colonization of America, wolves ran wild over the country in immense numbers, and were a source of great danger; but now, owing to wide-spread civilization, they have disappeared from the more settled localities and are chiefly found in Western wilds and prairie lands.

The Grey Wolf is the largest and most formidable representative of the Dog tribe on this continent. Its general appearance is truthfully given in our drawing. Its length, exclusive of the tail, is about four feet, the length of the tail being about a foot and a half. Its color varies from yellowish grey to almost white in the northern countries, in which latitude the animal is sometimes found of an enormous size, measuring nearly seven feet in length. The fur is coarse and shaggy about the neck and haunches, and the tail is bushy. They abound in the region east of the Rocky Mountains and northward, and travel in packs of hundreds in search of prey. Bisons, wild horses, deer and even bears fall victims to their united fierceness, and human beings, too, often fall a prey to their ferocious attacks.

The Coyote, or Common Prairie Wolf, also known as the Burrowing Wolf, as its name implies inhabits the Western plains and prairies. They are much smaller than the Grey Wolf, and not so dangerous. They travel in bands and unitedly attack

whatever animal they desire to kill. Their homes are made in burrows which they excavate in the ground. The Texan Wolf inhabits the latitude of Texas and southward. It is of a tawny red color and nearly as large as the grey species, possessing the same savage nature.

In April or May the female wolf retires to her burrow or den, and her young, from six to ten in number, are brought forth.

The wolf is almost as sly and cunning as the fox, and the same caution is required in trapping the animal. They are extremely keen scented, and the mere touch of a human hand on the trap is often enough to preclude the possibility of capture. A mere footprint, or the scent of tobacco juice, they look upon

with great suspicion, and the presence of either will often prevent success.

The same directions given in regard to trapping the fox are
equally adapted for the wolf. The trap (size No. 4, page 141)
should be smoked or smeared with beeswax or blood, and set in
a bed of ashes or other material as therein described, covering
with moss, chaff, leaves or some other light substance. The
clog should be fully twice as heavy as that used for the fox.
Some trappers rub the traps with "brake leaves," sweet fern, or
even skunk's cabbage. Gloves should always be worn in handling the traps, and all tracks should be obliterated as much as
if a fox were the object sought to be secured.

A common way of securing the wolf consists in setting the
trap in a spring or puddle of water, throwing the dead body of
some large animal in the water beyond the trap in such a position
that the wolf will be obliged to tread upon the trap, in order to
reach the bait. This method is described both under the head
of the Fox and the Bear.

Another plan is to fasten the bait between two trees which
are very close together, setting a trap on each side and carefully concealing them as already directed, and securing each to
a clog of about twenty pounds in weight. The enclosure described on page 144 is also successful.

There are various scent or trail baits used in trapping the
wolf. Oil of Assafœtida is by many trappers considered the
best, but Oil of Rhodium, powdered fennel, fenugreek and
Cummin Oil are also much used. It is well to smear a little of
the first mentioned oil near the traps, using any one of the other
substances, or indeed a mixture of them all, for the trail. This
may be made by smearing the preparation on the sole of the
boots and walking in the direction of the traps, or by dragging
from one trap to another a piece of meat scented with the sub
stance, as described under the head of Mink.

The wolf is an adept at feigning death, playing "'possum"
with a skill which would do credit to that veritable animal itself.

A large dead-fall, constructed of logs, page 17, when
skilfully scented and baited, will often allure a wolf into its
clutches, and a very strong twitch-up, with a noose formed of
heavy wire, or a strip of stout calf hide, will successfully capture the crafty creature.

In skinning the wolf the hide may be removed either by first
ripping up the belly, or in a circular piece, as described in connection with the fox, both methods being much used. The

board and hoop stretchers used in preparing the skin are described on pages 273 and 275.

THE PUMA.

The puma, commonly known also as the panther or cougar, is
the largest American representative of the Cat tribe, and for this
reason is often dignified by the name of the "American
Lion." It is found more or less abundantly throughout the
United States; and although not generally considered a dangerous foe to mankind, it has often been known in the wild districts to steal upon the traveller unawares, and in many instances human beings have fallen a prey to the powerful claws and
teeth of this powerful animal.

The life of the puma is mostly in the trees. Crouching upon
the branches it watches for, or steals, cat-like, upon its prey.
Should a solitary animal pass within reach, the puma will not
hesitate in pouncing upon the unfortunate creature; but if a
herd of animals, or party of men, should be travelling together,
the caution of the brute asserts itself, and he will often dog their
footsteps for a great distance, in hopes of securing a straggler.
Birds are struck down by a single blow of the puma's ready
paw, and so quick are his movements that even though a bird
has risen on the wing, he can often make one of his wonderful
bounds, and with a light, quick stroke, arrest the winged prey
before it has time to soar beyond reach. The puma is a good
angler. Sitting by the water's edge he watches for his victims,
and no sooner does an unfortunate fish swim within reach, than
the nimble paw is outstretcned, and it is swept out of the water
on dry land, and eagerly devoured.

A puma has been known to follow the track of travellers for
days together, only daring to show itself at rare intervals, and
never endeavoring to make an attack except through stealth. The
animal will often approach cautiously upon a traveller until sufficiently near to make its fatal spring; but if the pursued party
suddenly turn round and face the crawling creature, the beast
becomes discomfited at once, and will retreat from the gaze,
which seems to it a positive terror. So long as a puma can be
kept in sight, no danger need be feared from the animal, but it
will improve every opportunity of springing unobservedly upon
a heedless passer by. The total length of the puma is six feet
and a half, of which the tail occupies a little over two feet. Its
color is of a uniform light tawny tint, fading into light grey on

the under parts, and the tip of the tail is black. The puma is one of the few members of the Cat tribe, which are without the usual spots or stripes so observable in the tiger and leopard. The lion has the same uniformity of color, and it is perhaps partly on that account that the panther is so often known as the American lion. In infancy the young pumas possess decided tiger-like markings, and leopard-like spots, but these disappear altogether as the animal increases in size. The cougar has

learned by experience a wholesome fear of man, and as civilization has extended throughout our country, the animals have been forced to retire from the neighborhood of human habitations and hide themselves in thick, uncultivated forest lands.

Sometimes, however, the animal, urged by fierce hunger, will venture on a marauding expedition for several miles, and although not an object of personal dread to the inhabitants, he often becomes a pestilent neighbor to the farmer, committing great ravages among his flocks and herds, and making sad havoc in his poultry yard. It is not the fortune of every puma, however, to reside in the neighborhood of such easy prey as pigs, sheep and poultry, and the greater number of these animals are forced to depend for their subsistence on their own success in chasing or surprising the various animals on which they feed.

When a puma is treed by hunters, it is said to show great skill in selecting a spot wherein it shall be best concealed from the gazers below, and will even draw the neighboring branches about its body to hide itself from the aim of the hunter's rifle. While thus lying upon the branches the beast is almost invisible from below, as its fur, when seen, harmonizes so well with the the bark which covers the boughs, that the one can scarcely be distinguished from the other.

The puma loves to hide in the branches of trees, and from this eminence to launch itself upon the doomed animal that may pass within its reach. It may, therefore, be easily imagined how treacherous a foe the creature may be when ranging at will among the countless trees and jungles of our American forests.

Although so stealthy and sly a creature the cougar possesses very little cunning and is easily trapped. The Gun trap, page 20, is commonly and successfully employed in South America in the capture of the jaguar, as our title illustration, page 15, represents, and it may also be used with the same success in trapping the puma. The Bow trap, page 23, and the dead-fall described in the early part of the book, will all be found to work admirably in the destruction of this treacherous beast.

The animal may be entrapped alive, should any of our young trappers dare to try the experiment.

There are two ways of accomplishing this. The first is by the aid of a huge coop of logs, as described on page 30 or 33, and the other by the Pit-fall, as exemplified on page 31. Huge twitch-ups may also be constructed, using very strong wire. The bait may consist of a fowl, sheep's head, or the heart of any animal. Fresh meat of any kind will answer the purpose, and in the case of the Pit-fall a live fowl is preferable to a dead one as it will attract the puma by its motions, or by its cackling, and thus induce him to *spring* upon his prey, which will precipitate him to the bottom of the pit and thus effect his capture.

They are commonly taken with the steel trap. The puma seldom leaves the vicinity of the carcass of an animal it has killed until it is all devoured. When such a carcass can be found the capture of the beast is easily effected. Set the trap, size No. 5, page 143, near the remains, and cover the carcass with leaves. The next visit of the animal will find him *more attached* to the place than ever,—so much so that he will be unable to " *tear himself away.*"

The skin of the puma is properly removed by first cutting up the belly as described under the Beaver, using great care about the head and face.   Use the hoop stretcher, page

THE CANADIAN LYNX.

The lynx represents another of the Cat tribe, and as its name implies is a native of the regions north of the United States, although sometimes found in upper Maine and on the lower borders of the great lakes.   It is commonly known throughout Canada as the Peshoo, or " Le Chat."

Our illustration is a truthful representation of the animal.   Its total length exceeds three feet, and its tail is a mere stub.   The fur is thick, and the hairs are long, the general color being grey, sprinkled with black.   The legs are generally darker than the body, and the ears are often edged with white.   The limbs and muscles are very powerful, the paws are very large for the size of the animal, and are furnished with strong white claws, which are imbedded in the fur of the feet when not in use, they are shown in our illustration.   The ears of the lynx form a distinct feature, by which the animal could be easily identified ; they are long and tipped with stiff projecting hairs, giving the creature a very odd appearance.

The peshoo can not be said to be a very dangerous animal, unless it is attacked, when it becomes a most ferocious antagonist.   The writer knew of a gentleman who was pounced upon and very nearly killed by one of these infuriated creatures, and there are many like instances on record.

The principal food of the lynx consists of the smaller quadrupeds, the American hare being its favorite article of diet.   It is a good swimmer, and a most agile climber, chasing its prey among the branches with great stealth and dexterity.   Like the wolf, fox, and many other flesh eating-animals, the lynx does not content itself with the creatures which fall by the stroke of its own talons, or the grip of its own teeth, but will follow the trail of the puma, in its nocturnal quest after prey, and thankfully partake of the feast which remains after its predecessor has satisfied its appetite.

While running at full speed, the lynx presents a most ludicrous appearance, owing to its peculiar manner of leaping. It progresses in successive bounds, with its back slightly arched, and all the feet striking the ground nearly at the same instant. Powerful as the animal is, it is easily killed by a blow on the back, a slight stick being a sufficient weapon wherewith to destroy the creature. For this reason the " Dead-fall " is particularly adapted for its capture, and is very successful, as the animal possesses very little cunning, and will enter an enclosure of any

kind without the slightest compunction, when a tempting bait is in view. The dead-fall should of course be constructed on a large scale, and it is a good plan to have the enclosure deep, and the bait as far back as will necessitate the animal being well under the suspended log in order to reach it. The bait may consist of a dead quadruped or of fresh meat of any kind.

The Gun trap, page 20, and the Bow trap, page 23, will also be found efficient, and a very powerful twitch-up, constructed from a stout pole and extra strong wire will also serve to good purpose. The lynx is not so prolific as many of the feline tribe, the number of its young seldom exceeding two, and this only once a year. The fur of the animal is valuable for the purposes to which the feline skin is generally adapted, and commands a fair price in the market. Those who hunt or trap the lynx will do well to choose the winter months for the time of their operations, as during the cold season the animal possesses a thicker and warmer fur than it offers in the summer months.

When the steel trap is used, it should be of size No. 4, page

141, set at the opening of a pen of stakes, the bait being placed at the back of the enclosure in such a position, as that the animal will be obliged to step upon the pan of the trap in order to reach it. Any of the devices described under "Hints on Baiting" will be found successful.

The skin of the animal may be removed as directed in the case of the fox, being drawn off the body whole, or it may be removed after the manner of the beaver, and similarly stretched.

THE WILD CAT.

This animal is one of the most wide-spread species of the Cat tribe, being found not only in America, but throughout nearly the whole of Europe as well as in Northern Asia. In many parts of the United States, where the wild cat was wont to flourish, it has become exterminated, owing to civilization and the destruction of forest lands.

Many naturalists are of the opinion that the wild cat is the original progenitor of our domestic cat, but there is much difference of opinion in regard to the subject. Although they bear great resemblance to each other, there are several points of distinction between the two; one of the most decided differences being in the comparative length of the tails. The tail of the wild cat is little more than half the length of that of the domestic cat, and much more bushy.

The color of the wild animal is much more uniform than in the great raft of "domestic" mongrel specimens which make night hideous with their discordant yowls, although we sometimes see a high bred individual which, if his tail was cut off at half its length, might easily pass as an example of the wild variety.

The ground tint of the fur in the wild cat is yellowish grey, diversified with dark streaks over the body and limbs, much after the appearance of the so-called "tiger cat." A row of dark streaks and spots extends along the spine, and the tail is thick, short and bushy, tipped with black and encircled with a number of rings of a dark hue. In some individuals the markings are less distinct, and they are sometimes altogether wanting, but in the typical wild cat they are quite prominent. The fur is rather long and thick, particularly so during the winter season, and always in the colder northern regions.

The amount of havoc which these creatures often occasion is surprising, and their nocturnal inroads, in poultry yards and sheep folds, render them most hated pests to farmers in the countries where these animals abound. They seem to have a special appetite for the *heads* of fowls, and will often decapitate a half dozen in a single night, leaving the bodies in otherwise good condition to tell the story of their midnight murders. The home of the wild cat is made in some cleft of rock, or in the hollow of some aged tree, from which the creature issues in the dark hours and starts upon its marauding excursions. Its family numbers from three to six, and the female parent is smaller than the male, the total length of the latter being three feet.

Inhabiting the most lonely and inaccessible ranges of rock and mountain, the wild cat is seldom seen during the daytime. At night, like its domestic relative, he prowls far and wide, walking with the same stealthy step and hunting his game in the same tiger-like manner. He is by no means a difficult animal to trap, being easily deceived and taking a bait without any hesitation. The wild cat haunts the shores of lakes and rivers, and it is here that the traps may be set for them. Having caught and killed one of the colony, the rest of them can be easily taken if the body of the dead victim be left near their hunting ground and surrounded with the traps carefully set and concealed beneath leaves moss or the like. Every wild cat that is in the neighborhood will be certain to visit the body, and if the traps are rightly arranged many will be caught. The trap No. 3, page 141 is generally used. We would caution the young trapper in his approach to an entrapped wild cat, as the strength and ferocity of this animal under such circumstances, or when otherwise "hard pressed," is perfectly amazing. When caught in a trap they spring with terrible fury at any one who approaches them, not waiting to be assailed, and when cornered or hemmed in by a hunter they will often turn upon their pursuer, and springing at his face will attack him with most consummate fury, often inflicting serious and sometimes fatal wounds. When hunted and attacked by dogs, the wild cat is a most desperate and untiring fighter, and extremely difficult to kill, for which reason it has been truthfully said that "if a tame cat has nine lives, a *wild cat* must have a dozen."

The twitch-up, erected on a large scale, is utilized to a considerable extent in England in the capture of these animals; and these, together with steel traps and dead-falls, are about the only machines used for their capture. We would suggest the garrote, bow and gun trap also as being very effective. The bait may consist of the head of a fowl or a piece of rabbit or fowl flesh: or, indeed, flesh of almost any kind will answer, particularly of the bird kind.

In skinning the wild cat the same directions given under the head of the Fox may be followed, or the pelt may be ripped up the belly and spread on a hoop stretcher, page 275.

THE BEAR.

There are several species of the Bear tribe which inhabit our continent, the most prominent of which are the Grizzly, and the Musquaw or common Black Bear. There is no other animal of this country which is more widely and deservedly dreaded than the grizzly bear. There are other creatures, the puma and wild cat, for instance, which are dangerous when cornered or wounded, but they are not given to open and deliberate attack upon human beings. The grizzly, however, or " Ephraim," as he is commonly termed by trappers, often displays a most unpleasant readiness to attack and pursue a man, even in the face of fire arms. In many localities, however, where hunting has been pursued to considerable extent, these animals have learned from experience a wholesome fear of man, and are not so ready to assume the offensive, but a " *wounded* " grizzly is one of the most horrible antagonists of which it is possible to conceive, rushing upon its victim with terrible fury, and dealing most tearing and heavy blows with its huge claws.

In length this formidable animal often exceeds eight feet, and its color varies from yellowish to brownish black, and some specimens are found of a dirty grey color.

The legs are usually darker than the rest of the body, and the face is generally of a lighter tint. The fore limbs of the animal are immensely powerful; and the foot of a full-grown individual is fully eighteen inches long, and armed with claws five inches in length. The grizzly inhabits the Rocky Mountain regions and northward, being found in considerable numbers in the western part of British America. Its hair is thick and coarse, except in the young animal, which possesses a beautiful fur.

All other creatures seem to stand in fear of this formidable beast. Even the huge bison, or buffalo, of the Western Prairies sometimes falls a victim to the grizzly bear, and the very imprint of a bear's foot upon the soil is a warning which not even a hungry wolf will disregard.

Its food consists of whatever animal it can seize, whether human or otherwise. He also devours green corn, nuts, and fruits of all kinds. In his earlier years he is a good climber, and will ascend a tree with an agility which is surprisingly inconsistent with the unwieldy proportions of his body.

The average weight of a full-grown grizzly is over eight hundred pounds, and the girth around the body is about eight feet.

The Black bear, or Musquaw, which we illustrate is common throughout nearly all the half settled-districts of North America. But as the fur and fat are articles of great commercial value, the hunters and trappers have exercised their craft with such skill and determination that the animals are gradually decreasing in numbers. The total length of the black bear is seldom more than six feet, and its fur is smooth and glossy in appearance. The color of the animal is rightly conveyed by its name, the cheeks only partaking of a reddish fawn color.

It possesses little of that fierceness which characterizes the grizzly, being naturally a very quiet and retiring creature, keeping itself aloof from mankind, and never venturing near his habitations except when excited by the pangs of fierce hunger. When pursued or cornered it becomes a dangerous antagonist; and its furious rage often results in fearful catastrophes to both man and beast. Nothing but a rifle ball in the right spot will check the creature, when wrought up to this pitch of fury, and an additional wound only serves to increase its terrible ferocity. Bear-chasing is an extremely dangerous sport; and there are few bear-hunters in the land, however skilful, but what can show scars from the claws or teeth of some exasperated bruin.

The food of the black bear is mostly of a vegetable character,

animal diet not being indulged in unless pressed by hunger. At such times it seems to especially prefer a young pig as the most desirable delicacy; and even full-grown hogs, it is said, are sometimes lifted from their pens and carried off in his deadly embrace.

Honey is his especial delight; and he will climb trees with great agility in order to reach a nest of bees, there being few obstacles which his ready claws and teeth will not remove where that dainty is in view. He is also very fond of acorns, berries, and fruits of all kinds.

The young of the bear are produced in January or February, and are from one to four in number. They are very small and covered with grey hair, which coat they retain until they are one year of age. The flesh of the bear is held in high esteem among hunters, and when properly prepared is greatly esteemed by epicures.

The fat of the animal is much used under the title of "Bear

grease," and is believed to be an infallible hair rejuvenator, and therefore becomes a valuable article of commerce.

The bear generally hibernates during the winter, choosing some comfortable residence which it has prepared in the course of the summer, or perhaps betaking itself to the hollow of some tree. Sometimes, in case of early snow, the track of the bears may be distinguished, and if followed will probably lead to their dens, in which they can be secured with logs until it is desired to kill them.

The black bear has a habit of treading in a beaten track, which is easily detected by the eye of an experienced hunter or trapper, and turned to good account in trapping the animal.

There are various modes of accomplishing this result. The bear Dead-fall, described on page 17, is, perhaps, the most commonly used, and the Pit-fall, page 31, and "Giant Coop" trap are also excellent. The Gun trap and stone dead-fall, page 20, we also confidently recommend. When a steel trap is used it requires the largest size, especially made for the purpose. It should be supplied with a short and very strong chain firmly secured to a very heavy clog or grappling-iron page 147. If secured to a tree or other stationary object, the captured animal is likely to gnaw or tear his foot away, if, indeed, he does not break the trap altogether by the quick tightening of the chain. The clog should be only heavy enough to be an *impediment*, and may consist of a log or heavy stone. The grappling-iron, however, is more often used in connection with the bear trap. It is a common method in trapping the bear to construct a pen of upright branches, laying the trap at its opening, and covering it with leaves. The bait is then placed at the back in such a position that the animal, on reaching for it, will be sure to put his foot in the trap.

An experienced trapper soon discovers natural openings between rocks or trees, which may be easily modified, and by the addition of a few logs so improved upon as to answer his purpose as well as a more elaborate enclosure, with much less trouble. Any arrangement whereby the bear will be obliged to tread upon the trap in order to secure the bait, is, of course, all that is required. The bait may be hung on the edge of a rock five feet from the ground, and the trap set on a smaller rock beneath it. He will thus be almost sure to rest his forefoot on the latter rock in order to reach the bait, and will thus be captured.

Another way is to set the trap in a spring of water or swampy spot. Lay a lump of moss over the pan, suspending the bait beyond the trap. The moss will offer a natural foot-rest, and the offending paw will be secured.

Bears possess but little cunning, and will enter any nook or corner without the slightest compunction when in quest of food. They are especially fond of sweets, and, as we have said, are strongly attracted by honey, being able to scent it from a great distance. On this account it is always used, when possible, by trappers in connection with other baits. These may consist of a fowl, fruit, or flesh of any kind, and the honey should be smeared over it. Skunk cabbage is said to be an excellent bait for the bear; and in all cases a free use of the Oil of Anise page 152, sprinkling it about the traps, is also advisable. Should the device fail, it is well to make a trail (see page 153) in several directions from the trap, and extending for several rods. A piece of wood, wet with Oil of Anise, will answer for the purpose.

The general method of skinning the bear consists in first cutting from the front of the lower jaw down the belly to the vent, after which the hide may be easily removed. The hoop-stretcher page 275, will then come into good use in the drying and preparing of the skin for market.

THE RACCOON.

Although allied to the Bear family, this animal possesses much in common with the fox, as regards its general disposition and character. It has the same slyness and cunning, the same stealthy tread, besides an additional mischievousness and greed. It is too common to need any description here, being found plentifully throughout nearly the whole United States. The bushy tail, with its dark rings, will be sufficient to identify the animal in any community. Raccoon hunts form the subject of many very exciting and laughable stories, and a " coon chase," to this day is a favorite sport all over the country. The raccoon, or " coon," as he is popularly styled, is generally hunted by moonlight. An experienced dog is usually set on the trail and the fugitive soon seeks refuge in a tree, when its destruction is almost certain. Hence the term " treed coon," as applied to an individual when in a dangerous predicament. Besides possessing many of the peculiarities of the fox, the " coon " has the additional accomplishment of being a most agile and expert climber, holding so firmly to the limb by its sharp claws as to defy all attempts to shake it off.

The home of the raccoon is generally in a hollow tree ; the young are brought forth in May, and are from four to six in number.

In captivity this animal makes a very cunning and interesting pet, being easily tamed to follow its master, and when dainties are in view becomes a most adroit pickpocket. Its food is extensive in variety, thus making it quite an easy matter to keep the creature in confinement. Nuts and fruits of all kinds it eagerly devours, as well as bread, cake and potatoes. It manifests no hesitation at a meal of rabbit, rat, squirrel, or bird, and rather likes it for a change, and when he can partake of a dessert of honey or molasses his enjoyment knows no bounds. Frogs, fresh water clams, green corn, and a host of other delicacies come within the range of his diet, and he may sometimes be seen digging from the sand the eggs of the soft-shelled turtle, which he greedily sucks. We cordially recommend the coon as a pet. He becomes very docile, and is full of cunning ways, and if the young ones can be traced to their hiding-place in some hollow tree, and secured, if not *too* young, we could warrant our readers a great deal of real sport and pleasure in rearing the little animals and watching their ways

In cold climates the raccoon lies dormant in the winter, only venturing out on occasional mild days ; but in the Southern States he is active throughout the year, prowling about by day and by night in search of his food, inserting his little sharp nose into every corner, and feeling with his slender paws between stones for spiders and bugs of all kinds. He spies the innocent frog with his head just out of the water, and pouncing upon him, he despatches him without a moment's warning. There seems to be no limits to his rapacity, for he is always eating and always hungry. The print of the raccoon's paw in the mud or snow is easily recognized, much resembling the impression made by the foot of a babe.

The best season for trapping the coon is late in the fall, winter, and early spring, or from and between the months of October and April. During this time the pelts are in excellent condition Early in the spring when the snow is disappearing, the coons come out of their hiding places to start on their foraging tours ; and at this time are particularly susceptible to a tempting bait, and they may be successfully trapped in the following manner :—

Take a steel trap and set it on the edge of some pool, or stream where the coons are known to frequent : let it be an inch or so under the water, and carefully chained to a clog. The bait may consist of a fish, frog, or head of a fowl, scented with Oil of Anise, and suspended over the traps about two feet higher, by the aid of a sapling secured in the ground. (See title page at the head of this section.) The object of this is to induce the animal to jump for it, when he will land with his foot in the trap. Another method is to construct a V shaped pen,

set the trap near the entrance, and, fastening the bait in the angle, cover the trap loosely with leaves, and scent the bait as before with the anise. The trap should be at such a distance from the bait that the animal, in order to reach it, will be obliged to tread upon the pan, which he will be sure to do, his greed overcoming his discretion. Any arrangement whereby the animal will be obliged to tread upon the trap in order to reach the bait will be successful.

The beaten track of the coons may often be discovered in soft ground, and a trap carefully concealed therein will soon secure its victim. Another method is to set the trap near the coon tracks, spreading a few drops of anise on the pan and covering the whole with leaves. The coon, attracted by the scent, will feel around in the leaves for the bait, and thus "put his foot in it."

In the South they construct a coon trap from a hollow log, either having the ends supplied with lids, which fall just like the Rat trap page 106 as the animal passes through, or else constructed with nooses, similar to the Box-snare, page 56. Box traps of a style similar to that described on page 103 are also excellent, and a strong twitch-up, of any of the various kinds we have described, will be found to work admirably.

Many of the suggestions in trapping the mink, page 190, will be found equally serviceable in regard to the coon.

The skin of this animal should be removed as recommended for the fox, and similarly stretched. It may also be skinned by first ripping up the belly, and spread on a hoop .stretcher. page 275.

THE BADGER.

The American Badger is mostly confined to the North-western parts of the United States, and it is a curious little animal. In size its body is slightly smaller than the fox Its general color is grey, approaching to black on the head and legs. There is a white streak extending from the tip ot the animal's long nose over the top of the head and fading off near the shoulders. The cheeks are also white, and a broad and definitely marked black line extends from the snout back around the eyes ending at the neck. The grey of this animal is produced from the mixture of the varied tints of its fur, each hair presenting a succession of shades. At the root it is of a deep grey; this fades into a tawny yellow, and is followed by a black, the hair being finally tipped with white. The fur is much used in the manufacture of fine paint brushes, a good "Badger blender" being a most useful accessory in the painter's art. The badger is slow and clumsy in its actions, except when engaged in digging, his capacities in this direction being so great as to enable him to sink himself into the ground with marvellous rapidity. The nest of the animal is made in the burrow, and the young are three or four in number. His diet is as variable and extensive as that of the coon, and consists of anything in any way eatable. Snails, worms, rats, mice and moles, seem to have a particular attraction for him ; and he seems to take especial delight in unearthing the stores of the wild bees, devouring honey, wax and grubs together, and

caring as little for the stings of the angry bees as he would of
the bills of so many mosquitoes, the thick coating of fur
forming a perfect protection against his winged antagonists.
The badger is very susceptible to human influence, and can be
effectually tamed with but little trouble. Although his general
appearance would not indicate it, he is a sly and cunning animal,
and not easily captured in a trap of any kind. He has been
known to set at defiance all the traps that were set for him, and

to devour the baits without suffering for his audacity. He will
sometimes overturn a trap and spring it from the under side,
before attempting to remove the bait. Although not quite as
crafty as the fox, it is necessary to use much of the same
caution in trapping the badger, as a bare trap seldom wins
more than a look of contempt from the wary animal.
    The usual mode of catching the creature is to set the trap
size No 3 at the mouth of its burrow, carefully covering it
with loose earth and securing it by a chain to a stake. Any of
the methods used in trapping the fox will also be found to
work admirably. The dead-fall or garrote will also do good
service. Bait with a rat, mouse, or with whatever else the
animal is especially fond, and scent with Oil of Anise or Musk.
In early spring, while the ground is still hard, badgers are
easily captured by flooding their burrows. After being satisfied that the animal is in its hole, proceed to pour in pailfull
after pailful of water at the entrance. He will not long be able

to stand this sort of thing, and he may be secured as he makes his exit at the opening of the burrow.

The skin should be removed whole, as in the case of the fox, or as described for the beaver, and stretched as therein indicated.

THE BEAVER.

The Beaver of North America has now a world-wide reputation for its wonderful instinct and sagacity. The general appearance of this animal is that of a very large muskrat with a broad flattened tail, and the habits of both these animals are in many respects alike. The beaver is an amphibious creature and social in its habits of living, large numbers congregating together and forming little villages, and erecting their dome-like huts like little Esquimaux. The muskrat has this same propensity, but the habitation of the beaver is on a much more extensive scale. These huts or " Beaver lodges," are generally made in rivers and brooks, although sometimes in lakes or large ponds. They are chiefly composed of branches, moss, grass and mud, and are large enough to accommodate a family of five or six. The form of the " lodges " is dome-like, and it varies considerably in size. The foundation is made on the bottom of the river, and the hut is built up like a mound, often twenty feet in diameter and projecting several feet above the surface of the water. The walls of this structure are often five or six feet thick, and the roofs are all finished off with a thick layer of mud laid on with marvellous smoothness. These huts form the winter habitations of the beavers, and as this compost of mud, grass and branches becomes congealed into a solid mass by the severe frosts of our northern winter, it can easily be seen that they afford a safe shelter against any intruder and particularly the wolverine, which is a most deadly enemy to the beaver. So hard does this frozen mass become as to defy even the edges of iron tools, and the breaking open of the " Beaver houses " is at no time an easy task. Beavers work almost entirely in the dark ; and a pond which is calm and placid in the day time will be found in the night to be full of life and motion, and the squealing and splashing in the water will bear evidence of their industry. Lest the beavers should not have a sufficient depth of water at all seasons, they are in the habit of constructing veritable dams to ensure that result. These dams display a wonderful amount of reason and skill, and, together with the huts, have won for the beaver a reputation for engineering skill which the creature truly deserves. In constructing these ingenious dams the beavers, by the aid of their powerful teeth, gnaw down trees sometimes of large size, and after cutting them into smaller pieces float them on the water to the spot selected for the embankment. In swift

streams this embankment is built so as to arch against the current, thus securing additional strength, and evincing an instinct on the part of the animal which amounts almost to reason. In cutting down the trees the beaver gnaws a circular cut around the trunk, cutting deepest on the side toward the water, thus causing the trunk to fall into the stream. The first step in constructing the embankment is to lay the logs down cautiously in the required line of the dam, afterwards weighting them with heavy stones, which the beavers by their united efforts roll upon them. The foundation of the embankment is often ten feet in width, and is built up by continued heaping of branches, stones and mud, until it forms a barrier of immense strength and resisting power. In many cases, through a lapse of years, and through a consequent accumulation of floating leaves, twigs, and seeds of plants, these embankments become thickly covered with vegetation, and, in many cases in the Hudson Bay country, have even been known to nurture trees of considerable dimensions. The broad flat tail of the animal serves a most excellent purpose, in carrying the mud to the dams or huts, and in matting and smoothing it into a solidity.

The entrances to the various huts are all beneath the water, and they all open into one common ditch, which is purposely dug in the bed of the river, and is too deep to be entirely frozen. In the summer time the huts are vacated, and the beavers make their abode in burrows on the banks of the stream, which serve as a secure retreat at all times, and particularly in winter when their houses are molested. The Indians of the Northwest are aware of this fact, and turn it to good account in the capture of the animals.

When the beaver's village is in a small creek, or brook, it is first necessary to stake the water across both above and below the huts. The next thing is to ascertain the exact spots of the burrows in the banks, and when we consider the river is covered with ice, this seems a rather difficult problem. But this is where the Indian shows his skill. He starts upon the ice, provided with an ice chisel secured to a long, stout handle. With this he strikes upon the ice, following the edge of the stream. The sound of the blow determines to his practiced ear the direct spot opposite the opening of the burrows, and at this point a hole a foot in diameter is made through the ice. Following the edge of the bank he continues his search, and in like manner cuts the holes through the ice until all the retreats are discovered. While the expert Indians are thus engaged, the "squaws" are occupied in the more laborious work of breaking open the houses, and the beavers, alarmed at the invasion of their sanctums, make for the banks, and the ready huntsmen stationed at the various holes, watch for their victims beneath the openings, until a violent motion or discoloration of the water betrays their passage beneath. The entrance to the holes in the bank are then instantly closed with stakes and the beaver is made prisoner in his burrow. When the depth of the burrow will admit, the arm of the hunter is introduced, and the animal pulled out, but otherwise a long hook lashed to a pole is employed for this purpose. Scores of beavers are sometimes taken in this way in a few hours. Spearing is also often successfully resorted to, and when the ice is thin and transparent the beavers may be clearly observed as they come to the surface, beneath the ice, for air.

The general color of the animal is reddish brown, this tint being imparted principally by the long hairs of the fur. There is an inner and softer down of a grey color, which lies next the skin, and which is the valuable growth of the fur. The total length of the animal is about three feet and a half, the flat, paddle-shaped, scale-covered tail being about a foot in length.

The young are brought forth in April or May, from three to seven at a litter, and take to the water when a month old. The first four years in the beaver's life is spent under the "maternal roof," after which period they shift for themselves. To trap the beaver successfully, requires the utmost caution, as the senses of the animal are so keen, and he is so sagacious withal, that he will detect the recent presence of the trapper from the slightest evidences. The traps should be washed clean and soaked in ley, before using, and thereafter handled with gloves, as a mere touch of the finger will leave a scent which the acute sense of the beaver will easily perceive. All footprints should be carefully obliterated by throwing water upon them, and some trappers say that the mere act of spitting on the ground in the neighborhood of the traps has been known to thwart success.

Almost the only bait used in trapping the beaver is the preparation called "barkstone' by the trappers, or "castoreum" in commerce. This substance is fully described on page 150 under the head of "Scent Baits."

To the barkstone the trapper is mostly indebted for his success, and the effect of its odor on the beaver is something surprising. Our best trappers inform us that these animals will scent this odor for a great distance, and will fairly "squeal with delight," not being easy until the savory bait is discovered, which almost invariably results in capture.

Taking advantage of this curious propensity, the trapper always carries a supply of castoreum in a closed vessel.

There are various ways of trapping the beaver, of which we shall present the best. An examination of the river bank will easily disclose the feeding place of the beavers, as evinced by the absence of the bark on the branches and trunks of trees. At this spot, in about four inches of water, set your trap, which should be a Newhouse No. 4. Weight the end of the chain with a stone as large as your head, and, if possible, rest it on the edge of some rock projecting into deep water, having a smaller rope or chain leading from the stone to the shore. A small twig, the size of your little finger, should then be stripped of its bark, and after chewing or mashing one end, it should be dipped in the castoreum. Insert this stick in the mud, between the jaws of the trap, letting it project about six inches above the water. The beaver is soon attracted by the odor of the bait, and in reaching for it, his foot is caught in the trap. In his fright he will immediately jump for deep water, thus dislodging the stone, which will sink him to the bottom, and thus drown him. The smaller chain or rope will serve as a guide to the trap, and the victim may be drawn to the surface. Another plan is to set the trap in about a foot of water, chaining it fast to a stout pole securely driven in the mud further out in the stream, and near deep water. Bait as before. The trap being thus fastened will prevent the efforts of the animal to drag it ashore, where he would be certain to amputate his leg and walk off. There is another method, which is said to work excellently. The chain is secured to a very heavy stone, and sunk in deep water, and the trap set and baited near shore, in about a foot of water. This accomplishes the same purpose as the pole first described, and is even surer, as the animal will sometimes use his teeth in severing the wood, and thereby make his escape. In the case of the stone a duplicate rope or chain will be required to lift it in case of capture.

The trap may be set at the entrance to the holes in the banks, two or three inches under water, implanting the stick with the castoreum bait directly over the pan, a few inches above the water. If the water should be deep near this spot, it is an excellent plan to weight the end of the chain with a large stone with a "leader" from it also, as already described. Insert two or three sticks in the bank beneath the water, and rest the stone upon them.

When the beaver is caught he will turn a somersault into deep water, at the same time dislodging the stone, which will sink him. No sooner is a break ascertained in the dam than all the beavers unite in fixing it, and this peculiarity of habit may be turned to account in trapping them. Make a slight break in the dam, five inches across, beneath the water. On the under side of the break, and of course, on the inside of the dam, the trap should be set. The beavers will soon discover the leak, and the capture of at least *one* is certain. The trap may be also set where the beavers are wont to crawl on shore, being placed several inches below the water in such a position that they will step on it when in the act of ascending the banks. Where the weighted stone is not used, the sliding pole page 145 should always be employed, as it is necessary to drown the animal, to prevent amputation and escape.

The food of the beaver consists chiefly of the bark of various trees, together with aquatic plants. The fur is valuable only in the late fall, winter, and early spring.

In skinning the beaver, a slit is made from the under jaw to the vent, after which it is easily removed. It should be tacked to a flat board, fur side in, or stretched by means of a hoop, as described on page 275.

THE MUSKRAT.

The muskrat, or musquash, is very much like a beaver on a small scale, and is so well-known throughout the United States that a detailed description or illustration will hardly be necessary. Reduce the size of the beaver to one foot in length, and add a long flattened tail, instead of the spatula-shaped appendage of this animal, and we will have a pretty good specimen of a muskrat. The body has that same thick-set appearance, and the gnawing teeth are very large and powerful. Like the beaver, the muskrat builds its dome-like huts in ponds or swamps, which it frequents; and although not as large as those of the beaver they are constructed in the same manner and of the same materials. Muskrats are mostly nocturnal in their habits; they are tireless swimmers, and in the winter travel great distances beneath the ice; all of which peculiarities are like the beaver. Their food is quite variable, consisting of grass and roots, oats, corn and other grain, apples and nuts, and even tomatoes, turnips, carrots, mussels and clams, whenever these can be found.

The muskrat is a native of all of the Eastern, Western, and Middle States, and also the Southern States, with the exception of Georgia, Alabama and Florida. They are also found in Canada and the Arctic regions, and in the North-west. They are hunted and captured as a means of support to the native tribes of Indians who sell or trade the furs to Eastern dealers. The fur somewhat resembles that of the mink in texture, although not as fine, and the color varies from dark brown above to grey beneath. It is in its best condition during the winter, especially in March. The animal possesses a musky smell, from which it takes its name. It is said by many that the flesh of the animal, when carefully prepared, becomes quite palatable food.

Their houses are so nearly like those of the beaver that a

second description is scarcely necessary. They are often five or six feet in height, and the entrances are all under water Dozens of these huts may often be seen in ponds and marshes, and sometimes they exist in such numbers as to give the appearance of a veritable Esquimaux village. These houses are used only in the winter season. In general the muskrat lives in burrows, which it excavates in the banks of ponds or streams, bringing forth its young, from three to nine in number, in the nest, which it forms at the end of the tunnel. They are very prolific, producing three litters a year. Like the beaver, otter and mink, the muskrat can travel long distances under the ice with only one supply of fresh air, and its method is certainly very interesting. Before plunging beneath the ice the animal fills its lungs with air, and when under the water it swims until it can no longer hold its breath. It then rises up beneath the ice, empties its lungs, the air remaining in bubbles beneath the ice. In a short time this air absorbs sufficient oxygen from the water and ice as to be life-sustaining, when the animal again inhales it and proceeds on its journey. It is by this means that the beaver, muskrat and mink are enabled to travel such great distances beneath unbroken ice, and it is certainly a very novel and interesting method. Where the ice is thin and transparent these animals are sometimes captured through the means of this habit. A heavy stroke on the frozen hut will drive its occupants to the water, and their course may easily be followed through the ice. If one of them is tracked, he will presently be seen to stop at the surface of the water for fresh oxygen, as already described. The bubbles will soon appear, and if the hunter immediately strikes with an axe or heavy stick directly on the spot, the submerged animal will be literally driven away from its breath, and will of course drown in a very few minutes. A short search will soon reveal the dead creature, after which he may be taken out through a hole cut in the ice. Otter and mink are sometimes taken in the same way. In many localities great numbers of muskrats are also captured by spearing, either through the ice or through the walls of their houses. In the latter case, two are often taken at once. This method is quite uncertain and unreliable, as the walls of the hut are often so firmly frozen as to defy the thrust of the hardest steel, and a fruitless attempt will drive the inmates from their house at once. The spear generally used consists of a single shaft of steel about eighteen inches in length and half an inch in diameter, barbed at the point, and is feruled to a

solid handle five feet long. In spearing through the hut the
south side is generally selected, as being more exposed to the
heat of the sun.   Great caution is necessary, as the slightest
noise will drive out the inmates.   The spear should be thrust
in a slanting direction, a few inches above the surface of the
ice.   Where many houses exist it is well to destroy all but one.
Into this the whole tribe will centre, and by successive spearing they may all be captured.   When the spear has been
thrust into the house, it must be thus left until a hole is cut
with a hatchet, through which to remove the game.   Spearing
through the ice is a better method, but for general service there
is no means of capture more desirable than by trapping.   The
steel trap No. 1 or 2 is the size particularly adapted for the
muskrat, and may be set in various ways.   The most common
method is to set the trap under two inches of water on the projecting logs or stones on the border of the streams where the
"signs" of the animal indicate its recent presence.   The trap
should of course be secured by a chain, ringed to a sliding
pole, page 145, which will lead the animal into deep water
when captured, and thus effect its speedy death by drowning.
In this case bait is not necessary.   If their feeding grounds
can be discovered, or if their tracks indicate any particular
spot where they crawl ashore at the water's edge, at this point
a trap may be set with good success.   In this instance it is well
also to set it under water, baiting with a piece of turnip, par-
snip, apple, or the like, suspended a few inches above the
pan of the trap.   Late in the fall, when collecting their building
material, they often form large beds of dried grasses and sticks,
and a trap set in these beds and covered with some loose substance, such as grass, chaff, or the like, will often secure the
animal.   The trap, in this case should be attached to a spring-
pole, page 145 as the muskrat is a wonderful adept at self-
amputation, when its escape depends upon it.

The trap is sometimes set in the interior of the house, and
may be accomplished by first breaking an opening in the wall,
near the ice, the trap being inserted and set, afterwards covering it with the loose grass and moss, which is generally abundant in the interior of these huts.   When this is done, the chain
should be secured to a stick on the outside, and the hole re-
paired.   No spring or sliding-pole is necessary in this method, as
the animal when caught will immediately run for the water, and
the weight of the trap will sink and drown its prisoner.

Scent baits are sometimes used in trapping the muskrat, the

musk taken from the female animal being particularly valued. The Oils of Rhodium and Amber, page 151 are also successfully employed by many trappers ; a few drops of either in the neighborhood of the trap, or directly upon it, being sufficient.

Although steel traps are most generally used, there are several other devices which are equally if not even *more* desirable. Chief among these is the barrel trap, commonly and successfully employed in many parts of New England, where these animals often exist in such numbers as to render their destruction a matter of necessity.

The above trap consists merely of an old barrel, sunk to its upper edge in the river bank, and about half filled with water. On the surface of the water a few light pieces of wood are floated, over which the bait, consisting of carrot, sweet apple, or turnip, is placed. A trail is then made by dragging a piece of scented meat from the barrel in various directions, and a few pieces of the bait are also strewn along these trails. The muskrats will thus be led to the barrel, and will be certain to jump in after the tempting morsels, and their escape is impossible. No less than a dozen muskrats have been thus caught in a single barrel in one night, and a few of these traps have been known almost to exterminate the musquashes in localities where they had previously existed in such numbers as to become a pestilence to the neighborhood.

A barrel trap constructed on the principle described on page 131 is also equally effective, although rather more complicated in construction. The Twitch-up is often used, and possesses the advantage of a trap and spring-pole combined. Box traps, page 103, are also to be recommended.

The skin of the muskrat may be removed in the same manner as hereinafter described for the otter, with the exception of the tail. This is considered the best method. It may also be taken off flat by ripping from the under jaw to the vent, and peeling around the eyes and mouth, letting the skin of the legs come off whole, without cutting.

Another common method consists in cutting off the feet, and then ripping with a knife from the front of the lower jaw down the neck and belly to a point a little beyond the forelegs. The lips, eyes, and ears are then carefully skinned, and the hide is stripped backwards from the body. In the latter method the bow-stretcher, page 274, is used.

THE OTTER.

The fur of this animal is of such exquisite softness and beauty as to be in great demand for commercial purposes, bringing a very high price in the fur market.

The otter cannot be said to be a common animal, although it is found throughout the United States and Canada, being rather more plentiful in the cold northern localities than in the southern latitudes. It is an amphibious animal, and can remain for a long time beneath the water. In size it is larger than a cat, and it possesses a tapering tail some eighteen inches in length. Its fur is of a rich brown color, and the hair is of two kinds, the one a close, fine, and exquisitely soft down, which lies next

the skin, and which serves to protect the animal from the extremes of heat and cold, and the other composed of long shining coarser hairs, which permit the animal to glide easily through the water. In producing the beautiful otter furs of fashion these long hairs are plucked out, leaving only the softer down next the hide. The food of the otter mostly consists of fish, for the pursuit of which he has been admirably endowed by nature. His body is lithe and supple, and his feet are furnished with a broad web, which connects the toes, and is of infinite service in propelling the animal through the water when in search of his finny prey. His long, broad and flat tail serves as a most effectual rudder, and the joints of his powerful legs are so flexible as to permit of their being turned in almost any direction.

The habitation of the otter is made in the banks of the river which it frequents, or sometimes in a hollow log or crevice beneath rocks. The animal generally prefers to adopt and occupy a natural hollow or deserted excavation, rather than to dig a burrow for itself. The nest is composed of dry rushes, grasses and sticks, and the young, three or four in number, are produced in early spring.

The *track* which the otter makes in the mud or snow is easily distinguished from that of any other animal, on account of the "seal" or impression which is made by a certain ball on the sole of the foot. Otter hunting is a favorite sport in England, and indeed in the northern parts of our own country. Hounds are used to pursue the animal, and on account of the powerfully scented secretion with which the creature is furnished by nature, its track is readily followed. When attacked, the otter is a fierce and terrible fighter, biting and snapping with most deadly energy and never yielding as long as life remains in the body. The bite of an angry otter is extremely severe, and for this reason we would caution the amateur trapper on handling the animal should one be taken alive.

Although so fierce and savage when attacked, the otter is easily tamed when taken young, and can be taught to catch fish for the service of its master, rather than for the gratification of its own palate.

In the winter when the snow is on the ground, the otter navigates by sliding, and when on the ice he may often be seen to run a few steps and then throw himself on his belly and slide the distance of several feet. They are very fond of playing in the snow, and make most glorious use of any steep snow-covered bank, sloping toward the river. Ascending to the top of such an incline they throw themselves on the slippery surface and thus slide swiftly into the water. This pastime is often continued for hours, and is taken advantage of in trapping the playful creatures. A short search will reveal the place where they crawl from the water on to the bank, and at this spot, which will generally be shallow, a steel trap should be set, on the bed of the river, about four inches under water. The trap should be secured by a stout chain, the latter being ringed to a sliding pole, page 145, which will lead the animal when caught into deep water. If deep water is not near at hand, the spring pole, page

144, may be used, the object of either being to prevent the animal from gnawing off its leg and thus making its escape.

The trap may also be placed at the top or the slide, two or three feet back of the slope, a place being hollowed out to receive it and the whole covered with snow. To make success more certain a log may be laid on each side of the trap, thus forming an avenue in which the animal will be sure to run before throwing itself on the slope. Care should be taken to handle nothing with the bare hands, as the otter is very keen scented and shy. Anoint the trap with a few drops of fish oil or otter musk, see page 151. If none of these are handy, ordinary musk will answer very well.

The trap may also be set and weighted with a heavy stone and chain, as described for trapping the beaver. Another method still is to find some log in the stream having one end projecting above water. Sprinkle some musk on this projecting end and set the trap on the log in three or four inches of water, securing it firmly by a chain, also beneath the water.

A rock which projects over the stream may also be utilized in the same way as seen in the page title at the opening of this section. Smear the musk on the edge which juts into the water, and secure the trap by the chain as before. When the animal is caught he will fall or jump into the water, and the weight of the trap and chain will sink him. In every case it is necessary to obliterate every sign of human presence by throwing water over every foot print, and over everything with which the naked hands have come in contact. Where the traps are thus set in the water it should be done while wading or in a boat. In the winter when the ponds and rivers are frozen over the otters make holes through the ice at which they come up to devour their prey. Where the water is a foot deep beneath any of these holes the trap may be set in the bottom, the chain being secured to a heavy stone. When the otter endeavors to emerge from the hole he will press his foot on the trap and will thus be caught. If the water is deep beneath the hole the trap may be baited with a small fish attached to the pan, and then carefully lowered with its chain and stone to the bottom. For this purpose the Newhouse, No. 3, , is best adapted, as the otter is in this case caught by the head.

The beaten track of the animal may often be discovered in the snow in the winter time, and a trap carefully sunk in such a furrow and covered so as to resemble its surroundings, will be likely to secure the first otter that endeavors to pass over it. A trap set at the mouth of the otter's burrow and carefully covered is also often successful, using the sliding pole, page 145, to lead him into deep water.

Every trapper has his pet theories and methods of trapping all the different animals, and the otter has its full share. We have given several of the *best* methods ; and any one of them will secure the desired result of capture, and all of them have stood the test of time and experience.

The skin of the otter should be removed whole, and the operation may be performed in the following manner : Slit down the hind legs to the vent; cut the skin loose around the vent, and slit up the entire length of the tail, freeing it from the bone. With the aid of the knife the skin should now be peeled off, drawing it backward and carefully cutting around the mouth and eyes before taking it from the head.

With the fur thus inside, the skin is ready for the stretcher as described on page 273, and the tail should be spread out and tacked around the edges.

THE MINK.

This animal, as will be seen by our illustration, has a long, slender body, something like the weasel, to which scientific family it belongs. It inhabits the greater part of North America, and is also found abundantly in Northern Europe. The color of its fur varies considerably in different individuals, the general tint being a rich, dark brown. The chin and throat are light colored, sometimes white, and this spot varies considerably in size in different individuals, sometimes extending down on the throat to a considerable distance. The total length of the animal is from thirteen to sixteen inches, its size being variable.

The fur of the mink is excellent in quality, and has for many years been one of the "fancy furs" of fashion, a good prime skin often bringing from ten to twelve dollars. The introduction of the fur seal, however, and the universal demand for this as well as otter fur, has somewhat thrown the mink into comparative shade, although extra fine skins will still command high prices.

The mink is an aquatic animal, inhabiting small rivers and streams, and living somewhat after the manner of the otter. It has a most wide range of diet, and will eat almost anything which is at all eatable. Fishes, frogs, and muskrats are his especial delight, and he will occasionally succeed in pouncing upon a snipe or wild duck, which he will greedily devour. Craw fish, snails, and water insects of all kinds also come within the range of his diet, and he sometimes makes a stray visit to some neighboring poultry yard to satisfy the craving of his abnormal hunger. A meal off from his own offspring often answers the same purpose ; and a young chicken in the egg he considers the ne plus ultra of delicacies. The voracity of this animal is its leading characteristic, and is so largely in excess of its cunning or sagacity that it will often run headlong into a naked trap.

Its sense of smell is exceedingly well developed, and through this faculty it is often enabled to track its prey with ease and certainty. The mink lives in burrows, in steep banks, or between rocks or the roots of trees, and the young, five or six in number, are brought forth in May.

The chief occupation of the mink consists in perpetual search for something to eat, and, when so engaged, he may be seen running along the bank of the stream, peering into every nook and corner, and literally "leaving no stone unturned" in its eager search. Taking advantage of this habit, it becomes an easy matter to trap the greedy animal. Set your trap, a New-house No 2, in an inch of water near the edge of the stream, and directly in front of a steep bank or rock, on which you can place your bait. The bait may be a frog, fish, or head of a bird, suspended about eighteen inches above the water, and should be so situated that in order to reach it, the mink will be obliged to tread upon the trap. The trap may also be set in the water and the bait suspended eighteen inches above it, by the aid of a switch planted in the mud near the trap. It is a good plan to scent the bait with an equal mixture of sweet oil and peppermint, with a little honey added. If there is deep water near, the sliding pole, page 145, should be used, and if not, the " spring pole " in every case, in order to prevent the captured mink from becoming a prey to larger animals, and also to guard against his escape by amputation, which he would otherwise most certainly accomplish.

The trap may be set on the land, near the water's edge, baiting as just described, and lightly covered with leaves or dirt. Any arrangement of the trap whereby the animal is obliged to tread upon it in order to secure the bait, will be found effectual.

The trap may be set at the foot of a tree, and the bait fastened to the trunk, eighteen inches above it. A pen, such as is described on page 144, may be constructed, and the trap and bait arranged as there directed. Minks have their regular beaten paths, and often visit certain hollow logs in their runways. In these logs they leave unmistakable signs of their presence, and a trap set in such a place is sure of success.

Some trappers set a number of traps along the stream at intervals of several rods, connecting them by a trail, see page 153, the mink being thus led directly and almost certainly to his destruction. This trail is made by smearing a piece of wood with the " medicine " described at page 153, and dragging it on the line of the traps. Any mink which crosses this trail will follow it to the first trap, when he will, in all probability, be captured. A dead muskrat, crow, fish, or a piece of fresh meat dragged along the line answers the same purpose. The beaten tracks of the mink may often be discovered, and a trap set in such a track and covered with leaves, dirt or the like, will often be successful.

Minks may also be easily caught in the dead-fall. Garrote trap or a twitch-up, baiting with fish, muskrat, flesh, or the head of a bird, of which the animal is especially fond. A liberal use of the " medicine " is also desirable.

The fur of the mink is in its best condition in the late autumn, winter, and early spring, and the animal should be skinned as described for the fox.

THE PINE MARTEN.

This animal belongs to the tribe of "weasels," and is closely allied to the celebrated sable, which it greatly resembles. The pine marten is so called because it inhabits the northern climates where pine forests abound, and spends much of its life in the trees in search of its prey. Its general appearance is truly represented in our illustration, its fur being of a rich brown color, with a lighter or white patch on the throat. Its total length, including the tail, is about twenty-eight or thirty inches, of which the tail represents ten inches. It is mostly confined

to the forests in the far north, and is comparatively rare further south than the latitude of Maine and the lakes. The fur of the pine marten is of considerable value, particularly if the animal be killed in the winter. A really fine skin is but little inferior to the celebrated sable, and is hardly distinguishable from it. The hair is long and glossy, and the under fur is beautifully soft and very thick. The dark colored skins are the most valuable. Although so nearly like the sable, the same comparison does not exist in regard to their proportionate market values, the marten fur bringing a much lower price.

The marten is a shy and wary animal, withdrawing itself as far as possible from the sight of man, and building its habitation in the tops of trees, often seizing on the ready nest of some squirrel or bird, and adapting it to its purposes.

It is a night prowler, and in the dark hours it traverses the trunks and branches of the trees in search of its prey. It moves with wonderful stealth and activity, and is enabled by its rapid and silent approach to steal unnoticed on many an unfortunate bird or squirrel, seizing it in its deadly grip before the startled creature can think to escape. Coming across a bird's nest, it makes sad havoc with the eggs or young, often adding the parent bird to his list of victims. Rabbits, partridges, and mice also fall into the marten's "bill of fare," and the list is often further increased by a visit to a poultry yard, when the animal murders and eats all it can and kills the rest for sport. In pouncing upon its prey, the marten invariably seizes its victim by the throat, often dispatching the luckless creature with a single bite.

The martens generally are said to be very susceptible to human influence when taken young, and are very lively in a state of domestication. They are among the most graceful of animals, and in place of the disagreeable scent which renders many of their tribe offensive, this creature possesses an odor which is quite agreeable, and for this reason is often called the sweet marten in contradistinction to the foul marten or pole cat of Britain, which is like unto our skunk in the disgusting stench which it exhales.

The dead-fall and Garrote traps are very successful in trapping the marten. They should be set several rods apart, in the forest or on the banks of streams, and a trail established by dragging a dead or roasted crow, entrails of a bird, or fresh meat from one trap to another, as described in relation to the mink, page 190. The twitch-up may also be used, and possesses the additional advantage of acting as a spring pole, thus holding the captured victim out of reach of larger animals, to which it might otherwise become a prey. Any of the varities described under the title of "twitch-up" will answer the purpose, and a little experimenting will soon prove which one will be the most successful for this particular animal. The bait may consist of a bird's or fowl's head, fish, liver, or any fresh meat or entrails.

The common box trap, page 103, or the box snare, page 56, may also be used to good purpose, but the former will need to be carefully watched lest the enclosed prisoner gnaw his way out and thus escape.

When the steel trap is employed, it should be of the size of Newhouse, No. 2½, set on the ground beneath some rock, and covered with leaves, rotten wood, or earth, and the bait fastened or suspended about eighteen inches above it, in such a position that the animal will be obliged to step upon the trap in order to reach it. An enclosure may be constructed of stones piled together, the trap being set and covered in the opening and the bait secured at the back. A staked pen, such as is described on page 143, with the trap and bait arranged as there directed, also works well. Wherever or however the trap is set, the bait should be so placed that the animal cannot possibly climb on any neighboring object to reach it. The hollow of a tree trunk forms an excellent situation for the trap, and the same hollow may also be baited at the back and a dead-fall constructed across its opening. The box or barrel pit-fall, described on page 127, is said to be very successful in trapping the marten, always baiting it with the platform secure for a few days before setting for capture. The same methods directed for the capture of the mink are also useful in trapping the marten. The animal should be skinned as described for the fox.

THE FISHER.

This animal is classed among the martens, and is principally to be found in Canada and the Northern United States, where it is known as the black cat, or woodshock. In our natural histories it is described under the name of the pekan.

In general habits, this species resembles the other martens, but its body inclines more to the weasel shape. The fur is quite valuable, and much resembles the sable.. Its color is generally of a greyish brown, the grey tint being found chiefly on the back, neck, head and shoulders, the legs, tail, and back of the neck being marked with dark brown. Like the marten, the fisher prowls by night, frequenting swampy places in quest of food.

It builds its habitation in hollow trees, and in burrows, which it excavates in the banks of rivers or streams, and its young (generally twins) are produced in early spring. The trapping season for the fisher commences at about the middle of October, and extends to the middle of May, after which time the fur decreases in value.

In trapping the fisher, the same plans may be used as for the marten and mink, as these animals much resemble each other in general habits. The steel trap arranged in an artificial or natural enclosure, or otherwise so set as that the animal will be obliged to step on it in order to reach the bait, will be successful and the use of composition "scent bait," described on page 153 will be found to enhance success. In every case where the steel trap is used the spring pole, page 144, should always be employed, for the reasons already described.

Dead-falls, garrotes, box-traps, twitch-ups, or pit-falls, may all be employed to good advantage. Bait with a fish or bird, or fresh meat of any kind, and connect the various traps by a trail, as described for the mink and marten.

Remove the skin as directed for the fox, and stretch as described on page 273.

THE SKUNK.

This disgusting animal has won the unenviable but deserving reputation of being the most foul-smelling creature on the face of the globe. He belongs to the weasel tribe, and all these animals are noted for certain odors which they possess, but the skunk is pre-eminent in the utter noisomeness of the horrid effluvium which it exhales.

This scent proceeds from a liquid secretion which collects in a gland beneath the insertion of the tail, and the animal has the power to eject or retain it at will.

It must have been given to the creature as a means of defence, for there seems to be no animal that can withstand the influence of its fetid stench. Dogs are trained to hunt the animal, but until they have learned from experience the right method of attacking the fetid game, and have discovered the whereabouts of the animal's magazine of amunition, they are of little use to the hunter, and are only too glad to plunge into some neighboring brook, or roll in some near earth, in hopes of ridding themselves of the stench which almost distracts them. The offensive propensities of the skunk are only exercised when the animal is alarmed or frightened. There are generally certain "premonitory symptoms" of attack which the creature usually exhibits, and it is well to retire from his "shooting range" as soon as they are observed.

When the animal is ready to discharge his battery, he suddenly elevates his large bushy tail, over his body, and turns his back on his enemy. The result of the discharge fills the air for a great distance around, and man and beast fly from the neighborhood of the indescribable and fetid effluvium, which fairly makes one's nostrils *ache*.

A single drop of this disgusting secretion on the clothes is enough to scent the whole garment, and it is almost impossible to rid the tainted fabric from the odor.

It is extremely acrid in quality, and if a very small quantity fall upon the eyes, it is very apt to produce permanent blindness.

Dogs, in their first experiences with the skunk, are frequently thus blinded, and there are well authenticated instances of

human beings who have been deprived of their sight through their close proximity to an infuriated skunk.

The writer, in his extreme youth, learned, through dear experience, the putrid qualities of this noisome quadruped. It was on one bright Sunday, in New England, and he was out in his Sunday clothing, gathering wild strawberries. He suddenly discovered a pretty little playful animal with bushy tail, romping in the grass near him. The creature was seemingly gentle, and showed no inclination to run away, and the pet-loving nature of the writer prompted an irresistible desire to capture so pretty a creature. Encouraged by its gentle manner, he eagerly ran towards the tempting prize, and grasping it by the bushy tail, which the animal had raised perpendicularly, as if for a

handle, the pretty creature was locked in the affectionate em·
brace of its youthful admirer. But alas ! he soon repented his
rashness, and the treacherous "pet" was quickly flung away,
leaving its victim in such a foul state of overwhelming astonish-
ment as can be more easily imagined than described.

Every article of clothing worn on that eventful Sunday had
to be buried, and it took weeks of Sundays before the odor
could be thoroughly eradicated from the hair and skin of the
individual who wore those Sunday garments. After this adventure, the youth became more cautious with respect to pretty little playful animals, with black and white fur and bushy tails.

There is hardly a farmer in the country but what has had
some amusing or serious experience with the skunk, and almost
every trapper has, at one time or another, served as a target for
his shooting propensities. Natural histories are replete with
anecdotes of which this animal is the mephitic hero, and vol-
umes might be filled to the glory of his strong-smelling qualities.

Perhaps it is through the prejudice of the writer that he can·
not enthusiastically recommend the skunk as a domestic pet;
but it is neverthless asserted, on good authority, that these animals, when reared from the young, become very interesting and
playful in the household, and completely shut down on their
objectionable faculties.

Our illustration gives a very good idea of the animal, and it
is so unlike any other creature that a further description will not
be necessary. The prevailing colors are white and black; but
these vary much in proportion, the animal sometimes being
almost totally white, or altogether black. The fur is long, and
comparatively coarse, being intermixed with long, glossy hairs,
and is most valuable in the black animal. The body of the
creature is about a foot and a half in length, exclusive of the
tail, which adds about fourteen inches more.

The skunk is generally nocturnal in its habits, secreting itself
during the day in hollow trees, or crevices in rocks, or wood-
piles. At night it ventures forth in quest of its food, which
consists chiefly of grasshoppers, worms and other insects, wild
fruit and such small animals in the shape of frogs, mice and
birds as it can capture. The poultry yard often offers an irresistible temptation, and both fowls and eggs often serve to ap·
pease his appetite.

The skunk is common throughout the greater part of North
America, and in many localities the numbers increase very

rapidly unless checked. The young are brought forth in burrows or holes in rocks during April or May, and are from six to
nine in number.

"Skunk fur" does not sound well when thought of   in connection with a set of fashionable furs ;   and for this reason the
pelt of this animal is dignified by the name of Alaska sable by
all dealers in the article.   When known by this fancy title it
suddenly becomes a very popular addition to fashion's winter
wardrobe, and is one of the leading furs which are exported to
meet the demand of foreign countries.   Foul as the animal is,
it seldom soils its own fur with its offensive fluid ; and when
carefully skinned the fur is as saleable as that of any other
animal.

The Skunk is trapped in a variety of ways ; and as the animal
is not cunning, no great skill is required.   The steel trap is
most commonly used, as other wooden varieties,   box traps or
dead-falls, for instance, are apt to absorb and retain the stench
of the animal.   In using the steel trap the size No. 2   should
be taken.   It may be set at the entrance to their burrows or in
their feeding grounds.   It should be covered with loose earth
or chaff, or some other light substance, and baited with small
bits of meat, dead mice, or eggs placed around it.   The enclo-
closure illustrated on page 143 also answers well, and in all
cases the spring pole, page 144, should be used.   The dead-fall,
page 107, is often employed, and the twitch-up, page 43, is a
particularly effective contrivance for their capture, often preventing the evil consequences of the odor by causing instant
dislocation of the neck, and this without injuring the fur.   A
stroke upon the backbone near the tail, by producing paralysis
of the parts, also prevents the animal from using his offensive
powers, and a dead-fall so constructed as to fall upon the animal
at this part will accomplish the same effect.   To manage this it
is only necessary to place the bait far back in the enclosure, so
that the skunk on reaching it will bring the rear portion of his
body beneath the suspended log.   The scent of the skunk is as
we have said, almost ineradicable, but we would recommend
chloride of lime as the most effectual antidote.

It is also said by some trappers that the odor may be dissi-
pated by packing the garment in fresh hemlock boughs, letting
it thus remain for a couple of days.   This is certainly a valuable hint if true, and is well worth remembering.

For skinning the skunk, see Beaver, Otter and Fox.

THE WOLVERINE.

This, one of the most ferocious as well as detestable of American animals, is principally found in British America and the upper portion of the United States. It has won a world wide reputation for its fierceness and voracity, and on this account is popularly known as the Glutton. It is not confined to America, but is also found in Siberia and Northern Europe.

The general appearance of this animal, ugly in disposition as in appearance, is truthfully given in our illustration. It is not unlike a small bear in looks, and was formerly classed among that genus.

The general color of the wolverine is dark brown. The muzzle, as far back as the eye-brows, is black, and the immense paws partake of the same hue. The claws of the animal are long and almost white, forming a singular contrast to the jetty fur of the feet. So large are the feet of this animal, and so powerful the claws, that a mere look at them will tell the story of their death dealing qualities, a single stroke from one of them often being sufficient for a mortal wound. Although the wolverine is not as large as the bear, its foot prints in the snow are often mistaken for those of that creature, being nearly of the same size.

The glutton feeds largely on the smaller quadrupeds, and is a most determined foe to the beaver during the summer months; the ice-hardened walls of their houses serving as a perfect protection against his attacks in the winter time.

To the trapper of the north the wolverine is a most detested enemy, following the rounds of the traps and either detaching the baits or tearing away the dead animals which have fallen a prey to them. The trapper's entire circuit will be thus followed in a single night, and where the veritable "glutton" does not care to devour its victim it will satisfy its ferocious instinct by scratching it in pieces, leaving the mutilated remains to tell the story of its nocturnal visit.

The wolverine is a dangerous foe to many animals larger than itself, and by the professional hunter it is looked upon as an ugly and dangerous customer.

There are several methods of trapping this horrid creature, and in many localities successful trapping of other animals will be impossible without first ridding the neighborhood of the wolverines. Dead-falls of large size will be found to work successfully, baiting with the body of some small animal, such as a rat or squirrel. A piece of cat, beaver or muskrat flesh is also excellent, and by slightly scenting with castoreum success will be made sure. Several of these traps may be set at intervals, and a trail made by dragging a piece of smoked beaver meat between them. The gun trap, as described on page 20, will also do good service in exterminating this useless and troublesome animal.

Steel traps of size No. 3 or 4 are commonly used to good purpose. They may be arranged in any of the various methods already described, the plan of the enclosure, page 143, being particularly desirable. In all cases the trap should be covered with leaves, moss or the like, and the bait slightly scented with castoreum. Like all voracious animals, the perpetual greed of the wolverine completely overbalances its caution, and thus renders its capture an easy task.

The home of the animal is generally in a crevice or cave between rocks, and its young, two or three in number, are brought forth in May.

In removing the skin, it may be ripped up the belly, or taken off whole, as described for the fox.

THE OPOSSUM.

The opossum is found more or less throughout nearly all the United States. In size it equals a large cat, the tail being about

fifteen inches long, very flexible and covered with scales. The general color of the fur is grayish-white, slightly tinged with yel-

low, and the legs are of a brownish hue, which color also sur-
rounds the eyes to some extent.

The fur is comparatively soft and wooly, and thickly sprinkled
with long hairs, white at the base and brown at the tips.

The nature and habits of the animal are very interesting.   Its
nest is made in some sheltered hollow in an old fallen or live
tree, or beneath overhanging roots or rocks, and composed of
moss and dead leaves.   The young are produced in several litters during the year, and when born are transferred by the
mother to a pouch situated in the lower front portion of her
body.   Here they remain and are nourished by the parent until
they are five weeks old, at which time they emerge and travel
with their mother, and their little ring tails do them good service in holding fast to their guardian.   It is an amusing sight to
see a family of young 'possums thus linked together, and so "attached to each other."

The opossum is a voracious and destructive animal, prowling
about during the hours of darkness and prying into every nook
and corner in hope of finding something that may satisfy the
cravings of imperious hunger.   Rats, mice, nuts, berries, birds,
insects and eggs are all devoured by this animal; and when not
content with these he does not hesitate to insinuate himself
into the poultry yard, and make a meal on the fowls and young
chickens.   His fondness for fruit and Indian corn often leads
him to commit great havoc among plantations and fruit trees, and
his appetite for the fruit of the persimmon tree is proverbial.
While feeding on these fruits he frequently hangs by his tail, as
seen in our illustration, gathering the persimmons with his fore
paws and eating them while thus suspended.   He is a most agile
climber, and his tenacity and terminal resources in this direction
are admirably depicted in that well known Methodist sermon, as
follows: "An' you may shake one foot loose, but 'tothers thar;
an' you may shake all his feet loose, but he laps his tail around
the lim' an' he clings forever."

He is an adept at feigning death, "playing 'possum" so skilfully as frequently to deceive an expert.

"'Possums" are hunted in the Southern States much after the
manner of coons; and to the negroes a "'possum hunt" signi-
fies most unbounded sport.

Though cunning in many ways, the opossum is singularly
simple in others.   There is hardly any animal more easily captured; for it will walk into the clumsiest of traps, and permit
itself to be ensnared by a device at which an American rat
would look with utter contempt.

The dead-fall, garrote, or stout snare may all be employed, being baited with any of the substances already described. The steel trap 2½ or 3 is most commonly used, being set in the haunts of the animal, and slightly scented with musk.

See Fox and Beaver, for directions for skinning, stretching, etc., etc.

THE RABBIT.

The rabbit or "cotton tail," as he is familiarly termed, is too well-known to need any description here. From Maine to Texas our woods abound with these fleet-footed little creatures, of which there are several American species. They are the swiftest of all American quadrupeds, and have been known to clear over twenty feet in a single leap. They are all natural burrowers, although they often forego the trouble of excavating a home when one can be found already made, and which can be easily modified or adapted to their purposes. The common rabbit of New England often makes its home or "form," beneath a pile of brush or logs, or in crevices in rocks. Here it brings forth its young, of which there are often three or four litters a year. The creature becomes a parent at a very early age, and by the time that a rabbit is a year old it may have attained the dignity of a grand parent.

The food of the rabbit consists of grasses, bark, leaves, bulbs, young twigs, buds, berries and the like, and of cultivated vegetables of all kinds, when opportunity favors. When surprised in the woods it manifests its alarm by violently striking the ground with its feet, causing the peculiar sound so often noticed at their first jump. The animal is fond of pursuing a beaten path in the woods, and is often snared at such places. Its enemies, beside man, are the lynx, and other carnivorous animals, hawks, owls, and even the domestic cat.

The rabbit is a favorite game with all amateur sportsmen, and the devices used in its capture are multitudinous. It is by no means a difficult animal to trap, and a glance through the second and fourth sections of our book, will reveal many ingenious snares and other contrivances, commonly and successfully used.

The Box trap, page 103, is perhaps the most universal example of rabbit trap, but the Self-setting trap, page 110, and Double-ender, page 109, are also equally effective where the animal is desired to be taken alive. If this is not an object, the snare is to be recommended as simple in construction and sure in its result.

The above constitute the only devices commonly used for the capture of the rabbit, the steel trap being dispensed with. On page 109 will be found additional remarks concerning the rabbit, and many hints no baiting, etc., are also given under the heads of the various traps above alluded to.

The skin of the rabbit is very thin and tender, and should be carefully removed, either as described for the fox, or in the ordinary method, by incision up the belly. Full directions for curing and tanning the skins will be found under its proper head in a later portion of this work.

THE WOOD-CHUCK.

This animal also called the marmot, is so well-known to most of our readers, that a detailed description will not be necessary, suffice it to say that the general color is brownish grey above, changing to reddish brown on the under parts. The head, tail and feet partaking of a darker color. The length of the animal is about a foot and a-half, exclusive of the tail, which is four inches long.

The woodchuck is a clumsy looking animal, and anything but active in its movements. It is very unintelligent, and is always too ready to use its powerful teeth on the hand of any one who may attempt to handle it. It is naturally a timid animal, but when cornered or brought to bay, it fights most desperately.

The woodchuck is an expert excavator, and where the animals exist in large numbers great damage is done by their united burrowing. They generally remain in their burrows during the day, only venturing out casually to see what is going on, and keeping near their entrance. Towards evening they start out to feed, devouring certain grasses and weeds, and also pumpkins and green corn with avidity, ever and anon sitting upright on their haunches, to see if the coast is clear. In case they are surprised in their meal, they hurry home in a pell-mell sort of a way, giving as much the appearance of rolling as running, but, nevertheless, getting over the ground with fair speed for such an unwieldly animal. The skin is loose and very tough, and possesses no commercial value, being principally used for whiplashes. Their burrows are generally on the slope of a hill, and often at the foot of a rock or tree. These tunnels vary from ten to thirty feet in length, sloping downward from the opening, afterward taking an upward turn and terminating in a roomy chamber, in which the animal sleeps in winter and where the young from three to eight in number are brought forth. The woodchuck is found throughout nearly the whole of the United States, and is especially abundant in New England, where it is a decided nuisance. It is found as far south as Tennessee, and westward to the Rocky Mountains. The flesh of the woodchuck is by many much esteemed as food, particularly in the Fall. When used for this purpose, the animal should be skinned and carefully cleaned immediately after death, taking especial care to remove the masses of fat which lie inside of the legs, as these, if allowed to remain, are sure to taint the flesh in cooking.

The animals are easily caught by setting the traps at the entrance of their burrows, and carefully covering them with loose earth, no bait being required. They may also be captured by the aid of a spring-pole, with noose attached, the pole being bent down and caught under a notched stick, and the noose being arranged at the opening of the burrow, see page 43, the Woodchuck in passing in or out will become entangled in the noose, and in his efforts to escape the pole will be loosened from the peg, thus lifting the animal in mid-air. Woodchucks are also sometimes drowned out of their holes, and the turtle is often put to good use for the purpose of smoking the animals from their subterranean dwellings. A ball of wicking saturated with kerosene is attached by a wire to the tail of the reptile. When the ball is ignited the creature is introduced into the entrance of the hole, and of course in fleeing from its fiery pursuer it traverses the full length of the burrow, and as another matter of course drives out its other occupants, which are shot or captured as they emerge.

The woodchunk's skin is generally taken off as described for the muskrat, and stretched accordingly.

THE GOPHER.

This remarkable little animal somewhat resembles the Mole in its general appearance and habits. It is also commonly known as the Canada Pouched Rat, and is principally found west of the Mississippi and northward. It is a burrowing ani-mal, and like the Mole drives its subterranean tunnels in all di-rections, throwing up little hillocks at regular intervals of from five to twenty feet. Its body is thick set and clumsy and about ten inches long, and its Mole-like claws are especially adapted for digging. Its food consists of roots and vegetables, and its long and projecting incisors are powerful agents in cutting the roots which cross its path in making its burrow. The most striking characteristic of the animal, and that from which it takes its name, consists in the large cheek pouches which hang from each side of the mouth and extend back to the shoulders. They are used as receptacles of food which the animal hurriedly gathers when above ground, afterward returning to its burrow to enjoy its feast at its leisure. It was formerly very commonly and erroneously believed that the Gopher used its pouches in conveying the earth from its burrow, and this is generally supposed at the present day, but it is now known that the animal uses these pockets only for the conveyance of its food.

The color of the fur is reddish-brown on the upper parts, fading to ashy-brown on the abdomen, and the feet are white.

In making its tunnels, the dirt is brought to the surface, thus making the little mounds after the manner of the mole. After having dug its tunnel for several feet the distance becomes so great as to render this process impossible, and the old hole is carefully stopped up and a new one made at the newly excavated end of the tunnel, the animal continuing on in its labors and dumping from the fresh orifice. These mounds of earth occur at intervals on the surface of the ground, and although no hole can be discovered beneath them, they nevertheless serve to indicate the track of the burrow, which lies several inches beneath.

The Gopher is a great pest to western cultivators, and by its root feeding and undermining propensities does entensive injury to crops generally. They may be successfully trapped in the following manner: Strike a line between the two most recent earth mounds, and midway between them remove a piece of the sod. By the aid of a trowel or a sharp stick the burrow may now be reached. Insert your hand in the tunnel and enlarge the interior sufficiently to allow the introduction of No. (o) steel trap. Set the trap flatly in the bottom of the burrow, and then laying a piece of shingle or a few sticks across the excavation replace the sod. Several traps may be thus set in the burrows at considerable distances apart, and a number of the animals thus taken. The traps are sometimes inserted in the burrows from the hillocks, by first finding the hole and then enlarging it by inserting the arm and digging with the hand beneath. The former method, however, is preferable.

The skin of the Gopher may be pulled off the body either by cutting up the hind legs, as described in reference to the Fox, or by making the incision from the lower jaw down the neck, as decided for the muskrat, a simple board stretcher being used.

THE MOLE.

Of all the mammalia the Mole is entitled to take the first place in the list of burrowers. This extraordinary creature does not merely dig tunnels in the ground and sit at the end of them, as is the case with many animals, but it forms a complicated subterranean dwelling place with chambers, passages and other arrangements of wonderful completeness. It has regular roads leading to its feeding grounds; establishes a system of communication as elaborate as that of a modern railway, or,.to be more correct, as that of the subterranean network of the sewers of a city. It is an animal of varied accomplishments. It can run tolerably fast, it can fight like a bull-dog, it can capture prey under or above ground, it can swim fearlessly, and it can sink wells for the purpose of quenching its thirst. Take the mole out of its proper sphere, and it is awkward and clumsy as the sloth when placed on level ground, or the seal when brought ashore. Replace it in the familiar earth and it becomes a different being, full of life and energy, and actuated by a fiery activity which seems quite inconsistent with its dull aspect and seemingly inert form.

We all know that the mole burrows under the ground, raising at intervals the little hillocks or "mole hills" with which we are so familiar; but most of us little know the extent or variety of its tunnels, or that the animal works on a regular system and does not burrow here and there at random. How it manages to form its burrows in such admirably straight lines, is not an easy problem, because it is always done in black darkness, and we know of nothing which can act as a guide to the animal. As for ourselves and other eye-possessing creatures, the feat of walking in a straight line with closed eyelids is almost an impossibility, and every swimmer knows the difficulty of keeping a straight course under water, even with the use of his eyes.

The ordinary mole hills, so plentiful in our fields, present nothing particularly worthy of notice. They are merely the shafts through which the quadruped miner ejects the material which it has scooped out, as it drives its many tunnels through the soil, and if they be carefully opened after the rain has consolidated the heap of loose material, nothing more will be discovered than a simple hole leading into the tunnel. But let us strike into one of the large tunnels, as any mole catcher will teach us, and follow it up to the real abode of the animal. The hill under which this domicile is hidden, is of considerable size, but is not very conspicuous, being always placed under the shelter of a tree, shrub, or a suitable bank, and would scarcely be discovered but by a practiced eye. The subterranean abode within the hillock is so remarkable that it involuntarily reminds the observer of the well-known "maze," which has puzzled the earliest years of youth throughout many generations. The central apartment, or "keep," if we so term it, is a nearly spherical chamber, the roof of which is almost on a level with the earth around the hill, and therefore situated at a considerable depth from the apex of the heap. Around this keep are driven two circular passages or galleries, one just level with the ceiling and the other at some height above. Five short descending passages connect the galleries with each other, but the only entrance into the keep is from the upper gallery, out of which three passages lead into the ceiling of the keep. It will be seen therefore that when the mole enters the house from one of its tunnels, it has first to get into the lower gallery to ascend thence into the upper gallery, and so descend into the central chamber. There is, however, another entrance into the keep from below. A passage dips downward from the centre of the chamber, and then, taking a curve upwards, opens into one of the larger burrows or high roads, as they may be fitly termed. It is a noteworthy fact that the high roads, of which there are several radiating in different directions, never open into the gallery opposite one of the entrances into the upper gallery. The mole therefore is obliged to go to the right or left as soon as it enters the domicile before it can find a passage to the upper gallery. By the continual pressure of the moles upon the walls of the passages and roof of the central chamber, they become quite smooth, hard, and polished, so that the earth will not fall in, even after the severest storm.

The use of so complicated a series of cells and passages is extremely doubtful, and our total ignorance of the subject affords another reason why the habits of this wonderful animal should be better studied.

About the middle of June the moles begin to fall in love, and are as furious in their attachments as in all other phases of their nature. At that time two male moles cannot meet without mutual jealousy, and they straightway begin to fight, scratching, tearing, and biting with such insane fury that they seem unconscious of anything except the heat of battle. Indeed the whole life of the mole is one of fury, and he eats like a starving tiger, tearing and rending his prey with claws and teeth, and crunching audibly the body of the worm between the sharp points. Magnify the mole to the size of the lion and you will have a beast more terrible than the world has yet seen. Though nearly blind, and therefore incapable of following its prey by sight, it would be active beyond conception, springing this way and that way as it goes along, leaping with lightness and quickness upon any animal which it meets, rending it in pieces in a moment, thrusting its blood-thirsty snout into the body of its victim, eating the still warm and bleeding flesh, and instantly searching for fresh prey. Such a creature would, without the least hesitation, devour a serpent twenty feet in length, and so terrible would be its voracity that it would eat twenty or thirty of such snakes in a day as easily as it devours the same number of worms. With one grasp of its teeth and one stroke of its claws, it could tear an ox asunder; and if it should happen to enter a fold of sheep or enclosure of cattle, it would kill them all for the mere lust of slaughter. Let, then, two of such animals meet in combat, and how terrific would be the battle! Fear is a feeling of which the mole seems to be utterly unconscious, and, when fighting with one of its own species, he gives his whole energies to the destruction of his opponent without seeming to heed the injuries inflicted upon himself. From the foregoing sketch the reader will be able to estimate the extraordinary energies of this animal, as well as the wonderful instincts with which it is endowed.

The fur of the mole is noted for its clean, velvety aspect; and that an animal should be able to pass unsoiled through earth of all textures is a really remarkable phenomenon. It is partly to be explained by the character of the hair, and partly by that of the skin. The hair of the mole is peculiar on account of its want of " set." The tops of the hairs do not point in any particular direction, but may be pressed equally forward or backward or to either side. The microscope reveals the cause of this peculiarity. The hair is extremely fine at its exit from the skin, and gradually increases in thickness until it reaches its full width when it again diminishes. This alternation occurs several times in each hair, and gives the peculiar velvet-like texture with which we are all so familiar. There is scarcely any coloring matter in the slender portion of the hair, and the beautiful changeable coppery hues of the fur is

owing to this structure. Another reason for the cleanliness
of the fur is the strong, though membranous muscle beneath the skin. While the mole is engaged in travelling, particularly in loose earth, the soil for a time clings to the fur;
but at tolerably regular intervals the creature gives the skin a
sharp and powerful shake, which throws off at once the whole
of the mould that has collected upon the fur. Some amount of
dust still remains, for, however clean the fur of a mole may
seem to be, if the creature be placed for an hour in water, a
considerable quantity of earth will be dissolved away and fall
to the bottom of the vessel. The improvement in the fur after
being well washed with soft tepid water and soap, is almost
incredible. Many persons have been struck with such admira-
tion for the fur of the mole, that they have been desirous of
having a number of the skins collected and made into a waistcoat. This certainly can be done, but the garment thus made
is so very hot that it can only be worn in winter. Such garments are very expensive, and owing to the tender quality of
the skin, possess but little lasting powers. There is also a
wonderfully strong smell about the mole; so strong, indeed,
that dogs will sometimes point at moles instead of game, to the
great disgust of their masters. This odor adheres obstinately
to the skin, and even in furs which have been dried for more
than ten years, this peculiar savor has been noticed.

We have given much space to the mole, not particularly on
account of its particular usefulness to the trapper, but because
of its many claims to our notice. If the creature were a rare
and costly inhabitant of some distant land, how deep would be
the interest which it would incite. But because it is a creature
of our country, and to be found in every field, there are but few
who care to examine a creature so common, or who experience
any feelings save those of disgust when they see a mole making
its way over the ground in search of a soft spot in which to
burrow.

In many localities this interesting animal exists in such numbers as to become a positive nuisance, and the invention of a
trap which would effectually curtail their depredations has been
a problem to many a vexed and puzzled farmer.

Mole traps of various kinds have found their way into our
agricultural papers, but none has proved more effectual than
the one we describe on page 119. An arrangement of the
figure four, page 107, is also sometimes employed with good
success. In this case the bait stick crosses the upright stick

close to the ground, and rests over the burrow of the mole, the
earth being previously pressed down to the surrounding level.
The stone should be narrow and very heavy, and of course no
bait is required.

The pieces should be set carefully, and so adjusted that the
lifting of the soil beneath the stick as the mole forces its way
through the compressed earth will dislodge the bait stick and
let down the stone with its crushing weight.

Another method consists in embedding a deep flower pot in
one of the main tunnels of the animal, and carefully replacing
the soil above. The mole in traversing his burrow thus falls
into the pit and is effectually captured. This is a very ingenious mode of taking the animal, and rewarded its inventor
with seven moles on the first night of trial.

There are a number of other devices said to work excellently,
but the above we believe to be the most effectual of all.

There are several species of American moles, the star-nosed
variety being familiar to most of us. The most common moles
are the shrew moles, with pointed noses. The silver mole is a
large species, of a changeable silvery color, found on the
Western prairies. The Oregon mole is nearly black, with purplish or brownish reflections.

The most beautiful of all the moles is found at the Cape of
Good Hope. It is of about the size of the ordinary American
species, and its soft fur glistens with brilliant green and golden
reflections. The fur of this species is probably the most wonderful and beautiful in the whole animal kingdom.

SQUIRRELS.

There are many species of squirrels found in the United
States, but their fur is of little value, and of trifling importance
in the fur trade ; the squirrel fur of our markets being that of
a small grey European variety. Squirrels, as a class, possess
much the same peculiarities and habits. Their claws are particularly adapted for life among the trees ; their tails are long
and bushy, covering over the backs of the animals when in a
sitting posture. They are all lithe and quick of movement,
and their senses of sight and hearing are especially keen. They
are constantly on the alert, and are full of artifice when pursued. Their food consists chiefly of nuts, fruits, and grain, but
when pushed by hunger, there is no telling what they will not
eat. They generally provide for the winter months by laying

up a store of the foregoing provisions, either in holes in trees
or interstices in the bark, or in cavities under ground. The
shag-bark hickory offers an especial inducement to these provident creatures in the numerous crevices and cracks throughout the bark. It is not an uncommon thing to find whole handfuls of nuts carefully packed away in one of these cracks, and

a sharp stroke with an ax in the trunk of one of these trees
will often dislodge numbers of the nuts. The writer has many
a time gone "nutting" in this way in the middle of winter with
good success. The nests of squirrels are generally built in
trees, either in a crotch between the branches or in some deserted woodpecker's hole. Some species live in burrows in
the ground, and those individuals who are lucky enough to
be in the neighborhood of a barn often make their abode
therein, taking their regular three meals a day from the gran-
ary. In many localities these animals thus become a perfect
pest to the farmers, and their destruction becomes a matter of
urgent necessity.
   Squirrels, although resembling each other much as regards

their general habits, differ considerably in the size and color of the different species.

The principal varieties found on our continent are :—

The large grey squirrel, which is common in the Eastern and Middle States, and which is about two feet in length, including the tail. The common red squirrel, or chicaree, smaller than the foregoing, and found more or less all through the United States. The black squirrel, which is about the size of the grey, and found in the north-eastern part of the United States, near the great lakes. In the Southern States there is a variety known as the fox squirrel, about the size of the red squirrel, and quite variable in color. The Middle States furnishes a species called the cat squirrel, rather smaller than the preceding. Its tail is very broad, and its color varies from very light to very dark grey.

The ground squirrel, or chipmuck, with its prettily striped sides, is common to most of our readers, its general color being red and the stripes being black and white.

Another burrowing species, known as the Oregon or downy squirrel, is found in the Territory from which it takes its name, and also northward in British America. In size it resembles the chipmuck, and its color is light red above, pure white beneath, and silver grey at the sides.

The beautiful silky variety, known as the flying squirrel, with its grey chinchilla-like fur and loose skin, is found throughout the United States east of the Mississippi.

Louisiana and Texas furnish the golden-bellied squirrel, which is about twenty inches in length, with tail golden yellow beneath, and golden grey above. The sooty squirrel is also found in this locality, being about the same size as the last mentioned, and black above and brownish red beneath.

There are other varieties in California known as the woolly, soft-haired, and weasel squirrels; and in the Western States we find the large red-tailed squirrels, which are about the size of the large grey variety of the Eastern and Middle States.

Squirrels, as a tribe, are much sought for as pets, and most of the species are easily tamed.

Box traps of various kinds are used in taking them alive. The varieties on pages 103, 106 and 110 are especially adapted for this purpose, and should be set either in the trees or on the ground, and baited with an apple, a portion of an ear of corn, or of whatever the animal is particularly fond.

When the animals exist in such numbers as to become a de-

structive nuisance to the farm, the small-sized steel trap, No. o,
arranged with bait hung above it, will work to good advantage.
Twitch-ups are also successful, and we might also recommend
the traps on pages 107, 116 and 128 as worthy of trial when the
animal is not desired to be captured alive.

Squirrels may be skinned either by ripping up the belly, or
in a whole piece, as described in regard to the fox.

We pause before going further into the mysteries of trapping
in connection with the animals which we are about to consider,
as they are generally exempt from the wiles of the trapper's art,
coming more properly in the field of the hunter or sportsman. The idea of trapping a deer, for instance, seems barba-
rous indeed; but are not all the ways of deceiving and killing
these splendid animals equally so? Are not the various strate-
gies and cunning devices of the sportsman, by which these noble
creatures are decoyed and murdered, equally open to the same
objection? As far as barbarity goes, there is to us but little
choice between the two methods; and, generally speaking, we
decry them both, and most especially do not wish to be understood as encouraging the trapping of these animals, except
where all other means have failed, and in cases where their capture becomes in a measure a matter of necessity. This is often
the case in the experience of professional trappers. The life
of the trapper during the trapping season is spent almost entirely in the wilderness, often many miles from any human
habitation; and at times he is solely dependent upon his gun or
trap for his necessary food.

Sometimes in a dry season, when the leaves and twigs
crackle under foot, the rifle is as good as useless, for it becomes
impossible to approach a deer within shooting range. And
there are other times when ammunition is exhausted, and the
trapper is thus forced to rely only on his traps for his supply of
food. In such circumstances, the necessities of the trapper
are paramount, and the trapping of deer, in such straits, as the
most desirable food is rather to be recommended than con-
demned. The same remarks also in a measure apply to the
moose and prong-horn antelope, as well as to several other animals hereinafter mentioned, as they are generally considered
more in the light of the hunter's than the trapper's game.

THE DEER.

There are upwards of eight varieties of this animal which inhabit North America. The common red or Virginian deer is found throughout the United States. The stag or Wapiti deer is now chiefly confined to the country west of the Mississippi and northward to British America. The moose we shall speak of hereafter. The Rocky Mountain mule deer, and the long-tailed deer of the same locality, are two more species, and there are also the black-tailed deer and the reindeer, the latter of which is a native of British America. The scope of our volume will not of course admit of detailed directions for trapping each variety, but, as the habits of all the species are in a measure similar, our remarks will apply to them in general, and particularly to the red or Virginian deer, which is the most important to American trappers.

The trap for taking deer should be large, strong, and covered with spikes. The Newhouse (No. 4) is particularly adapted, and is especially arranged for this purpose.

When the path of the deer is discovered on the border of a stream or lake, the trap should be set beneath the surface of the water, near the tracks of the animal, and covered by a handful of dried grass thrown upon it. When thus set, it may either be left to run its chances, or success, further insured by the following precaution: In winter the principal food of the deer consists of the twigs, buds, and bark of various forest trees, and particularly those of the basswood and maple. In the season when the traps are set as above described, a most tempting bait is furnished by a large branch of either of those trees, freshly cut, and laid near the trap. The deer in feeding are thus almost sure to be captured. There are certain glands which are located on the inner side of the hind legs of the deer, and which emit a very strong and peculiar odor. The scent of these glands seems to attract the animal, and for this reason are cut out and used by trappers as a scent-bait. In the case already described, it is well to rub the glands on the twigs of the trees, thus serving as an additional attraction to the bait. There is still another method of trapping deer, which is commonly employed in the winter time. The trap is sunk in the snow at the foot of a tree, and the bait, consisting of an ear of corn or a few beards of other grain, is fastened to the tree, above the trap, three or more feet from the ground. The animal, in reaching for the bait, places its foot in the trap and is secured.

When first caught, the deer becomes very wild and violent; so much so that if the trap were chained or retarded by a heavy clog, the chain, or even the trap itself, would most likely be broken. The weight of a trap of this size is generally a sufficient impediment, no clog, or at best a very light one, being required. The first frantic plunge being over, the entrapped creature immediately yields and lies down upon the ground, and is always to be found within a few rods of where the trap was first sprung upon him. During the winter the traps may also be set in the snow, using the same bait already described. It is a common method to fell a small tree for the purpose, setting the traps beneath the snow, around the top branches. The deer, in browsing in the tender twigs or buds, are almost certain to be captured. Dead-falls of different kinds are sometimes used in trapping the deer, with good success; using the scent bait already described, together with the other bait. The food of the deer during the summer consists of nuts, fruits, acorns, grass, berries, and water plants, and when in convenient neighborhood of cultivated lands, they do not hesitate to make a meal from the farmer's turnips, cabbages, and grain.

As we have said, the winter food consists chiefly of the twigs of trees. When the snow is deep the deer form what are called "yards," about such trees as they particularly select for their browsing. These yards are made simply by tramping down the snow, and large numbers of the deer are often thus found together. As the supply of food is consumed, the yard is enlarged, so as to enclose other trees for browsing, and where deep snows abound throughout the winter, these enclosures often become quite extensive in area. Panthers, wolves, and wolverines take especial advantage of these, and easily secure their victims. By wolves especially entire herds of deer are thus destroyed, and whole yards depopulated in a single night. Panthers secrete themselves in the trees above the boughs overhanging the "yards," and, with stealthy movements, approach and pounce upon their unsuspecting prey. The bloodthirsty wolverine secretes himself in the nooks and by-ways to spring upon its tawny victim unawares. These, together with man, form the principal foes of the deer, and we can truthfully assert that the *hunter* is much more its enemy than the *trapper*.

As we do not wish to encourage the wanton trapping of this noble creature, it would perhaps be well for us to devote also a few words in describing the various modes of hunting the animal, adopted by the "professional sportsmen" throughout the land. The most common method is that called "still hunting," most generally pursued in winter. The hunter is shod with deer-skin or other soft sandals, and starts out with his rifle and ammunition. Finding the fresh track of the deer, he cautiously and noiselessly follows up the trail, keeping a sharp lookout ahead. A practised deer-hunter becomes very skillful and accurate, and the animal is nearly always tracked to discovery, when he is shot. The deer's sense of smell is extremely acute, and, when in shooting range, it is very necessary to approach them in the face of the wind, the direction of which may be easily determined by holding the finger in the mouth for a moment, afterward pointing it upward toward the sky. The cool side of the finger will indicate the direction from which the wind blows, and toward that direction the deer should always be approached, or as far toward that direction as possible. It will sometimes happen that the hunter will surprise the buck, doe, and fawn together. In order to secure the three, shoot the doe first. The buck and fawn will remain near the spot. The buck should next be shot, and then the fawn, the charge being aimed at the breast. Never approach a wounded deer without reloading the gun, as he is often more frightened than hurt, and is likely to start and run away, unless prevented by another shot. During the snow season, deer are always watchful of their back track. They are generally at rest during the day, starting out late in the afternoon on their usual ramblings, which they continue through the night. During the dark hours they love to resort to the water side in quest of aquatic plants, and are here often taken by hunters, many of which consider "night hunting" the favorite and most exciting sport. It is pursued in the following manner: The hunter requires a boat or canoe, page 261, a good rifle, and a lamp. The lamp, with a screen or reflector behind it, is placed at the bow of the boat. One hunter takes the oar, and, with noiseless paddle, propels or sculls the boat from the stern. The armed hunter crouches behind the light, with the muzzle of his rifle projecting beyond the screen sufficiently to easily show the forward sight on the tip of the barrel. A dark lantern is sometimes used as a light. The eyes of the deer shine very perceptibly at night, and his presence on the banks is thus easily detected. If he is noiselessly approached, he will remain transfixed by the effect of the light from the boat, and he may be neared even to a very close range, when he is easily despatched. Hundreds of deer are thus taken during the summer and autumn. Deer are also chased by dogs until they are forced to take refuge in the nearest rivers or lakes, when the hunter in his canoe overtakes and shoots them. Another method is frequently employed in the hunting of the deer. These animals are very fond of salt, and with it they are often decoyed to a spot where the hunter lies in wait tor them. These places are called " deer licks," or salting places, and can be made as follows : Select a locality where deer are known to frequent, and place a handful of salt either on a smooth spot of ground or in the hollow of a log. A section of a log is sometimes slightly dug out at one end and the other inserted in the earth, the salt being placed in the hollow. The hunter secretes himself in a neighboring tree, sometimes erecting a bench or scaffolding for comfort, and, provided with gun and ammunition, he awaits the coming of the deer. Hunters say that a deer seldom looks higher than his head, and that a sportsman on one of these scaffoldings, even though he is clumsy in his movements, is seldom noticed by the animal.

The salt lick is also utilized for night hunting. A head-lantern is generally required. This can be made in the following manner : Construct a cylinder of birch bark or paste-board or any like substance, ten inches in height, and of sufficient size to fit closely on the head. A circular partition should next be firmly inserted at about the middle of the cylinder, and the centre of the partition should be provided with a socket for the reception of a candle. On this end of the cylinder a piece should now be cut to admit of the passage of light from the candle on that side. Having this fire-hat at hand wait patiently for the game. When a significant noise is heard light the candle and place the cylinder on the head, with the open cut in front, thus directing the light toward the ground. As the deer approaches, his fiery eyes will easily be seen, and the light from the candle will shine sufficiently on the rifle to clearly reveal the sights and admit of a sure aim. There is still another method of night hunting by the salt lick. The rifle is aimed directly at the salted spot, and thus firmly fixed—this preparation being made in the day-time. When night approaches, the hunter finds a piece of phosphorescent wood or "fox fire," and places it on the ground, at a point which he has previously determined to be on a direct line of the aim of his gun. The "fox fire" is plainly seen from the tree, and as soon as it is darkened he knows that it is obscured by the deer, and he pulls the trigger and kills his game.

Deer are hunted at all seasons of the year, *but ought not* to be hunted during the summer. The sport legitimately begins in September, when the buck begins to harden his horns, and when his flesh is in its best condition for food. In October the deer is more shy, and during this month and after, the sport is at its height. The deer should be skinned from an incision down the belly, and the hide spread on a hoop stretcher, page 275.

THE MOOSE.

We have already given so much space to the hunting of the deer that we shall be obliged to cut short our remarks on the Moose, particularly as it is a representative of the same family.

This animal is the largest of the Deer tribe, being seven or eight feet in height and often weighing over fifteen hundred pounds. It is supplied with immense flat spreading horns, sometimes expanding to the distance of six feet between the tips. It is found in Maine, Oregon and Washington Territories, and in the neighborhood of the great lakes, and inhabits the regions as far north as the Arctic Sea. Its color is yellowish brown. The fur is thicker in winter than summer, and on the neck of the animal the hair is very coarse and hangs in an immense tuft of over a foot in length. The flesh is most excellent food and is much esteemed by trappers. The habits of the moose are in most respects identical with the deer, already described, and like them they form " yards " during the winter season.

In the North the moose is hunted on snow-shoes by the natives, and in summer they are shot like the deer. They are often very dangerous and terrible creatures to hunt, and the utmost care and skill, as described in regard to the deer, is required on the part of the hunter in order to avoid detection through the exquisite sense of smell which the animal possesses. The moose is easily trapped. The Newhouse, No. 6, is especially adapted for the purpose, and it should be chained to a clog of stone or wood of over fifty pounds in weight. Set the trap in the "yard," or beneath the snow where the moose frequents, or in the summer, or fall seasons, as described for the deer, using the same methods in regard to baiting, etc.

Skin after the manner of cattle, and stretch the hide on a hoop-spreader.   Page 275.

ROCKY MOUNTAIN SHEEP.

These creatures are natives of the entire range of the Rocky Mountains, and are especially prized on account of the superior quality of their flesh as food. They are much larger and more powerful than the domestic sheep, and the ram is provided with enormous curved horns. The wool of the animal is intermixed with coarse grey hairs, and the general appearance of the fur is russet grey, with the exception of the rump and under parts, which are of a dirty white color. The animal is generally very wary and retiring, and inhabits the most secluded and inaccessible mountain regions and rocky cliffs.

They are easily captured by the steel trap (No. 5) set in their haunts. The dead-fall is also used in some instances. Remove the skin as described for the deer.

THE BUFFALO.

The Buffaloes or Bison of the Western plains is too well known to need description. They travel in migrating herds of thousands, and are found from Texas to British America. Their food consists chiefly of grass, of which the "Buffalo grass" is their great delight. They graze and travel through the day and rest by night. They are more the game of the hunter than the trapper, although the largest side Newhouse would effectually secure one of the animals. The Buffalo is generally hunted on horseback, the usual method being that of stealing into the drove while grazing, always moving against the wind in order to avoid being scented. The flesh is palatable and by many much relished. The Buffalo skins of commerce are furnished by the cows. The bull skins are almost devoid of fur on the hinder parts, the hair being confined to the huge heavy mass on the hump and mane. Skin the animal as described for the Moose.

THE PRONG HORN ANTELOPE.

This sole American representative of the Antelope tribe we believe is seldom trapped ; but as it is a well-known animal on the Western plains, a short mention of it is required here. In general shape this creature bears considerable resemblance to the deer, the form of the horn being its chief peculiarity, each one of which is provided with a single prong, from which the animal takes its name, of Prong Horn. The color of the body is brownish-yellow, with the exception of the rump and belly which are almost white. The Antelopes generally travel in herds, and are much hunted by the Indians who surround them and destroy them with heavy clubs. Like the deer, their sense of smell is especially keen and the same caution is required in hunting them. In size they are about the same as the Virginian Deer. They are wonderfully graceful in all their movements, and are even more fleet of foot than the deer. These Antelopes inhabit the Western Prairies and wooded borders from New Mexico northward, and their flesh is much esteemed as an article of diet. They may be caught in their feeding places, as recommended for the deer, using the same sized trap.

The dead fall is also efficacious in their capture, and they are also sometimes taken in large pit-falls covered over with light sticks and leaves, to resemble the natural surroundings. On this false covering, the bait, consisting of green corn or other vegetables, is strewn and a high wall of logs or stones is erected around it, in order that the animal will be obliged to *jump* slightly in order to reach the bait.

Remove the hide as recommended for the deer.

SHOOTING AND POISONING.

Until the introduction of the steel-trap, shooting was a common method of taking fur bearing animals, and even to the present day it is quite prevalent in some localities. Any one who has had any experience with the fur trade must have learned that furs which are "shot," are much affected in value. Some furriers will not purchase such skins at any price; and they never meet with any but a very low offer. "Trapped furs" and "shot furs" are terms of considerable significance in the fur trade, and any one who wishes to realize from a profitable sale of his furs, should use his gun as little as possible. A shot grazing through the fur of an animal cuts the hairs as if with a knife, and a single such furrow is often enough to spoil a skin. It is these oblique grazing shots which particularly damage the fur, and an animal killed with a *shot gun* is seldom worth skinning for the value of its pelt. If firearms are used, the rifle is preferable. If the animal chances to be hit broadside or by a direct penetrating bullet, the two small holes thus made may not particularly effect the value of its skin, although even then the chances are rather slight.

Trapped furs are of the greatest value.

The use of poison is objectionable as a means of capture in animals especially desired for their fur. Strychnine is the substance generally employed, and unless its victim is skinned *immediately* after death the pelt becomes considerably injured by the absorption of the poison. It has the effect of loosening the fur and the hair sheds easily.

The poison is principally used in the capture of Wolves and animals considered in the light of vermin. For a wolf or fox, the poison is mixed with lard or tallow and spread on pieces of meat, or a small amount of the powder is inclosed in an incision in the bait. The amount sufficient for a single dose may be easily held on the point of a knife blade, and death ensues in a a very few moments after the bait is taken. For a Bear the dose should be a half thimbleful, and it should be deposited in the centre of a piece of honey comb, the cells being emptied of their honey for that purpose.

Other animals may be taken by proportionate quantities of the poison, but for general purposes we discourage its use.

THE

CAMPAIGN.

BOOK VII.

CAMPAIGN LIFE IN THE WILDERNESS.

 T has been the author's object in the preparation of this book not simply to content the reader with a mere superficial knowledge of so-called "Amateur trapping," but to carry him further into the art professionally considered, and for this reason we present in the following chapter a full catalogue of the trapper's outfit, containing detailed descriptions of all the necessaries for a most thorough campaign, including boats and canoes, log cabins, shanties and tents, snow shoes and camp furniture of all kinds, together with numerous and valuable hints on trapper's food.

PLAN OF CAMPAIGN.

The first thing to be considered in reference to a campaign is the selection of a trapping ground, and it is always desirable to choose a locality where travel by water can be resorted to as much as possible. Otter, mink, beaver and muskrat are among the most desirable game for the trapper, and as these are all amphibious animals, a watered district is therefore the best on all accounts. Lakes, ponds, and streams, bordered by wild woods, form the best possible grounds for general trapping, and the mountain lakes of the Adirondacks and Alleghenies, and all similar regions are especially desirable on this account. Almost any wild country, intersected with streams, lakes, and rivers, is apt to abound with game, and some trappers confine their labors to the borders of a single lake, and adjoining forest. This plan is especially to be recommended to the amateur, as much of the travelling to and fro can be done by boat, the labor being thus much lightened. Having decided upon the seat of operations, the young trappers should immediately set to work at building their shanties and boats. The home shanty is of the greatest importance, and should be constructed first. Select some flat bit of land near the water and clear it of brush wood, or other rubbish and proceed to work as described on page 242. A good axe is the only tool required by an experienced trapper in the construction of such a shanty. Should the trapping lines be very extensive, additional *bark* shanties, page 245, will require to be made at intervals along the line, for sleeping stations and shelters in case of storm. The professional trapper generally attends to the building of his shanties and boats before the trapping season commences, and thus has everything in readiness for his campaign. If in a birch bark country the Indian canoe, page 260, is the most desirable craft, on account of its lightness and portability. The dug-out, or bateau, described on page 259, will also do good service.

The trapping season begins in October, and everything should be in readiness at this time, so that the trappers may devote all their time strictly to business.

The route of the professional trapper often extends over fifty miles, and the number and weight of traps and provisions which these rough-and-ready individuals often carry as personal luggage is most astounding. Fifty or sixty pounds apiece is considered a *fair* burden, and they deem no one a fit physical subject for a campaign who cannot at least manage thirty pounds with comparative ease. The number of the trapping party generally consists of from two to four. A few days prior to the opening of the trapping season, the party start out, laden with their burden of traps and provisions, and deposit them at intervals along the line, the provisions being mainly kept in the "home shanty." Several trips may be necessary to complete these preparations, unless the trapping ground is readily accessible by wagon or boat, in which case the transportation is much easier.

The "home shanty" is generally built only when the trapping grounds are far in the wilderness, miles away from civilization. If the line extends from the outskirts of some town or village, such a hut may be dispensed with. It is used principally as a storehouse for furs, provisions, ammunition, tools, and other valuables, and also serves as a point of rendezvous, or a home, for the trappers, one of the number being generally left in charge to "keep shanty" while his companions are on their tramps in search of game. If desired, a boy may be taken along for this especial purpose. In every case, some such guardian is very necessary, and particularly in wild districts, abounding in wolves and bears, as these animals have an odd trick of breaking into unguarded shanties, and often make sad havoc with its stores. Steel traps are almost exclusively used by the professional trapper, and the supply for a single campaign will often exceed one hundred and fifty. Many of the traps described in the early part of this work are also used, and for the amateur who has not the ready cash to lay out in steel traps, are decidedly to be recommended and will be found very efficient. From thirty to fifty traps would be a fair number for an ordinary amateur trapping season, and the probable cost of such a lot would be from $15 to $25. The sizes of the traps will depend upon the game sought, No. 2½ being a good average. With this supply, relying somewhat on dead-falls, twitch-ups, and the various other devices described in our early pages, we can guarantee lively sport, of course, presuming that good judgment has been used in the selection of a trapping ground. In later articles, under the proper headings, we give full details concerning food and cooking utensils, shelter and bedding, as well as many other requisites for the trapper's comfort. To complete the list he should provide himself with a good sharp axe, and hatchet, and if the log canoe is in anticipation he will also require the other tools mentioned on page 259 an oilstone being carried in order to keep the various tools in good repair ; an auger, saw, and some large nails are also to be desired, and a small parcel containing needles, thread, pins, scissors, etc., will be found indispensable. "Cleanliness is next to Godliness," and there are no more luxurious necessities in camp life than a piece of soap and a clean towel. For light it is advisable to carry a supply of candles, or a lantern with a can of oil. The latter is, of course, more bulky, and for a campaign wholly on foot is hardly to be recommended on this account.

Each trapper should be provided with a stout jack-knife, pocket-compass, and a supply of matches, a number of these being always carried on the person to provide for the emergencies to which the hunter is always subject.

One of the party should carry a double-barrelled shot-gun and another a rifle, or both may be combined in a single weapon. A revolver is also a desirable acquisition. Purified neats-foot oil should be used on the fire-arms, and in lieu of this, some trappers use the melted fat of the grouse for the same purpose. A good supply of fishing tackle is almost indispensable, and with these valuable equipments the young trapper may defy the wilderness with all its hazards. With his traps, gun and rod, together with his store of provisions, he may look forward to a larder well stocked and may calculate on an appetite which will do it justice.

The list of portable provisions and cooking utensils best adapted for a campaign are given under their proper title, and will be found to cover all the wants of the most fastidious. The stove is the most cumbersome article, but trappers generally dispense with its use altogether, looking at it rather in the light of a luxury as well as a nuisance. The open camp fire will answer every purpose, both for cooking and for comfort in cold weather.

For clothing it is desirable to carry at least two suits, in order to have a "change." They should be of woolen, and from the *hunter's* point of view, should be of a sombre shade, so as to be as inconspicuous as possible. The use of high-top boots is to be deprecated, as they are tiresome and unwieldy. Short boots, with thick, iron-pegged soles, are generally preferred by trappers, and in order to render them soft, pliable, and waterproof they may be soaked or smeared with a hot mixture, composed of one part rosin, two parts beeswax, and three parts tallow. Simple tallow, or even the fat of the deer, is sometimes used for the same purpose.

Calculating on a successful campaign, a supply of board-stretchers, page 273, will be needed for the curing of the skins, and if our adventurous enthusiasts should extend their experience along into the winter, the toboggan and snow-shoes will come into good use for convenient winter travel.

The trapping season properly commences in October and ends in April. The pelts of fur bearing animals are in their best condition during this time, and in the winter are in their prime. The various modes of setting and baiting traps for all our leading animals are clearly set forth in another part of this volume. And in the accompanying engravings will be found life like representations of each species.

In a trapping campaign it is an excellent plan to select a central point for the home shanty, extending the trapping lines in several directions therefrom, following the borders of the lakes or streams for the otter, beaver, mink and muskrat; and setting a few lines inland for the capture of martens, racoons, foxes, etc.

For an amateur campaign this a most excellent and convenient arrangement, the lines may extend all the way from one to five miles each, and connect at their edges, the whole ground plan resembling the form of a wheel, the shanty corresponding to the hub, and the trapping lines the spokes, the tire representing the circuit connecting the various lines. Where the latter extend over many miles it is well to construct bark shanties at the limits. Let each trapper take a certain "spoke," and follow it to its terminus, returning on the adjacent line. On his arrival at the shanty he should immediately set to work skinning the animals taken, and stretching their furs. Full directions for skinning the various game are given under their respective titles, and the curing of skins is treated in detail in another chapter of this work. We also present a table of the comparative values of the various American furs at the present date of publication. Of course these values are constantly varying, but the table will serve at least to gauge the relative values of common and scarce furs. Great care should always be used in removing the skins from the various animals, as the final value of the fur much depends upon this. They should not be removed from the stretchers until perfectly dry, and should then be laid in a cool, airy place. When near a village or settlement it is advisable to send "into town" every few days with a batch of furs for safe keeping, and particularly so when the skins are valuable, and in cases where the home shanty is left unguarded. The value of prime otter or mink pelt is a matter of no small importance, and a good trapping ground furnishes a rare field for light fingered prowlers who are well posted on the market price of raw furs, and who are constantly on the lookout for such prizes, either in the shape of the prepared skin, or on the back of the live animal. These "trap robbers," or poachers, are the pests of trappers, and many have learned from dear experience the advisability of placing their choice furs beyond the reach of the marauders.

The hut in which they are stored is nearly always kept guarded, and, where this is impracticable, the skins are hid in hollow trees, or carried to some near settlement, as we have already mentioned.

If the campaign proves successful and promises well for another season, it is customary to hide the traps beneath rocks, thus saving the labor of a second transportation. In order to keep the traps from rusting, it is well to cover them with oat or buckwheat chaff. The rock should be first rolled from its resting place, and a bed of the chaff made beneath it, in which the traps should be covered, the rock being afterwards replaced. In a few such places all the traps may be effectually stored away, and they will be found in prime order and ready for business on the following season.

In the months of September and October trappers are much annoyed by gnats and mosquitoes, and, as a preventive against the attacks of these pests, we give on page 255 some valuable receipts, which have stood the test of time, and are still the most effective remedies. The "smudge," consisting of a smouldering pile of birch bark is also used where the insects infest the tents or shanties by night. The bark should be dry, and should not be allowed to blaze. The smudge is generally placed at the entrance of the tent, and the trapper may then take his choice between smoke or mosquitoes, both cannot exist together, and a tent infested with the blood-thirsty pests may be effectually cleared in a few minutes by the introduction of smoking brand for a few seconds. If the tent is now closely buttoned and the smudge kept burning directly outside, there will be no further trouble with the mosquitoes, and the odor of the smoke is, after all, but a slight annoyance and to some is even enjoyable after being once accustomed to it. When the home shanty is infested, it may be cleared in the same way, and by the aid of two or more smudges on the windward side may be kept free from the insects.

FOOD AND COOKING UTENSILS.

The professional trapper on a campaign depends much upon his traps for his food, and often entirely contents himself with the subsistence thus gained. We *encourage* and *believe* in "roughing it" to a certain extent, but not to that limit to which it is often carried by many professional "followers of the trap" throughout our country. The course of diet to which these individuals subject themselves, would often do better credit to a half civilized barbarian than to an enlightened white man, and when it comes to starting on a campaign with no provision for food excepting a few traps, a gun, and a box of matches, and relying on a chance chip for a frying-pan, he would rather be "counted out." In ordinary cases we see no necessity for such deprivation, and, on the other hand, we decry the idea of transporting a whole kitchen and larder into the woods. There is a happy medium between the two extremes, whereby a light amount of luggage in the shape of cooking utensils and closely packed portable food, may render the wild life of the trapper very cozy and comfortable, and his meals a source of enjoyment, instead of a fulfilment of physical duty. What with the stock of traps, necessary tools, blankets, etc., the trapper's burden is bound to be pretty heavy, and it becomes necessary to select such food for transportation as shall combine the greatest amount of nutriment and the least possible weight, and to confine the utensils to those absolutely necessary for decent cooking.

The trapper's culinary outfit may then be reduced to the following items, and in them he will find a sufficiency for very passable living.

One of the most nutritious and desirable articles of food consists of fine sifted Indian meal; and it is the only substantial article of diet which many trappers will deign to carry at all.

By some it is mixed with twice its quantity of wheat flour, and is thus used in the preparation of quite a variety of palatable dishes. One or two pounds of salt pork will also be found a valuable addition ; boxes of pepper and salt and soda should also be carried. With these simple provisions alone, relying on his gun, traps and fishing tackle for animal food, the young trapper may rely on three enjoyable meals a day, if he is anything of a cook. Pork fritters are not to be despised, even at a hotel table ; and with the above they can be made to suit the palate of the most fastidious.

Indian meal is a valuable accessory with cooks generally, and to the trapper it often becomes his great " staff of life." If our young enthusiast desires to try his hand at roughing it to the fullest extent, compatible with common sense and the strength of an ordinary physical constitution, he may endeavor to content himself with the above portable rations ; but with anything less it becomes too much like starvation to arouse our enthusiasm. For cooking utensils, a small frying-pan and a deep tin basin are indispensable ; and a drinking cup is also to be desired. The kind known as the telescope cup, constructed in three parts, which close within each other, when not in use, possesses great advantages on account of its portability. With these one can get along pretty decently.

The pork fritters already mentioned form a favorite dish with trappers generally, and can be made in the fol-

lowing way; have at hand a thick batter of the Indian
meal and flour; cut a few slices of the pork, and fry them in the
frying-pan until the fat is tried out; cut a few more slices of
the pork; dip them in the batter and drop them in the bubbling
fat, seasoning with salt and pepper; cook until light brown and
eat while hot. The question now arises, "What shall we eat
them with?" If you are "roughing it," such luxuries as plates
and knifes and forks are surely out of the question; and you
must content yourself with a pair of chop sticks "a la Chinee,"
or make your jackknife do double purpose, using a flat chip or
stone as a plate. A small tin plate may be added to the list of
utensils if desired, but we are now confining ourselves to the
"lowest limit" of absolute necessities. That wholesome dish
known as "boiled mush," may come under the above bill of fare;
and fried mush is an old stand-by to the rough and ready trapper. In the first case the Indian meal is slowly boiled for one
hour, and then seasoned as eaten. It is then allowed to cool,
and is cut in slices and fried in fat. Indian meal cakes are
easily made by dropping a quantity of the hot mush in the frying-pan, having previously stirred in a small quantity of soda,
and turning it as soon as the lower side is browned. A Johnny
cake thus made is always appetizing, and with the addition of
a little sugar, it becomes a positive luxury. Hoe cakes, so
much relished by many, can be made by mixing up a quantity
into a thick mass, adding a little soda. Bake in the fire on a
chip or flat stone. The trapper's ground is generally in the
neighborhood of lakes or streams, and fresh fish are always to
be had. They may be cooked in a manner which would tempt
a city epicure; and when it comes to the cooking of a fresh
brook trout, neither a Prof. Blot nor a Delmonico can compete
with the trapper's recipe. The trout is first emptied and cleaned
through a hole at the neck, if the fish is large enough to admit
of it; if not, it should be done by a slit up the belly. The interior should be carefully washed and seasoned with salt and
pepper; and in the case of a large fish, it should be stuffed with
Indian meal. Build a good fire and allow the wood to burn
down to embers; 'lay the fish in the hot ashes and cover it with
the burning coals and embers; leave it thus for about half an
hour, more or less, in proportion to the size of the fish (this may
be easily determined by experiment); when done, remove it
carefully from the ashes, and peel off the skin. The clean
pink flesh and delicious savor which now manifest themselves
will create an appetite where none before existed. All the deli-

cate flavor and sweet juices of the fish are thus retained, and
the trout as food is then known in its perfection.

By the ordinary method of cooking, the trout loses much of its
original flavor by the evaporation of its juices; and although a
delicious morsel in any event, it is never fully appreciated excepting after being roasted in the ashes, as above described.

The other method consists in rolling the fish in the Indian
meal and frying it in the frying-pan with a piece of the salt
pork. Seasoning as desired.

Partridges, ducks, quail, and other wild fowl are most delicious when cooked in the ashes as described for the trout. The
bird should be drawn in the ordinary manner, and the inside
washed perfectly clean. It should then be embedded in
the hot coals and ashes, the feathers having been previously
saturated with water. When done, the skin and feathers will
easily peel off, and the flesh will be found to be wonderfully
sweet, tender, and juicy. A stuffing of pounded crackers and
minced meat of any kind, with plenty of seasoning, greatly im-
proves the result, or the Indian meal may be used if desired.
A fowl thus roasted is a rare delicacy. A partridge, squirrel,
pigeon, woodcock, or any other game can be broiled as well in
the woods as at home, using a couple of green-branched twigs
for a spider or "toaster," and turning occasionally. For this
purpose the bird should be plucked of its feathers, cleanly
drawn and washed, and spread out by cutting down the back.
Venison, moose, or bear meat, can be deliciously roasted in
joints of several pounds before a good fire, using a green birch
branch as a spit, and resting it on two logs, situated on opposite
sides of the fire. The meat can thus be occasionally turned
and propped in place by a small stick, sprinkling occasionally
with salt and pepper. The above manner of making the fire is
that adopted by most woodsmen. Two large green logs, of
several feet in length, being first laid down at about three feet
distant, between these the fire is built, and when a kettle is used
a heavy pole is so arranged as to project and hold it over the
fire. A cutlet of venison fried in the pan is delicious, and a
"Johnny cake" cooked in the fat of this meat is a decided
dainty.

With the above hints for a "rough and ready" campaign,
we think the young trapper ought to be able to get along quite
comfortably.

We will now pass on to the consideration of what the average professional trapper would call "luxuries." The stock of these depends much upon the location of the trapping ground. If accessible by wagon or boat, or both, they may be carried in unlimited quantities, but when they are to be borne on the back of the trapper through a pathless wilderness of miles, the supply will, of course, have to be cut short. When two or three start out together it becomes much easier, one carrying the traps and tools; another the guns, cooking utensils, etc.; the third confining his luggage to the food. One of the most necessary requisites for a journey on foot consists in a knapsack or large square basket, which can be easily strapped to the back of the shoulders, thus leaving the hands free. Matches are absolutely indispensable, and a good supply should be carried. They should always be enclosed in a large-mouthed bottle with a close fitting cork, to prevent their being damaged by moisture. For further safety in this regard the matches may be rendered perfectly water-proof by dipping their ends in thin mastic or shellac varnish. If not at hand, this varnish can be easily made by dissolving a small quantity of either sort of gum in three or four times its bulk of alcohol. It is well to dip the whole stick in the solution, thereby rendering the entire match impervious to moisture. Lucifer matches are the best, and, when thus prepared, they may lay in water for hours without any injury. It is a fearful thing to find oneself in the wilderness, cold and hungry, and without the means of lighting a fire, and to prepare for such an emergency it is always advisable to be provided with a pocket sun glass. So long as the sun shines a fire is thus always to be had, either by igniting a small quantity of powder (which the trapper is always supposed to carry) or using powdered "touch wood" or "punk tinder" in its place. Fine scrapings from dry wood will easily ignite by the sun glass, and by fanning the fire and adding additional fuel it will soon burst into flame. In cloudy weather, and in the absence of matches, a fire may easily be kindled by sprinkling a small quantity of powder on a large flat stone, setting a percussion cap in its midst, and covering the whole with dry leaves. A smart strike on the cap with a hammer will have the desired result, and by heaping additional fuel on the blazing leaves the fire soon reaches large proportions. If the young trapper should ever be so unfortunate as to find himself in the wild woods, chilled and hungry, minus matches, powder, caps, and sun glass, he may as a last resort try the following: Scrape some lint or cotton from some portion of the garment, or some tinder from a dry stick, and lay it on the surface of some rough rock, white quartz rock if it can be found. Next procure a fragment of the same stone, or a piece of steel from some one of the traps, and strike its edge sharply, and with a skipping stroke into the further side of the tinder, the direction being such as will send the sparks thus produced into the inflammable material. Continue this operation until the tinder ignites. By now gently fanning the smoking mass it may easily be coaxed into flame. At least so our Adirondack guide told us last summer. The author has never had occasion to test the merits of the plan for himself, and has no special desire of being so placed, as that his life will hang upon its success. He presents it therefore as a mere suggestion without endorsing its practibility, and would rather prefer matches in the long run. The open fire generally serves both for purposes of warmth and cooking, but by many, a camp stove is considered a great improvement. Stoves of this character, and for this especial purpose, are in the market. They are small and portable, with pipe and furniture, all of which pack away closely into the interior. A fire is easily started in one of these stoves, and, by closing the damper, a slow fire may be kept up through the night. The stove is generally set up at the entrance of the tent, the pipe passing through the top, in a hole near the ridge pole. The furniture consists of three pots or kettles, which pack easily into each other, and when in the stove still leave ample room for a considerable amount of provisions.

The kettles are made of block-tin, and frying-pans also, as these are much more light and portable than those made of iron. The lid may be used as a plate, and for this purpose the handle consists of an iron ring, which will fold flat against the surface when inverted. Knives, forks, and spoons are easily stowed away in the stove or knapsack, and a coffee-pot should always be carried. There is a knife known as the combination camp-knife, which is much used by hunters and trappers, and contains a spoon, fork, knife, and various other useful appendages, in a most compact form. It costs from one to two dollars.

For provisions, potatoes will be found excellent, both on account of their portability and the variety of ways in which they may be served. They are healthy and nutritious, and always palatable. Beans are also very desirable for the same reasons. Wheat flour will form a valuable addition to the trapper's larder, and particularly so, if the "self-raising" kind can be had. This flour contains all the required ingredients for light bread and biscuit, and is sold by grocers generally, in packages of various sizes, with accompanying recipes. We strongly recommend it where a stove is employed; and to any one who is fond of biscuit, bread, or pancakes, it will be appreciated. Butter, lard, sugar, salt, pepper and mustard are valuable accessories, and curry-powder, olive oil, and vinegar will often be found useful. Olive oil is often used by camping parties with the curry powder, and also as a substitute for lard in the frying-pan. Pork, Indian meal and crackers, wheaten grits, rice, and oat-meal are desirable, and coffee and tea are great luxuries. For soups, Liebig's extract of beef is a most valuable article, and with the addition of other ingredients, vegetables or meat, the result is a most delicious and nutritious dish. This extract is obtainable at almost any grocer's, and full directions and recipes accompany each jar. Canned vegetables are much to be desired on account of their portability, and are never so delicious as when cooked over a camp fire. Lemonade is always a luscious beverage, but never so much so as to a thirsty trapper. A few lemons are easily carried and will repay the trouble.

All provisions, such as meal, flour, sugar, salt, crackers, and the like, should be enclosed in water-proof canvas bags, and labelled. The bags may be rendered water-proof either by painting, (in which case no *lead* or arsenic paints should be used) or by dipping in the preparation described on page 247. If these are not used, a rubber blanket, page 250, may be substituted, the eatables being carefully wrapped therein, when not in use. The butter and lard should be put up in air-tight jars, and should be kept in a cool place, either on the ground in a shady spot, or in some cool spring.

For a campaign on foot, the knapsack, or shoulder-basket, already alluded to on page 234, is an indispensable article. It should be quite large and roomy, say fifteen inches in depth and ten by twelve inches in its other dimensions. The material should be canvas, rubber cloth, or wicker, and, in any case, the opening at the top should have a water-proof covering extending well over the sides. The straps may consist of old suspender bands, fastened crosswise on the broad side of the bag. The capacity of such a knapsack is surprising, and the actual weight of luggage seems half reduced when thus carried on the shoulders. When three or four trappers start together, which is the usual custom, and each is provided with such a shoulder basket, the luggage can be thus divided, and the load for each individual much lightened.

Venison is the trapper's favorite food, and in mild weather it sometimes happens that the overplus of meat becomes tainted before it can be eaten. To overcome this difficulty the following process is resorted to, for the preservation of the meat, and the result is the well-known and high-priced "jerked venison" of our markets. The flesh is first cut into small, thin strips, all the meat being picked off from the bones. The pieces are then placed on the inside of the hide of the animal and thoroughly mixed with salt, a pint and a half being generally sufficient. The salt being well worked in, the fragments should be carefully wrapped in the hide, and suffered to remain in this condition for two or three hours. The meat is then ready to be dried,—"jerked."

Four forked poles should be first driven into the ground, about six feet apart, in the form of a square, the forks being four feet above ground. Lay two poles of green wood across the forks on the two opposite sides of the square, and cover the space between them by other poles laid across them, an inch or two inches apart. On to this mammoth gridiron the strips of flesh should now be spread, and a steady fire of birch or other clean, fresh wood should be kept steadily burning beneath for about twenty-four hours. At the end of this time the meat will have reduced much in size and weight. The salt will have been thoroughly *dried in*, and the flesh so prepared may be kept for almost any length of time. In its present condition it is excellent eating, and it is always at hand for frying, and may be cooked in a variety of ways. Moose and bear meat may be dried in a similar manner, using a proportionate amount of salt. Fish may also be prepared in the same way, for which purpose they should be scaled as usual and afterward spread open by cutting down the back, the bone being removed. We cordially recommend this method of preparing both flesh and fish, and no trapper's "recipe book" is complete without it.

In localities where wolves abound, the nocturnal invasions of these creatures often render the keeping of fresh meat a very difficult task, and in this connection it may be well to give directions for the preservation of game desired to be used either as fresh meat or for purposes of drying.

The spring-pole is most commonly and successfully used.

Select some stout sapling, bend it down, and cut off a limb several feet from the ground. Hang the meat in the crotch thus formed, and allow the tree to swing back. By dividing the meat into several parts it may thus all be protected. When a moose or deer is killed at such a time or place, or under such circumstances as render its immediate dressing impossible, its carcass may be defended against mutilation by another means. Wolves are naturally sly and sagacious, and have a wholesome fear of a trap. Any unnatural arrangement of logs and stones immediately excites their suspicion, and the trapper takes advantage of this wary peculiarity to good purpose. Laying his dead game near some fallen tree or old log he strews a few branches over the carcass, or perhaps rests a log over it. Sometimes he hangs the entrails of the animal over the body, on a forked stick, any one of which devices is said to have the desired result. The wolverine is another pest to the trapper, and not being so sly as the wolf, never hesitates to pounce upon any flesh within its reach. The former method, therefore, is always the safest plan for absolute protection against all animals.

The moose and deer are the favorite food of trappers in the country where these animals abound, and the trappers of the Far West find in the flesh of the Moufflon, or Rocky Mountain sheep, a delicacy which they consider superior to the finest venison. The prong-horn antelope of the Western plains is another favorite food-animal with hunters, and the various "small game," such as squirrels, rabbits, woodchucks, etc., are by no means to be despised. The author once knew a trapper who was loud in his praises of "skunk meat" for food, and many hunters can testify to its agreeable flavor when properly dressed and cooked. It is hard, to be sure, to get up much enthusiasm over a skunk, dead or alive, but where other food is not to be had we would discourage the young trapper from being too fastidious.

The buffalo, or bison, is the great resource of the trappers of the West. The tongue, tenderloin and brisket are generally preferred, but all the meat is eatable. The flesh of the cow is best. It much resembles beef, but has a more gamey flavor. In winged game there is no food superior to the flesh of the grouse, and the great number of the species and wide range of territory which they inhabit render them the universal food game of trappers throughout the world. The ruffed grouse or partridge, pinnated grouse or prairie hen, spruce or Canada grouse, and the cock-of-the-plains or sage cock, are familiar American examples of the family, and their near relatives, the ptarmigans, afford a valuable source of food to the trappers and hunters, as well as general inhabitants of our northern cold countries. Here they are known as "snow grouse," and there are several species. The willow ptarmigan is the most common, and in some localities exists in almost incredible numbers. Flocks numbering several thousand have been frequently seen by travellers in the Hudson's Bay territory ; and the surface of the snow in a desirable feeding ground, is often completely covered by the birds, in quest of the willow tops, which form their chief food during the winter season. The Indians and natives secure the birds in large numbers, by the trap described on page 75, and Hearne, the traveller and explorer of the Hudson's Bay region, asserts that he has known over three hundred to be thus caught in a single morning, by three persons.

Of water fowl, ducks and geese are especially to be recommended. The former are hunted with decoys and boats, and are sometimes trapped, as described on pages 94. The species are distinguished as sea ducks and river or inland ducks. The latter are considered the most desirable for food, being more delicate and less gamey in flavor than the salt-water, or fish-eating varieties. The mallard, teal, muscovy, widgeon, and wood-duck are familiar species of the inland birds, and the merganser and canvass-back are the two most esteemed salt-water varieties. Wild geese are common throughout North America, and may be seen either in the early spring or late fall migrating in immense numbers. They form a staple article of food in many parts of British America, and great numbers are salted down for winter supply. They are trapped in large numbers, as described on page 75, and are hunted with tame geese as decoys, the hunter being secreted behind a screen or covert, and attracting the game by imitating their cries.

Fish form an agreeable change to the trapper's diet, and may be caught by the hook and line, or by spearing. The latter method requires considerable practice and skill, but is very successful. The Indians of the North are great experts in the use of the spear, and the number of salmon taken by them annually is enormous. The spear generally consists of five or six steel prongs an inch apart and barbed at the ends. It is mounted on a heavy handle, and when it strikes its victim its grip is sure death. The spearing is generally performed either at the spawning beds or at the falls.

Salmon trout are generally speared in the night time by boat, the spawning ground, generally a gravel bank near the shore, being the seat of operations. A fire of pitch pine and birch bark is ignited on an elevated "jack" in the bow of the boat, the "jack" consisting of an ox-muzzle, or other concave wire contrivance which will hold the inflammable materials. This is secured to a post or crotched stick, as a prop, and the spearman stands near the burning mass with his spear in readiness. As his companion in the stern of the boat paddles, he keenly watches for his victim, and, seeing his opportunity, makes his lunge and lands his prize. To become a successful spearman requires much practice and no small degree of skill. To retain one's balance, acquire quickness of stroke, and withal to regulate the aim so as to allow for the refraction of the light in the water, all tend to invest the sport with a degree of skill which only experience can master.

Fishing through the ice in winter is a rare sport, and large numbers of brook and lake trout are often taken at this season by cutting holes through the ice and fishing with hook and line. The baits commonly used consist of cow's udder or hog's liver, these being especially preferred on account of their toughness. Angle worms are also excellent, and any kind of raw meat may be used if other bait is not to be had.

It is asserted by some sportsmen that bait scented with assafœtida is much more attractive to the fish, and will insure a capture which would otherwise be impossible. Sweet cicily and anise are also used for the same purpose. When the trout bite lively, fishing through the ice is a most exciting sport, and by the aid of "tip-ups" a single person may command a great number of lines. The winter resort of the brook trout is in water two or three feet deep, over sandy beds. The lake trout frequent deeper water.

The holes are made in the ice at intervals of one or two rods, and a line set in each hole.

The "tip-up" consists of a narrow strip of lath or shingle, with a hole bored through it near the large end. At this end the line is attached, and the hook thrown in the water. A branch is now inserted through the aperture, and its ends are rested across the opening in the ice. No sooner does the fish bite than the long end tips straight in the air, and thus betrays its captive. Ten or fifteen of these contrivances will often keep one pretty busy, and do good service. By some an ordinary cut fish pole, arranged on a crotch, is used instead of the tip-ups just described. Pickerel fishing through the ice is a favorite winter sport in many localities. The line should be about thirty feet in length, and the bait should consist of a small, live fish, hooked through the back. A small cork float should be attached to the line at such a distance as will keep the bait above the bottom, and the superfluous line should be laid in a loose coil near the hole, the end being attached to a small switch or bush, stuck up in the ice near by. The pickerel, on taking the bait, should be allowed to play out the whole line before being pulled in, as the fish requires this time to fully swallow his prey, after which the hook is sure to hold him firmly. Twenty or thirty lines may thus be attended at once, the bush or twig acting the part of a tip-up, or sentinel.

Pickerel spearing is another successful mode of capture during the winter months. A large hole is made in the ice, in about two feet of water, and covered by a spacious box or board hut, six or seven feet square, and provided with a door. The spearman, concealed within, lowers his bait, consisting of an artificial fish with silver fins, made especially for the purpose. This he continually twirls in the water, and as the pickerel approaches the bait, he gradually raises it, until the fish is decoyed nearly to the surface of the water, when a quick stroke of the spear secures his victim, and the line is again lowered. This is capital sport, and is very successful.

There is a very curious device for fishing by night commonly employed by some anglers, and sometimes known as the "lantern, or fish trap." Many kinds of fish are attracted by a light, but to use a light as a bait, submerged beneath the water, certainly seems odd. It may be done, however, in the following way: The "fish lantern" used for this purpose consists of a bottle containing a solution of phosphorus in sweet oil. Procure a piece of the stick phosphorus the size of a small cherry, and submerging in a saucer of water, proceed to cut it into small pieces. Have in readiness a three-ounce white glass bottle half filled with sweet oil. Drop the pieces of phosphorus into the oil and cork the bottle tightly. In the space of a few hours the phosphorus will have been completely dissolved, and the contents of the bottle will present a thick, luminous fluid, which in a dark room, will afford considerable light. This is the fish lantern. To use it, the cork is firmly inserted and the bottle, with fish line attached, is lowered through the hole in the ice. The water becomes luminous for several feet around, and the unusual brightness attracts the fish in large numbers. They are plainly, discernible, and are readily dispatched with the spear, or captured by a circular net, sunk on the bottom, beneath the luminous bait. This is certainly an odd way of catching fish, but it is often a very efficacious method.

It has not been our intention to enter very extensively into the subject of fishing, but only to give such hints as will be found especially useful and practical to the trapper in relation to his food. The above methods, together with those of trolling and fly-fishing, are those most commonly employed by trappers and hunters generally, and we commend them to the amateur.

We give, on page 120, a unique device for the capture of fish, which might also be found useful.

With the above general remarks on the campaign, together with what follows in the detailed articles on the subject, we think that the ground will have been completely covered. Every possible requirement has been anticipated, and every ordinary emergency forseen and provided against.

THE TRAPPER'S SHELTER.

The life of the professional trapper is a life of hardship and severe exposure, and a man not only requires considerable courage, but also great bodily vigor, in order to combat successfully the dangers of such a wild, adventuresome existence.

The cold and the storm not only imperil his life, but he is often exposed to the attacks of wild beasts. A shelter, therefore, in one form or another, becomes a necessity while it is always a decided comfort, in comparison to a campaign without it.

The reader will find below descriptions of the various shelters alluded to in other parts of this work, and used by trappers throughout the land.

The most substantial of these is the log shanty, commonly known among trappers as the "home shanty," on account of its being constructed as the only permanent shelter on the trapping line.

It is used as a "home," a place of rendezvous, and a storehouse for provisions, furs, and other necessities and valuables. Other temporary shelters, known as bark shanties, are also constructed along the trapping lines at intervals of five or ten miles, as resting places. These we describe under the proper title.

Although, to the amateur trapper, the log shanty is not likely to become a necessity, we will nevertheless describe its mode of construction, in order to satisfy our more earnest and adventurous readers, who aspire to a full taste of wild life.

Our illustration gives a very clear idea of such a shanty.

It may be constructed of any size, but one of about twelve

THE HOME SHANTY.

by ten feet will be found large enough for ordinary purposes. Select straight logs, about eight inches in diameter. The whole number required will be thirty-six. Of these one-half should be twelve feet in length and the other ten. These should now be built up in the square form, on a level piece of ground, laying the ends of the logs over each other, and securing them by notches at the corners, so deep as to allow the edges of the logs to meet. Lay two short logs first, and continue building until all the thirty-six logs are used, and we will now have four symmetrical sides about six feet in height. The place for the door should now be selected. The uppermost log should form its upper outline, and the two sides should be cleanly and straightly cut with a cross-cut saw. The window openings, one or more, may next be cut, commencing beneath the second log from the top, and taking in three beneath it. Replace the logs above, and on the ends of those thus cut, both in windows and doors, proceed to spike a heavy plank, driving two nails into each log, about five inches apart, one above the other. This will hold them firmly in place, and offer a close-fitting jam for the door, and neat receptacle for the window sashes, which latter may now be put in after the ordinary manner.

The gable ends should next be built upon the smaller sides of the hut. Commence by laying a long log (notched as before) across the top of the frame work, and about two feet inside the edge. This should of course be done on both sides of the hut, after which they should be overlapped at the corners with logs eight feet in length. Next lay two more long logs, parallel with the first two, and about a foot inside them, notching as before. The ends of these should be spanned with beams eight feet in length. Two more long logs are next in order—let them be one foot inside the last two. Overlap these with beams five feet and a half in length, and in the exact centre of these last pieces chop notches for a heavy log for a ridge pole. The gable outline, direct from the ridge pole to the eaves, should now be cut off by the aid of a sharp axe. This may be done either while the pieces are in position, or the line may be marked with a piece of chalk, and the logs taken down in order to accomplish it. The roof is now required. This should consist either of strips of bark or the rounded sides of logs split off and hollowed into troughs. The latter method is preferable, on account of its greater strength and durability, but the bark will answer the purpose very well, and is much more easily obtained. The manner of adjusting the roof pieces is clearly shown in our illustration. The first row is laid on with the hollow side up, securing them at top and bottom by nails driven through each into the ridge pole and eaves-log, care being taken that one of these pieces projects well over the gable, on both ends of the hut. These pieces are now overlapped by the second row, and with the addition of the large piece which covers them all at the ridge pole, the roof is complete, and will stand a heavy rain with little or no leaking. The crevices should now be stopped with moss, dried grass or clay, after which the log cabin is complete. When the bark roof is made, additional poles may be inserted beneath as props. They should be three or four inches in diameter, and run parallel with the ridge pole, at intervals on the slope, notches being cut to secure them.

Our engraving represents a chimney, which may be constructed if desired, but the necessity of this may be done away with by using a small camp stove, and making a small opening in the gable end of the hut for the passage of the pipe. If a stove should not be at hand, and our amateur should decide to "rough it" to the full extent, he may build his fire-place and chimney as follows : It will be necessary to cut away an opening in the logs at the gable end, as was done for the door and windows. This should be about three feet square, and the fire place should be built of stone and clay, or cement, to fill the opening, and project inside the hut.

The chimney may then be built up outside in the same manner, sufficiently high to overtop the gables.

Inside the hut overhead will be found abundant room for the hanging of the skins, and any number of cross-poles may be rested across the beams. There are facilities for the swinging of a hammock, if desired, and, in fact, a hut constructed like the foregoing is a perfect one in its way. There are other methods of building a log cabin, but we will content ourselves with what we consider the *best* way of all, and pass on to the

BARK SHANTY.

This is made by first driving into the ground two forked poles seven or eight feet in height and stout enough to sustain a ridge pole of moderate size. Against this ridge pole other poles should be rested at intervals of two feet, and sloping to the angle of forty-five degrees. The frame-work thus formed should now be covered with bark, commencing at the ground and allowing the edge of each piece to overlap the one beneath after the manner of shingles, in order to shed the rain in case of storm. Spruce or birch bark are excellent for this purpose, and the pieces may be secured with nails, and kept flat by the weight of another series of poles rested against them. The sides of the shelter should be treated similarly, the front being usually left open to face the fire, which the trapper generally builds a few feet distant. In constructing a bark shanty, it is well to select some spot protected from the wind, close to the foot of a mountain or in the midst of trees, always letting the open side face the direction most sheltered.

If desired, the front can be enclosed after the manner of the sides and top, but this is not required where the fire is used.

This style of shelter is represented in our page title to this section, and certainly looks very comfortable.

TENTS.

Shanties like the foregoing are in general use among the old veteran trappers of all countries, and even to the amateur there is a charm in a shelter constructed from the rude materials of the woods which the portable tents do not possess.

Tents, however, are much used both by professionals and amateurs, and are indeed valuable acquisitions to the trapper's outfit, and where time is valuable, do away with the labor which the construction of a hut or shanty involves.

Tents are of several kinds. Those most commonly used by the trapper are the house-tent, fly-tent, and half-tent, or shelter-tent.

The first of these is made for prop-poles and a ridge pole, closed on one end and buttoning up at the other. The sides are perpendicular for two or three feet, before the slope commences, and the stay-ropes are fastened to the eaves.

The fly-tent is generally a large, square piece of canvas, with ropes extending from opposite sides. This is thrown over a ridge pole, or over a rope extending between two trees, and the sides are held to the proper slope by tightening and pegging the side ropes to the ground. Fly-tents are also made with ends, which can be lowered, and the whole tent may be pegged close to the ground.

The shelter-tent, when erected, resembles, in general shape, the bark shanty already described. It consists of a strip of canvas, having each end cut off to a point. The tent is pitched over three slanting poles, and the ends are brought down and securely pegged. This is clearly shown in our illustration.

We do not propose giving any extended directions for making tents, as they are a staple article of trade, and, as a general thing, can be bought for a figure which would render their domestic manufacture of little saving or profit. The **shelter-tent**, however, is so useful an affair, and withal so very simple

made, that we will give a few directions in regard to its manufacture. It should be made from stout *cotton drilling*, or very heavy sheeting. Let the piece be about thirteen feet in length by six in width. Each end of the piece should now be cut to a rectangular point, commencing to cut at a distance of three feet from each corner. In order to render the cloth waterproof, it should now be dipped in a pail containing a solution of equal parts of alum and sugar of lead, a couple of handfuls of each, in tepid water. It should be allowed to remain several minutes in soak, being dipped and turned occasionally, after which it should be spread out to dry. This treatment not only renders the cloth impervious to rain, but the alum tends to make it fire-proof also. A spark from the fire falling upon a tent thus prepared, will often rest upon the cloth until it goes out, without doing the slightest damage.

The manner of pitching the tent has already been alluded to, and is clear from our illustration. The poles should be three or four in number, and seven feet in length, inserted in the ground at the angle denoted. The two outside poles should be seven feet apart, and the intermediate ones equally disposed. The tent piece should now be laid over the poles, and the ends brought down and pegged to the ground at the apex, and rear corners of each side through loops, which should have been previously attached to these parts. A tent, thus arranged, affords a safe shelter from the wind or a moderate storm, and with a bright fire in front, is warm and comfortable.

BEDS AND BEDDING.

Many a trapper does away with these commodities, merely rolling himself in a blanket and using his arm for a pillow ; but we do not propose to encourage or recommend any such half-way comfort as this, when by a very little labor a portable bed

can be prepared on which the weary hunter can rest as serenely as if slumbering on the congenial softness of a hair mattrass. A bed of this kind we illustrate, and it can be made in the following manner : Procure a large piece of canvas, sacking or other strong, coarse material six and a half feet square. If a single piece of this size cannot be found, several parts may be sewed together to the required dimensions. After which two opposite sides should be firmly stitched together, thus forming a bottomless bag, if we may be allowed to use the expression. Two stout poles seven or eight feet in length and as large as the wrist should now be cut. Insert them through the bag, allowing the ends to project equally on each side. These ends should now be rested on two logs, one placed across each end of the canvas. In order to hold the poles in place notches should be cut in the logs at such distances as will draw the bag to its full width. The interior of the canvas should now be filled with dried grass, leaves, moss or spruce boughs, after which the bedstead and bed is complete.

The yielding elasticity of the poles and the softness of the warm filling in the bag, give the effect of a spring and straw mattrass combined, lifting the sleeper above the cold, damp ground, and by the addition of a blanket above, insuring warmth on all sides. If the logs are not at hand four forked stakes may be used, driving them firmly into the ground at such distances as will draw the bag to its full width, when the poles are rested upon them. If by the weight of the body the forked props should tend to incline towards each other this trouble may be easily remedied by inserting short poles as braces between them. If desired a bed of this kind may be used as a hammock and hung in a tree without much trouble. It is only necessary to secure the long poles firmly at their full width by a stout brace pole at the ends, letting the latter be deeply notched at the tips in order to receive the bed supports. The joints should then be tightly bound with stout twine in order to prevent slipping, after which the bed may be hung in mid-air by ropes at each end, and the tired trapper may swing himself to sleep with perfect comfort and safety. For this purpose the ropes should be attached at the joints, using a loop of six feet for each end. In the centre of this loop a small one should be made by doubling the rope and winding twine about it, leaving only a small aperture. Through these small loops, by the aid of other ropes, the bed is attached to the tree. By using this precaution the unpleasant experience of being turned or dumped out of bed will be impossible. For bed clothes a woollen blanket should always be carried, and if convenient a large bag of thick Canton flannel is a most excellent acquisition.

Bags of this sort are in common use among amateur trappers, hunters and camping parties, and are very warm and comfortable. They should be nearly seven feet in length and of a "loose, easy fit." With one of these contrivances it is impossible to "kick the clothes off" and the warmth is continual in-

stead of " intermittent," and even on the bare ground it is said
to be sufficient protection.   Hammocks are also in very general
use, but we can confidently recommend the suspended bed
above described as decidedly preferable.

There are various kinds of hammocks in the market, from the
light fibred silk, weighing only a few ounces, to the large corded
variety of several pounds weight and capable of holding many
persons.   They are an established article of trade, and as the
details of their manufacture would be of little practical use to
the reader, we will leave them without further consideration.
They can be had at almost any sporting emporium, at comparatively small cost.

TENT CARPETING.

We have described a most excellent contrivance for a bedstead and recommend its use whenever possible ; but when the
bed is desired to be made on the ground the following method
is usually employed, by which the whole interior of the tent,
hut or shanty is carpeted with a soft, even covering of green.

Spruce or hemlock boughs are generally used, and should be
from the tips of the branches where the wood is not too large.
Commence at the back part of the shelter, and lay down a row
of the boughs with the butt of the branch towards the front.
Overlap these with another nearer row and continue the operation, laying the evergreen as evenly as possible until the whole
interior is smoothly covered.   The projecting ends at the front,
should now be secured by the weight of a medium sized log, or
by a pole pegged down firmly at intervals. A similar log should
now be laid at the back portion of the shelter over the tips of
the boughs after which the bed is complete, and will be found
easy and comfortable in proportion to the care and skill shown
in its construction.   A blanket should be thrown over the
boughs before reclining to rest, as the fresh green gives forth
considerable dampness.

If possible a rubber blanket should be used for this purpose.
These consist of thick Canton flannel, coated on one side with
Indian rubber, and are used with the rubber side down.   They
are warm and comfortable, and a valuable acquisition to the
trapper's outfit.   There is a thinner and cheaper variety, having
equal water-proof qualities but which does not possess the
warmth of the former.   Either will be found useful.

So much for beds and bedding.   If the reader will now turn

his attention to the following section, " The Trapper's Miscellany," he will find much in detail of what has only been alluded to in the present chapter, besides other hints of great value in reference to a trapping campaign.

THE TRAPPERS'

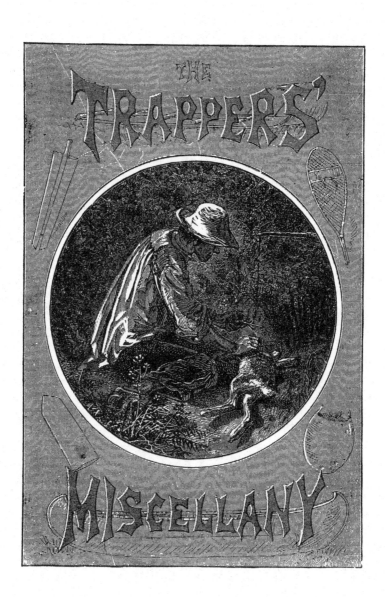

MISCELLANY

BOOK VIII.

THE TRAPPER'S MISCELLANY.

OUR enthusiastic novice, as he starts out into the wilderness, should not be unmindful of the swarms of blood-thirsty flies, gnats and mosquitoes, which infest the woods in the summer and early autumn, and are there lying in wait for him. These often become a source of great annoyance to the woodsman, and more often a source of positive bodily suffering.

Although trapping is not generally carried on during this season, the preparations for the coming campaign, including the building of shanties, transporting of traps, etc., are generally made at this time, and unless some perventive is used, the persecutions of the mosquitoes and other winged vermin, become almost unbearable.

INSECT OINTMENTS.

These insects seem to have a special aversion for the scent of pennyroyal—an herb growing commonly in sandy localities—and a single plant rubbed upon the face and hands will often greatly check their attacks.

The oil of pennyroyal is better, however, and an ointment made by straining one ounce of the oil into two or three ounces of pure melted lard, or mutton tallow, forms an excellent antidote. This may be carried in a little box or bottle, in the pocket, and applied as occasion requires. Plain mutton tallow is also a most excellent ointment for general use, and in the case of bruises or slight wounds, will give great relief.

Another preparation in very common use amongst hunters and woodsmen, although not quite as agreeable in odor, consists of a mixture of common tar and sweet oil, in equal parts. By some this liniment is considered superior to the other, inasmuch as it also prevents tanning, and is beneficial to the complexion.

During the night time, the tent or shanty often becomes swarmed with the winged pests, and their nocturnal assaults are proverbial for their pertinacity and severity. Their thirst for blood overcomes every other instinct, and pennyroyal often ceases to have any effect. Our Adirondack guide, in narrating his experience with these insect vampires, even says that on a certain night, becoming exasperated at their indomitable perseverance, and, getting tired of the monotonous occupation of spreading ointment, he arose, lit his candle, and drove the creatures out of the tent. He then buttoned up the opening, and retired to rest. A storm came up in the night, and so completely had his canvas been riddled by the bills of the mosquitoes, that the rain poured through his tent as through a sieve.

We have heard of the man who, when pursued by hungry mosquitoes, took refuge beneath a large chaldron, and, by the aid of a stone, clinched the blood-thirsty bills as they protruded in quest of his life-blood, until, by the united efforts of the winged captives, the chaldron was lifted and wafted out of sight, as if it were a feather.

One story is just as true as the other, and a summer in the Adirondack woods will tend to strengthen, rather than diminish, the belief in either.

The smoke of smouldering birch bark will effectually drive away the mosquitoes from the tents at night. This method is commonly known as "the smudge," and is more fully described in another part of this work.

The smell of the smoke is often unpleasant at first, but it is always preferable to the insect bites.

Mosquitoes are not the only vampires which infest our wooden lands. The "punkeys" and "midgets" can outstrip them for voracity, and the painful character of the wound which they inflict. The "punkey," or "black-fly," as it is called, is a small, black gnat, about the size of a garden ant, and the bite of the insect often results very seriously. The midget is a minute little creature, and is the most everlastingly sticky and exasperating pest in the catalogue of human torments. They fly in swarms of thousands, and go for their victim "en masse" and the face, hands and neck are soon covered as if with "hay seed." They stick where they first light, and commence operations immediately. All endeavors to shake them off are fruitless, and their combined attacks are soon most painfully realized. Their bites produce great redness and swelling, and the itching is most intolerable. Happily for the woodsman, the "smudge" and pennyroyal ointment are effectual preventives against the attacks of both midgets and black flies, as well as mosquitoes; and no one who values his life or good looks should venture on a woodland excursion in the summer months without a supply of this latter commodity. In conclusion, we would remark that, to the mosquito the blood of the intemperate seems to have a special attraction, and any one who wishes to enjoy comparative freedom from the attacks of these pests, should abstain from the use of alcoholic stimulants. It is a too prevalent idea among trappers that whiskey and rum are necessary adjuncts to a trapping campaign, and many a trapper would about as soon think of leaving his traps at home as his whisky bottle. This is all a mistake. Any one who has not sufficient strength of constitution to withstand the hardships and exposures of a trapping life, without the especial aid of stimulants, should stay at home. We are now alluding to the *habitual* use of such stimulants. It is always well to be provided with a flask of whisky or brandy, in case of illness, but it should only be resorted to in such an event. For a mere chill, we recommend the use of red pepper tea. A simple swallow of this drink, (made simply by soaking a red pepper in a cup of hot water) will restore warmth much quicker than three times the amount of any alcoholic stimulant. It is not our purpose to extend into a lengthened temperance lecture, but only to discourage the wide-spread idea that *stimulants* are *necessities* in the life of the trapper. Midgets, musquitoes and punkeys delight over a victim with alcohol in his veins, and while to a healthy subject the bites are of only brief annoyance, to the intemperate they often result in painful, obstinate sores.

In addition to the various ointments used, it is well to be provided with a head-net, such as we illustrate. Nets of this kind are specially made for sportsmen, and consist of a spiral wire framework, covered with mosquito netting, and of such a size as to slip easily on the head.

They are easily made, as our engraving would indicate.

A netting attachment for the hat is also an acquisition, especially in open woods, free from overhanging branches or dense thickets. Such a netting may be secured to the edge of the hat brim, and gathered with an elastic at the lower edge. This elastic will close snugly around the neck when in use, and at other times may be drawn above the brim and allowed to rest on top of the crown.

The portable hat brim, which we illustrate, is an article of trade in common use among sportsmen, and particularly the angler. Our engraving (a) shows the article separate. It is made of cloth, and is kept in its circular shape by a steel spring band at the circumference, between the two sides. It

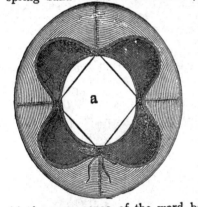

may be attached to any hat, and will act as a most effectual shelter to the rays of a hot sun.

The netting above alluded to may be attached to such a brim, and applied to the edge of the hat when desired. This is shown at (b), which also indicates the manner of adjustment of the brim. Such a brim will often do good service, and may be obtained at almost any sporting emporium at trifling cost. It is portable in every sense of the word, being easily bent and packed away in the pocket.

BOAT BUILDING.

Where trapping is carried on along
the banks of the lakes and rivers, a boat
of some kind becomes almost a positive
necessity.

The following examples represent
those in most general use. Perhaps
the most common form of the "rough
and ready" order of boats, is that
called the—

"DUG-OUT," OR LOG CANOE.

It's general appearance is well indicated by the accompanying illustration.
With the proper tools, one of these canoes is easily made. A sharp axe, an
adze, a shaving knife, a round edged
adze, and a small auger, are principally
necessary; and a cross-cut saw, broad-
axe, sledge, and large sized chisel, will
also be found useful.

In any case the log should not be
much less than two feet in diameter,
perfectly sound, and free from knots. If
this precaution is observed, the result
will be all the more satisfactory, and the
canoe can be cut so thin, as to render it
a light burden; being easily carried on
the shoulders.

A pine log is generally chosen for
a dug-out, on account of the lightness
of the wood, and the ease with which
it can be worked. Butternut, cotton-
wood and whitewood, are also excellent,
and indeed almost any sound log of
large size will answer the purpose.

For a dug-out of good size, the log
should be ten or more feet in length.
The first thing to be done is to cut a
flat surface on one side of the log, from
end to end. This indicates the bottom
of the canoe. On the upper side the wood should be hewn
away, in the curve shown on the upper outline of our illustration.

It is well to divide the log by notches into three equal lengths. In the centre division, the wood may be cut down to a straight line to a depth of about eight inches from the upper surface. The gradual curve to the bow and stern of the canoe should start from each end of this flat cut, and extend to the upper edge of the log, the guiding line being made on the sides of the log by a piece of chalk. The adze will come into good use in trimming off the wood on these curves. When this upper outline is accomplished, the log may be turned bottom side up, and the sides of the extremities rounded off. This may be done with an axe and adze, and when performed, the bottom curves should be made by chopping away the wood in the curves shown in the lower outline of our illustration. This curve should also be marked out with chalk, and should commence a little nearer the end of the log than the curve on the upper side. Shave off the wood to a blunt edge on this curve, at both bow and stern. The rough form of the canoe is now obtained, and by the aid of the draw-knife, or shaving-knife, it can be neatly and smoothly finished.

It is then ready to be "dug-out." The tools most useful for this purpose are the adze and axe, and sometimes the sledge and chisel. The digging out is of course the most tedious part; but with sharp tools it is a comparatively easy matter. When the great bulk of the wood is taken out, the interior should be finshed with a howel or round adze; and the sides may be worked to one inch and a half in thickness if desired. The writer once saw one of these canoes of most exquisite workmanship, being only one inch in thickness, and so light as to be easily lifted with one hand. Of course such perfection as this is not necessary for ordinary purposes ; although where the canoe is expected to be carried any great distance, it is well to thin it as much as possible. A gimlet or small auger may be used to gauge the thickness of the canoe, using it in the following manner : Supposing the required thickness of the wood is two inches, proceed to bore the hole from the inside of the canoe, and continue until the point of the gimlet or auger barely makes its appearance on the outside. Draw out the tool, and if the thickness measures more than is required, insert into the hole a slender piece of wood exactly two inches in length ; push it in as far as it will go, and you may safely work until you reach the end of it. By this method the thickness may be gauged in different parts of the boat sufficiently to acquire a fair average thickness, and there is no danger of

cutting through. The gimlet should be allowed to extend outside of the canoe only sufficiently to be detected, and the holes
thus made will seldom give any trouble as leaks. If, however,
this should be the case, a little putty or pitch will remedy the
difficulty.

The "dug-out" may be constructed of any size, and of any
desired shape, but the above is the usual type.

When leaks or cracks occur, they may be caulked with hemp,
and smeared with pitch, which will render them thoroughly water-
proof.

For lightness and portability there is no boat more desirable
or more unique than—

THE INDIAN OR BIRCH-BARK CANOE.

Where the white birch grows in perfection, and the trees attain a large size, the chief material of the birch bark canoe is at
hand; and although we ordinary mortals could not be expected
to attain to that perfection of skill which the Indians exhibit in
the manufacture of these canoes, we nevertheless can succeed
sufficiently well to answer all practical purposes. The Indian
canoes are often perfect marvels of skill and combined strength
and lightness. These half-civilized beings seem to take as naturally to the making of these commodities, as if it were almost
an hereditary habit with them; and few men, even with the most
exhaustive practice, can compete with the Indian in the combined
result of strength, lightness, durability, external beauty, and
nicety of work, which are the united characteristics of the
typical bark canoe.

The average length of the "Bark," as used by trappers, is
about twelve feet, but they may be constructed of any desired
dimensions, to the length of forty feet. A canoe of this size
will carry fifteen or twenty persons, and may be transported
with ease upon the shoulders of two strong men. The smaller
size, above mentioned, is capable of carrying two persons, and is
a light load for a single man.

In constructing the bark canoe the first requisite is the gunwale, or upper framework. This should consist of four strips
of cedar, ash, or other light, strong wood; two for each side of
the boat. For an ordinary sized canoe, their length should be
about twelve feet, width one inch, and thickness one-quarter of
an inch. They should be tied together in pairs at the ends, and
the two pairs then joined at the same place. The object of

these pieces is to give strength and form to the canoe, and to offer a firm security for the edges of the bark, which are secured between them. The gunwale being prepared, we are now ready for the birch bark. The bottom of a well made canoe should be in one large piece, as our illustration indicates, if possible. Select some large tree with the trunk free from knots or excrescences. Mark off as great a length as possible, and chop a straight cut in the bark through the whole length of the piece, after which it should be carefully peeled from the wood. It will sometimes happen, where large birches exist in perfection, that a single piece may be found of sufficient size for a whole canoe, but this is rather exceptional, and the bottom is generally pieced out, as seen in our drawing. This piecing may be accomplished with an awl and Indian twine, or by the aid of a large needle threaded with the same, sewing with an over-and-over stitch around the edge of each piece. Use as large pieces as are attainable, and continue to sew them on until the area of bark measures about four and a half feet in width by twelve feet in length, the dark colored sides of the bark all facing the same way. Next select a flat piece of ground, and mark off a distance of ten feet, or two feet less than the length of the gunwales. At each end of the space two tall stakes should be driven into the ground about three inches apart. Now turn the bark on the ground with its white side uppermost, and fold it loosely and evenly through the long centre. In this folded condition it should now be lifted by the upper edge and set between the stakes. There will then be about a foot of projecting bark beyond each pair of stakes. These ends should now be covered by folding another piece of bark over them, sewing the edges firmly to the sides of the rude form of the canoe, which now presents itself. When this is done, each end should be supported on a log or stone; this will cause the bottom line to sink downwards at about the proper curve. We are now ready for the gunwale. Lay it in the proper position, fitting the edges of the bark between the two strips on each side, and sewing around the whole with a winding stitch, exactly after the manner of the edge of an ordinary palm-leaf fan. The inside of the canoe should now be lined with long strips of cedar running through the entire length of the boat if possible, but if not, should be so cut as to neatly overlap at the ends. These pieces should be an inch or two in width, and from a quarter to half an inch-in thickness. The ribs are then to be put in. These are generally made from ash, one or two inches in width, and a quarter of an inch in thickness. Any light flexible wood will answer the purpose, and even barrel hoops when attainable will do very well. These ribs should be bent to fit the interior of the canoe crosswise, either close together, or with equal distances between them and the ends should then be firmly secured beneath the gunwales by a continuous loop-stitch through the bark. For a canoe of twelve feet in length, the width should be about two feet, and in order to keep the gunwales firm, two or more cross-pieces should be inserted, and lashed firmly at their ends as our illustration shows. The centre third of the length of the canoe should be parallel at the sides, and if two braces, two feet in length are placed at each end of this third, the shape will be about perfect. We now have a bark canoe of considerable strength and durability, and it only awaits to be made water-proof for final use. In order to accomplish this all the seams outside, and the entire interior of the canoe should, be smeared with pitch, after which its floating qualities may be tested with confidence. Should any leaks occur their where-abouts are easily detected, and an additional application of pitch will remedy the difficulty. The Indians in sewing their bark canoes use tamarack roots, fibrous plants, and grasses, in lieu of thread, and even with these inferior materials often attain to such perfection in compact sewing, as to render the use of pitch unnecessary for water-proof purposes. Such skill is rarely attained by the white man, and the art of making a water-proof canoe, even out of a single piece of bark, is by no means an easy task without the aid of tar or pitch.

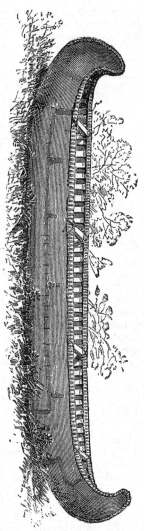

For the trapper we strongly recommend the birch "bark." With the above directions we are sure no one could go astray, and we are equally sure that a canoe made as we describe, would present advantages of lightness and portability which no other style of boat would possess. For temporary purposes, canoes can be made from basswood, hemlock, or spruce bark; but they are at best, very rude and clumsy in comparison with the birch bark. They are generally made after the principles of the above described; either sewing or nailing the edges of the bark together, and smearing every joint and seam profusely with pitch, and adding gunwales, lining, and ribs.

A LIGHT HOME-MADE BOAT.

The following gives an easy method of making a light and serviceable bateau, which any boy, with moderate ingenuity or skill, could easily construct:—

Select two boards, about three-quarters of an inch in thickness, eighteen or twenty inches in width, and twelve feet in length, which we will consider the required length of the boat. These boards should be well seasoned, and free from knots, and at least one of the sides should be straight.

Next, with the aid of a draw-shave, proceed to shape the ends of one of the boards, as seen on our diagram, (e) representing the forward, (g) the stern. The curve of the bow should commence at about four feet from the end, and take a rounded slope upward, leaving about ten inches of width at the end of the board (e). The stern should be cut at the angle shown at (g), commencing at about two and a half feet from the extremity of the board and continuing upward to about ten inches from the upper edge. The board thus shaped should now be laid evenly on the other, and the outline of the cut portions carefully scratched upon it, after which the second board should be cut in a similar manner as the first, so as to form an exact duplicate.

This being accomplished, the two should be laid evenly, one over the other, and the exact center of their long edges ascertained. Marking off about five inches on each side of this centre on both boards.

Next procure another board about ten inches in width, three feet in length, and perfectly squared at the ends. Nail each end of this piece securely and squarely in the space marked on each of the long boards. Then turn the pieces carefully over and

nail another board across the bottom, directly opposite the
first. We will now leave them and give our attention to the bow piece, which is the next requisite. This is shown at (*a*), and consists of a solid
piece of oak, or other hard wood, well seasoned, and
hewn out in the arrow shape, indicated in our illustration. It should first be cut three-cornered, the
inside face being about eight inches, and the other
two ten inches. Its length should be about eleven
inches, and its under side should be sloped off on a
line with the under curve of the bows. At about
five inches from the inner face, and on each side, a
piece should be sawn out, one inch in thickness, thus
leaving on each side a notch which will exactly receive
the side-boards of the boat, as seen at (*a*).

The piece being thus ready, the bow ends of the
boards should be drawn together, fitted in the notches
and securely spiked with large nails. A bow piece
of this kind adds greatly to the strength of a boat,
and will stand much rough usage. The board for
the stern should next be prepared. This should be
ten inches in width and two feet in length, and should
be securely nailed between the ends of the boards
at the stern, as shown at (*g*), being afterwards overlapped on the top by a board of similar size, as our
illustration shows, at (*c*). The bottom of the boat is
now easily made by nailing boards crosswise, sawing
off the projecting ends close to the curve of the
side-boards. After the pieces are all nailed in place,
the seams and crevices should be caulked with hemp,
using a blunt chisel, or hard wooden wedge, and a
mallet. The seats should now be put in, as these are
not only a matter of comfort, but of necessity, acting
as braces to the sides of the boat. They should be
two in number, one being placed three feet from the
stern and the other one foot beyond the brace board
originally nailed across the top of the boat. The
seats should be cut at the ends in a curve corresponding to the part of the boat in which they are
placed, and should be situated about a foot from the
bottom of the boat, their ends resting on short boards
beneath them against the sides of the boat. These
are indicated by the dotted lines (*h h*) in the diagram. When

thus resting they should be securely fastened in place by strong

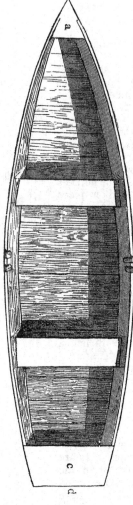

screws, driven through the sides of the boat into their ends (*f f*), allowing some one to sit on the seat meanwhile to keep it in place. Small cleats should now be tacked to the bottom of the boat, beneath the seat and underneath the seat itself, in order to keep the props in place ; after which the original brace board across the top of the boat may be knocked off and the bateau is complete and ready for service. A boat thus made is quite comely in shape, and may be painted to suit the fancy. Should a rudder be required, the broad board at the stern offers a good place of attachment, and oar-locks may be adjusted at the proper places. These may consist of a pair of cleats attached to the inside of the boat, as seen in the illustration. In case it may be found difficult to obtain the large single boards for the sides of the boat, two or more narrow ones will answer the purpose, although not as perfectly. In this case they should first be firmly attached together by cleats, securely screwed to the inside. When first put on the water the boat will probably leak in places, but if left to soak for a few hours the wood will generally swell sufficiently to completely close the crevices. If, however, the leak should continue, that particular part of the boat should be re-caulked and smeared with pitch. This latter substance is of great value to the trapper, not only in boat building but in the construction of his shanties and in other various ways. It will most effectually stop almost any leak in a canoe or boat, and of course should always be applied hot.

THE SCOW.

The bateau we have above described is built so as to allow for considerable speed in the water, either in rowing or sculling; but where this speed is not especially desired the pointed bows may be dispensed with, and the sides of the boat made perfectly straight. In this case the bottom takes equal slopes at the ends, and both bow and stern are of the same width, and an ordinary flat-bottomed boat with parallel sides is the result. In many cases a scow of this kind answers every purpose, and is certainly much more easily made.

We have thus described a few of the most common instances of boats used by trappers, and with our full description and illustrations no one can go astray. A boat of some kind is almost an indispensable requisite to the trapper, and any one of the foregoing will be found sufficient for all ordinary purposes.

A paddle may be used, and in shallow or muddy water a pusher or mud-stick will be found useful. This should consist of a pole seven or eight feet in length, supplied at the ends with an attachment of the shape of the letter U. This may be constructed in two pieces, firmly screwed to opposite sides of the end of the pole, and so formed as to present a curved crotch. Such a stick will be found very useful for pushing through weeds and muddy places. A simple pole trimmed so as to leave a crotch at the end will also answer the purpose very well.

SNOW-SHOES.

These commodities are almost indispensable to the trapper where he pursues his vocation in the winter time, during the prevalence of deep snows. When properly made they permit the wearer to walk over the surface of the snow with perfect ease; where, without them, travel would be extremely difficult if not impossible.

In the regions of perpetual snow, and also in Canada and neighboring districts, snow-shoes are very commonly worn. In the latter localities the " snow-shoe race " forms one of the favorite sports of the season, and young and old alike join in its mysteries. Like riding on the velocipede, walking on snow-shoes looks "easy enough," but we notice that a few somersaults are usually a convincing argument that the art is not as simple as it appears. The first experience on snow-shoes is apt to be at least undignifying, if not discouraging, and in order to get used to the strange capers and eccentricities of an ordinarily well-behaved snow shoe, it requires considerable patience and practice. There is no telling where, in an unguarded moment, they will land you, and they seem to take especial delight in stepping on each other and turning their wearer upside down. The principal secret of success (and one may as well know it at the start, as to learn it at the expense of a pint of snow down his back) consists in taking steps sufficiently long to bring the widest portion of the stepping shoe beyond that of the other, keeping the feet rather far apart and stepping pretty high. By observing these precautions, and trusting in Providence, much embarrassment may be saved, and an hour's effort will thoroughly tame the unruly appendages, which at best do not permit of much grace or elegance of gait.

To the moose hunter snow-shoes are often an absolute necessity, and trapping in many cases would be impossible without them. They are thus brought fully within the scope of our volume, and we give a few simple directions for their manufacture. Our illustration gives the correct shape of the shoe. The framework should consist of a strip of ash, hickory or some other elastic wood, bent into the form indicated and wound around the ends with twine or strips of hide. The length of the piece should be about six feet, more or less, in proportion to the size of the individual who proposes to wear the shoe. If the bending should prove difficult it may be rendered an easy matter by the application of boiling water. Across the front part two strips of stout leather, or other tough hide, are then fastened, and these further secured together by three or four bands on each side of the middle, as our drawing shows.

In the original Indian snow-shoe, from which our drawing was made, the net work was constructed from strips of moose hide, which were interlaced much after the manner of an ordinary cane-seated chair. Strips of leather, deer skin, or even split cane, above alluded to, may also be used, and the lacing may be either as our illustration represents, or in the simpler rectangular woof seen in ordinary cloth.

In order to attach the interlacing to the bow the latter should be wound with wide strips of cane, if it can be procured, or otherwise with strips of tough skin. The loops thus formed offer a continuous security, and the whole interior, with the exception of the space at the front between the cross pieces, should be neatly filled with the next work. It is well to run the first lines across the shoe, from side to side, passing through the windings of the bow. Across them, in the form of the letter X, the two other cords should be interlaced, after the manner shown in the cut. This forms a secure and not very complicated network, and is the style usually adopted by the Indian makers.

There is another mode of attaching the lace-work to the bow which is also commonly employed, and consists in a series of holes bored at regular intervals through the wood. The winding is thus dispensed with, but the bow is sometimes weakened by the operation, and we are inclined to recommend the former method in preference. In attaching the shoe, the ball of the foot should be set on the second cross piece, and there secured by a strip of hide, which should be first adjusted as seen in the engraving, being afterward tied over the foot and then behind the ankle.

Snow-shoes are made in other ways, but we believe that the typical Indian snow-shoe above described is the best.

THE TOBOGGAN OR INDIAN SLEDGE.

For winter traffic over deep snows there is no better sled in the world than the Indian toboggan. To the trapper during a winter campaign it is often an indispensable convenience, and without it the Indian hunters of the North would find great difficulty in getting their furs to market. All through the winter season the various trading posts of Canada are constantly visited by numbers of Indian trappers, many of whom have travelled hundreds of miles on their snow-shoes with their

heavily laden toboggans.   Arrived at their market they sell or
trade their stock of furs, and likewise dispose of their toboggans, reserving only their snow-shoes to aid them in their long
tramp homewards.

In Canada and northward the toboggan is in very extensive
use, both for purposes of traffic and amusement.   It is quite
commonly met with in the streets of various Canadian cities, and
is especially appreciated by the youthful population, who are
fond of coasting over the crust of snow.   For this purpose there
is no other sled like it, and a toboggan of the size we shall de-

scribe will easily accommodate two or three boys, and will glide
over a crust of snow with great ease and rapidity.   To the trapper it is especially valuable for all purposes of transportation.
The flat bottom rests upon the surface of the snow, and the
weight being thus distributed a load of two or three hundred
pounds will often make but little impression and can be drawn
with marvellous ease.   Our illustration gives a very clear idea
of the sled, and it can be made in the following way: the first
requisite is a board about eight feet in length and sixteen or
more inches in width.   Such a board may be procured at any
saw-mill.   Oak is the best wood for the purpose, although hickory, basswood or ash will do excellently.   It should be planed
or sawed to a thickness of about a third of an inch, and should
be free from knots.   If a single board of the required width is
not easily found, two boards may be used, and secured side by
side by three cleats, one at each end and the other in the middle, using wrought nails and clinching them deeply into the board
on the under side.   The single board is much to be preferred,
if it can be had.   The next requisites are seven or eight wooden
cross-pieces of a length equivalent to the width of the board.
Four old broom-sticks, cut in the required lengths, will answer

this purpose perfectly, and if these are not at hand other sticks of similar dimensions should be used. Two side pieces are next needed. These should be about five feet in length, and in thickness exactly similar to the cross pieces. Next procure a few pairs of leather shoe-strings or some strips of tough calf skin. With these in readiness we may now commence the work of putting the parts together. Begin by laying the cross pieces at equal distances along the board ; across these and near their ends lay the two side pieces, as seen in the illustration. By the aid of a gimlet or awl, four holes should now be made through the board, beneath the end of each cross piece, and also directly under the side piece. It is well to mark with a pencil, the various points for the holes, after which the sticks can be removed and the work much more easily performed. The four holes should be about an inch apart, or so disposed as to mark the four corners of a square inch. It is also necessary to make other holes along the length of the cross pieces, as seen in the illustration. The line on these can also be marked with the pencil across the board, and the holes made afterwards. These should also be an inch apart, and only two in number at each point, one on each side of the stick. When all the holes are made the board should be turned over, in order to complete preparations on the other side. The object of these various holes is for the passage of the leather shoe-strings for the purpose of securing the cross pieces firmly to the board. In order to prevent these loops from wearing off on the under side, small grooves should next be made connecting the holes beneath, thus allowing the leather string to sink into the wood, where it is securely protected from injury. A narrow chisel is the best tool for this purpose, the making of the grooves being much more easily and perfectly accomplished with this than with the jack-knife. When the under side is thus finished the board may be turned over and the cross pieces and sides again arranged in place as already described. Secure the pieces to the board by the leather strings through the various holes, always knotting on the upper surface, and taking care that the knots are firmly tied. The ends of all the cross pieces will require a double cross stitch through the four holes beneath, in order to secure the side pieces as well. This is plainly shown in the small diagram (*a*). The front end of each side piece underneath should now be sharpened to a point, to allow for the bend at the front of the toboggan. The cross piece at this end should be secured to the under side of the board, so that as it bends over it will appear on the upper edge, as our illustration shows. The board should next be bent with a graceful curve, and thus held in position by a rope or strip of leather at each extremity of the end cross piece and attached to the ends of the third cross piece, as seen in the engraving. If the bending is difficult and there is danger of breaking the board, the application of boiling water will render it pliable. The draw strings should then be attached to the ends of the second cross piece, and our toboggan is now complete.

It may now be laden with two or three hundred pounds of merchandize and will be found to draw over the surface of the snow with perfect ease. For coasting over the crust there is nothing like it. Such a toboggan as we have described will easily accommodate three boys, the one at the stern being provided with a sharp stick for steering, and the front occupant holding firmly to the draw strings. The toboggan is easily made, and will do good service either for traffic or sport.

CURING SKINS.

This department of the trapper's art is one of the most important and necessary, as affecting pecuniary profits. The value of a skin in the fur market depends entirely upon the care with which it is taken from the animal and afterward prepared, and without a knowledge on this subject the young trapper will in vain seek for high prices for his furs. Large quantities of valuable skins are sent to our markets annually by inexperienced amateur trappers, and in many cases rare and beautiful furs have been almost spoiled by want of care in skinning and curing. The rules are simple and easily followed, a little care being all that is necessary to insure most perfect success. In every case the skin should be removed shortly after death, or at least before it has become tainted with decay. Great pains should be taken in skinning. Avoid the adherence of flesh or fat to the skin, and guard against cutting through the hide, as a pierced skin is much injured in value. The parts about the eyes, legs and ears should be carefully removed. The various methods of skinning are described in our section on trapping, and in all cases the furs should be allowed to dry in a cool, airy place, free from the rays of the sun or the heat of a fire, and protected from rain.

Astringent preparations of various kinds are used by many trappers, but they are by no means necessary. The most common dressing consists of equal parts of rock salt and alum, dissolved in water. Into this a sufficient amount of coarse flour or wheat bran is stirred to give the mixture the consistency of batter, after which it is spread thickly over the skin and allowed to dry.

It is afterwards scraped off, and in some cases a second application is made. This preparation is much used in dressing beaver, otter, mink and muskrat skins, but as many of our most successful and experienced trappers do without it, we fail to see the advantage of using it, as it is only an extra trouble. The simplest and surest way is to stretch the skin and to submit it to a gradual process of natural drying without any artificial heat or application of astringents to hasten the result.

A very common mode of stretching skins consists in tacking them to a board, with the fur inwards, and allowing them to dry as already described.

This method does very well for small skins, but for general purposes the "stretchers" are the only means by which a pelt may be properly cured and prepared.

STRETCHERS.

The board stretcher is the simplest form and is in most common use among trappers for the smaller animals. These stretchers are of two kinds, the plain and the wedged. The plain stretcher consists of a piece of board a quarter of an inch in thickness, about eighteen inches long and six inches in width.

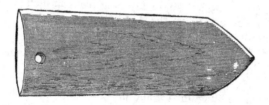

One end of this board is rounded off, as seen in our illustration, and the sides should also be whittled and smoothed to a blunt edge.

The board stretchers are used only for those skins which are taken off whole, that is, as described in the chapter on the otter. The skin should be drawn tightly over the blunt end of the board, and its edges either caught in notches cut in the edges of the square end or secured by a few tacks. This stretcher is particularly adapted to the skins of muskrats, minks and animals of a like size. They are known in New England as "shingle stretchers," and are much to be recommended on account of their lightness and the ease with which they can be made and carried.

The wedge stretcher is rather more elaborate than the foregoing, and is said to be an improvement.

The first requisite is a board of about three-eighths of an inch in

thickness, two feet or more in length, and three and a half inches at one end tapering to the width of two inches at the other. This end should now be rounded, and the edges of the board whittled off to a blunt edge, as already described in the foregoing, commencing near the centre of the board, and thinning to the edge, and finishing with the notches at the square end. Now, by the aid of a rip-saw, sever the board through the middle lengthwise.

The wedge is the next thing to be constructed, and should consist of a piece of wood the thickness of the centre of the board and of the same length, tapering from an inch in width at one end to half an inch at the other.

To use the stretcher the two boards are inserted into the skin, (the latter with the fur side inward). The wedge is then inserted between the large ends of the boards and driven in sufficiently to stretch the pelt to its full capacity, securing it in the notches by slight cuts in the hide, or by a tack or two at the edge. It should then he hung in a cool, airy place, and the pelt left to "season."

The bow stretcher is another contrivance very commonly used for small skins like the foregoing. When this is used the pelt should be skinned as described on page 185, the initial cut commencing at the lower jaw and extending down between the fore legs, all the feet being previously cut off. The bow may consist of a switch of any elastic wood, such as hickory, iron wood, elm or birch. It should be about three or more feet in length, and as large as a man's thumb at the butt end. By bending it in the shape of the letter U it may easily be inserted in the skin, the latter being fastened by catching the lip on each side into a sliver notch cut on each end of the bow, as our illustration indicates.

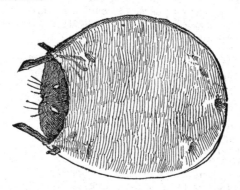

For large animals, such as the deer, bear, beaver, the hoop stretcher is generally employed.

THE HOOP STRETCHER.

This consists of a hoop made from one or more flexible switches tied together so as to form a circle. In order to be adapted to ' this mode of stretching, the skin should be flat, *i. e.* taken off as described on page 172, the initial cut extending from the lower jaw to the vent. The size of the hoop required depends upon the dimensions of the skin. Lay the latter upon some flat surface and so gauge the hoop as that it shall surround the pelt on all sides; after which the latter should be secured or laced to the hoop with twine at the edges. All loose parts should be drawn up, and the skin should everywhere be stretched like a drum head. When this is accomplished it is the custom with many trappers to apply the preparation described on page 273, particularly where the skin is thick and fatty. But we are rather disposed to discourage the use of any preparation whatever, in any case, as they are by no means necessary.

In using the board stretchers the fur should always be on the inside, and when the hoop or bow is used it should be placed in such a position that the air may circulate freely on both sides of the skin, which should not be removed until thoroughly dry.

TANNING SKINS.

In case some of our readers might desire to tan fur skins for their own domestic purposes, the subjoined directions will be found to be reliable, and for all ordinary requirements, sufficiently adequate.

For tanning with the hair on, the skin should first be cleaned, every particle of loose fat or flesh, being removed, and the useless parts cut away. When this is done, it should be soaked for an hour or two in warm water. The following mixture should then be prepared: Take equal parts of borax, saltpetre, and sulphate of soda, and with them mix water sufficient to produce the consistency of thin batter.

This preparation should be painted thickly on the flesh side of the skin, after which these sides should be doubled together and the pelt left in an airy place.

A second mixture should next be prepared. This should consist of two parts sal soda; three parts borax; four parts castile or other hard soap: all to be melted together over a slow fire. At the end of twenty-four hours, after the application of the first mixture, the second should be applied in a similar manner, and the fur again folded and left for the same length of time. Next, make a mixture equal parts of salt and alum, dissolved in warm water and thickened with coarse flour to the consistency of thin paste. Spread this thickly over the skin and allow it to dry, after which it should be scraped off with the bowl of a spoon. The skin should be tightly stretched during the operation, in order to prevent too great shrinkage. A single application of the last-named dressing, is generally sufficient for small skins; but a second or third treatment may be resorted to if required, to make the skin soft and pliable, after which it should be finished off with sand-paper and pumice stone. A skin may be thus dressed as soft as velvet, and the alum and salt will set the hair securely.

The above directions are excellent, for all general purposes, but we subjoin, in addition, a few other valuable hints and specific recipes in common use. Every trapper has his own peculiar hobby in regard to his tanning process, and the recipes are various and extensive. The above is one of the most reliable for general use. A common mode of tanning mink and muskrat skins is given in the following :—

TO TAN MINK AND MUSKRAT SKINS.

Before tanning, the skin should always be thoroughly cleansed in warm water, and all fat and superfluous flesh removed. It should then be immersed in a solution made of the following ingredients : Five gallons of cold soft water ; five quarts wheat bran ; one gill of salt ; and one ounce of sulphuric acid. Allow the skins to soak in the liquid for four or five hours. If the hides have been previously salted, the salt should be excluded from the mixed solution. The skins are now ready for the tanning liquor, which is made in the following way : into five gallons of warm, soft water, stir one peck of wheat bran, and allow the mixture to stand in a warm room until fermentation takes place. Then add three pints of salt, and stir until it is thoroughly dissolved. A pint of sulphuric acid should then be poured in gradually, after which the liquor is ready. Immerse the skins and allow them to soak for three or four hours. The process of "fleshing" is then to be resorted to. This consists in laying the skin, fur side down, over some smooth beam, and working over the flesh side with a blunt fleshing tool. An old chopping knife, or tin candlestick, forms an excellent substitute for the ordinary fleshing knife, and the process of rubbing should be continued until the skin becomes dry, after which it will be found to be soft and pliable. The skin of the muskrat is quite tender, and the fleshing should be carefully performed.

HOW TO TAN THE SKINS OF BEAVER, OTTER, RACCOON, AND MARTEN.

These should be stretched on a board and smeared with a mixture composed of three ounces each, of salt and alum ; three gills of water, and one drachm of sulphuric acid. This should be thickened with wheat bran or flour, and should be allowed to dry on the skin, after which it should be scraped off with a spoon. Next, take the skin from the board, roll it with the fur inside. and draw it quickly backward and forward, over a smooth peg, or through an iron ring. The skin should then be unfolded and rolled again the opposite way, and the operation repeated until the pelt is quite soft and flexible. This is a good way of softening all kinds of skins, and the above preparation will be found excellent for all ordinary purposes. The muskrat skin may be treated in the same manner as the above, if desired, and the process directed on the muskrat skin may also be applied to the pelts of the other animals.

To remove the fur for a simple tanned skin, the hide should be immersed in a liquid composed of—soft water, five gallons ; slaked lime, four quarts ; and wood ashes, four quarts. Allow the skin to soak for a couple of days, after which the fur will readily slip off.

Another method—Take equal parts wood ashes and slaked lime, and add water to the consistency of batter. Spread this over the inside of the skin, roll it up, and place it in a pail, covering it with water. Here let it remain from one to five days, or until the hair will shed easily, after which it should be finished with the fleshing knife and velveted with sand paper.

OBSERVATIONS ON THE HISTORY OF FURS AND THE FUR TRADE.

In all cold climates, man has availed himself liberally of the warm covering with which nature has clothed the animals around him; but the wealth of the most favored nations has drawn to them the most beautiful furs, in whatever part of the world they are procured. Skins of animals were among the first materials used for clothing. Before Adam and Eve were driven from the Garden of Eden, they were furnished with coats of skins. The ancient Assyrians used the soft skins of animals to cover the couches or the ground in their tents, and the Israelites employed badger's skins and ram's skins, as ornamental hangings for the Tabernacle. The ancient heroes of the Greeks and Romans, are represented as being clothed in skins. Æneas, wearing for an outer garment, that of the lion, and Alcestes being formidably clad in that of the Libyan Bear. Herodotus speaks of those living near the Caspian Sea wearing seal skins, and Cæsar mentions that the skin of the reindeer formed in part the clothing of the Germans. In the early period, furs appear to have constituted the entire riches of the Northern countries, and they were almost the only exports. Taxes were paid on them, and they were the medium of exchange. So it was also in our own Western territories in the latter part of the last century, and is to the present day, to a great extent, among the Indians. In the eleventh century, furs had become fashionable throughout Europe, and the art of dyeing them, was practiced in the twelfth. In the history of the Crusades, frequent mention is made of the magnificent displays by the European Princes, of their dresses of costly furs, before the Court at Constantinople. But Richard I. of England, and Philip II. of France, in order to check the growing extravagance in their use, resolved that the choicer furs, ermine and sable amongst the number, should be omitted from their kingly wardrobes. Louis IX. followed their example in the next century, but not until his extravagance had grown to such a pitch, that *seven hundred and forty-six* ermines were required for the *lining* of one of his *surcoats.* In these times, the use of the choicer furs, as those of the sable, ermine, gris, and Hungarian squirrel, was restricted to the royal families and the nobility, to whom they served as distinctive marks and badges of rank. These privileged persons applied them lavishly to their own use, and the fashion extended to the princes of other less civilized nations. Their royal use soon extended to Tartary, and the tents of the Khan were bedecked with the most rich and costly furs. In the following century, furs were commonly worn in England until their use was prohibited by Edward III., to all persons whose purse would not warrant a yearly expenditure of £100.

The early fur trade of Western Europe, was conducted through the merchants on the south coast of the Baltic, who received goods from the ports of Livonia. In the sixteenth century, a direct trade was opened between the English and Russians; and a company of the former, protected by the Czar, established trading posts on the White Sea, and a warehouse at Moscow, whence they sent trading parties to Persia and the countries on the Caspian Sea. The Czar sent rich presents of beautiful furs, to Queen Mary and Queen Elizabeth; but the latter prohibited the wearing of any but native furs, and the trade soon declined and was abandoned. In the 17th century, Siberia was conquered by the Russians, and its tribute was paid in furs. Large quantities were also furnished to China, but the choicest kinds—the precious ermine, the brilliant, fiery foxes, and the best sables, were taken to Moscow, for the use of the princes and nobles of Russia, Turkey, and Persia.

In our own country, the early settlers of the Northern provinces, soon learned the value of the furs of the numerous animals which peopled the extensive rivers, lakes, and forests of these vast territories. They collected the skins in abundance, and found an increasing demand for them, with every new arrival of immigrants from the mother country. Trinkets, liquors, and other articles sought for by the native tribes, were shipped to Quebec, and from thence up the St. Lawrence to Montreal, which soon became the great trading post of the country. The various tribes of Indians were stimulated by trifling compensation, to pursue their only congenial and peaceful occupation; and the French settlers, readily assimilating to the Indian habits, became themselves expert hunters, trappers, and explorers.

The business prospered, and the English soon became interested and secured a share of the valuable trade. Many wealthy and influential parties, connected with the government of Great Britain,—Prince Rupert and Lord Ashley, among the number—became deeply interested in this source of revenue; and after a successful enterprise, they obtained from Charles II., a charter of incorporation, giving to them full possession of the territory within the entrance of Hudson's Straits, not already granted to other subjects, or possessed by those of any other Christian prince or State. In this charter was included the monopoly, of all trade in these regions, and thus we see the origin of the Great Hudson's Bay Company, which is to-day, one of the largest organizations of its kind on the globe. The territory they claimed, extended from Hudson's Bay, west to the Pacific, and north to the Arctic Ocean, excepting that occupied by the French and Russians. They soon formed settlements upon the various rivers which empty into Hudson's Bay, and carried on their operations with immense vigor and success. They met with much opposition and open hostility from the French, and were subjected to vast expenses and losses, but in spite of all, they continued to prosper. Their forts or factories were extended further into the interior of British America, and their power was supreme throughout the country, and in a great measure over the Indians, whom they employed to collect their skins. In the course of time, the French Canadians organized themselves into a united band, under the name of the North West Company, and established their headquarters at Montreal. Their operations were carried on with great energy and profit, and many factories were built in the western portion of the Province. The company thus soon became a formidable competitor with the Hudson's Bay Company, and for a period of two years, an actual state of war existed between them. This condition of affairs finally terminated in a consolidation of the two organizations, under the name of the Hudson's Bay Company, the privileges of which extended over all the territory formerly occupied by both.

Thus, we have the history of the famous Hudson's Bay Company, from its origin to its perfect organization. It is a most stupendous concern, and its annual shipment of furs, is something amazing. Their great sales take place in the month of March, in order to be completed before Easter; and again in September, every year at London, and are attended by purchasers from nearly all parts of the world. Leipsic, the famous fur mart of Germany, is also the scene of a great annual fair, for the sale of skins.

The importance of the fur trade in this country, led to the

early settlement of the Western territories of the United States;
and many a frontier city, like St. Paul, has been built up by
the enterprise of the trapper. Mackinaw and Montreal owe
much of their growth to the traffic of the fur trade; and many
a kingly fortune—John Jacob Astor's, for instance—has been
founded on peltry.

Besides the above fur sales in London a moderate portion of
those annually collected in the United States are retained for
use, amounting to about 150,000 mink and 750,000 muskrat
skins, besides a number of other furs which are manufactured
and worn.

The annual yield of raw furs throughout the whole world is
estimated at over twenty millions of dollars in value; and when
we include the manufactured articles therefrom, the amount will
swell to a hundred millions or over. This will serve to give
some idea of the immensity and value of the business.

American dealers divide our native furs into two classes, viz.,
home and *shipping* furs; the former being chiefly utilized in
our own country, while the latter are exported to all parts of
the world. New York City is the great fur mart and depot for
the shipping trade in this country, and the annual value of its
exports, in this one branch of trade is enormous.

The principal shipping furs are the silver, red and cross Fox,
Wild Cat, Raccoon, Fisher, Muskrat and Skunk.

Among the home furs are the Marten, Mink, Opossum, Wolf
and Muskrat, the latter being extensively used both here and
abroad.

In the following chapter will be found more detailed notes on
the leading American furs, including their various uses and the
different countries for which they are the especial staples.

In order to give the reader some idea of the variety and mag-
nitude of the yield of furs from our own country, we annex a
table (p. 282) showing the sales of the Hudson's Bay Company,
at London, in the year 1873.

MARKET VALUE OF FUR SKINS.

Below will be found an authentic table of the comparative
values of the various American furs at the present date of publication. The quotations are those of one of our largest fur
dealers, as published in "THE HAT, CAP AND FUR TRADE
REVIEW," the leading journal of the trade in America. Of
course these values are constantly varying—keeping pace with the
eccentricities of fashion and the demands of the fur trade; but

KINDS.	No. of Skins. March Sale.	No. of Skins. Sept. Sale.	Total No.	Price according to quality.	Estimated average price per skin.		
					£	s.	d.
Badger.........	2,700	....	2,700	1s. to 7s.		1	06
Bear	5,217	2,794	8,011	5s. to £8 10s.	5	0	00
Beaver.........	111,993	37,052	149,045	4s. 3d. to 38s. 6d.	1	00	00
Fisher.........	2,843	779	3,622	8s. to £3 5s.	2	10	00
Fox, Blue.......	90	....	90	18s. to £4.	2	10	00
" Cross......	1,818	471	2,289	5s. to £4.	1	10	00
" Kitt........	6,930	....	6,930	2s. 8d. to 28s. 10d.		3	00
" Red.......	6,914	1,383	8,297	4s. 6d. to 17s.		10	00
" Silver......	540	148	688	£3 10s. to £21.	10	00	00
" White.....	7,312	....	7,312	2s. to 14s. 9d.		7	00
Lynx..........	2,468	1,652	4,120	9s. 6d. to £1 14s.		18	00
Marten.........	47,878	18,955	66,833	10s. to £3 19s.	1	10	00
Mink..........	31,802	12,896	44,698	4s. to £1 8s. 6d.		15	00
Muskrat	651,498	116,488	767,896	3d. to 16d.		00	8
Otter..........	8,571	2,681	11,252	14s. to £3 18s.	2	10	00
" Sea.......	....	98	98	£4 10s. to £32.	15	00	00
Rabbit........	10,029	....	10,029	3d. to 4d.		00	3
Raccoon........	....	3,582	3,582	1s. to 3s. 3d.		2	6
Skunk..........	1,691	....	1,691	2s. to 7s.		4	00
Wolf..........	6,216	188	6,404	6s. to £2 15s.		15	00
Wolverine......	1,770	320	2,090	8s. to £1 1s.		15	00

the table will serve at least to gauge the relative values, as between the two extremes of common and scarce furs. The fur market is a great deal like the stock market. It is constantly fluctuating, and a fur which is to-day among the novelties, may next year find itself on the low priced list. The demand for furs of any kind is nearly always governed by fashion, and of course the value is estimated on the demand. If the convention of fur dealers should decide to usher in *Muskrat fur* as the leading and most fashionable article in that line, the fashion would create the demand, the demand would be in turn supplied by the trappers throughout the country, and in proportion as the Muskrat skins became scarce, so their value would increase. In this way a skin which may be worth fifty cents at one time may soon acquire a value of twenty times that amount. The comparative value of skins is, therefore, constantly varying more or less; but the annexed table (page 283) will be found useful for general reference, and for approximate

AMERICAN FUR SKINS—TABLE OF VALUES.*

	Prime.	Seconds.	Thirds.	Fourths.
Badger...............................	$1.00	$0.50	$0.10	$...... .
Bear, Black......	18.00	9.00	1.00	....
" Cub..................	10 00	5.00	1.00	....
" Brown	7.00	4.00	1.00	....
Beaver, California.............. .....per lb.	1.25	75	50	....
" Southern	1.00	75	40	....
" Upper Missouri.................	1.75	1.50	50	....
" Lake Supr. and Canada............	2.50	1.75	75	....
Cat, Wild.....	40	10	....	....
" House.............................	15	10	....	....
Deer, Florida.............. ....per lb	20	....	....	....
" Missouri...........................	20	....	....	....
Elk and Moose.....................per lb.	35	25	....	....
Fisher, Southern.....	7.00	5.00	1.00	....
" Eastern and Canada	10.00	8.00	2.00	....
Fox, Silver...........................	100.00	25.00	1.00	....
" Cross...	3.00	1.50	1.00	....
" Blue.............................	15.00	5.00	1.00	....
" White	3.00	1.50	....	....
" Red	1.75	1.00	75	25
" Gray.............................	3.00	1.50	50	25
" Kitt.............................	50	25	....	....
Lynx, Minnesota......................	2.50	1.00	....	....
" Canada........................	4.00	2.00	....	....
Marten, Dark..........................	10.00	6.00	2.00	....
" Small Pale	2.00	1.00	50	....
Mink, Southern.	1.00	50	25	10
" Western........................	1.25	1.00	50	10
" Middle States.................	2.00	1.25	50	10
" Minnesota......................	2.50	1.50	75	20
" New England......	3.50	1.75	1.00	20
" Quebec and Halifax	4.00	2.00	1.00	20
Muskrat, Southern.....................	28	25	15	5
" Western	30	28	18	6
" Northern......................	32	30	20	8
" Eastern	35	30	22	10
Opossum, Ohio.........................	30	20	10	....
" Southern....................	20	10	....	....
Otter, Southern.......................	5.00	3.00	2.00	50
" Northern......................	10.00	6.00	2.00	50
Rabbit	3	....	....	....
Raccoon, Southern.....................	50	30	15	5
" Western	1.00	50	20	5
" Michigan....................	1.25	80	30	5
Seal, Hair...........................	60	....	....	....
" Fur..............................	10.00	....	....	....
Skunk, Black Cased....................	1.00	60	40	10
" Half Stripe....................	60	50	25	10
" White	20	10	....	. ...
Wolf, Timber.........................	3.00	1.50	....	....
" Prairie.	1.00	75	....	....
Wolverine............................	5.00	2.00	....	....

* From the "Hat, Cap and Fur Trade Review."

figures, will probably answer every purpose for some time to come.

Notwithstanding all these advertised prices, the young trapper often experiences great difficulty in a profitable disposal of his furs. Like every other business, the fur trade runs in its regular grooves, and the average furrier will often pay an experienced professional five dollars for a skin for which he would not offer a *dollar* to an amateur. This certainly seems discouraging, but the knowledge of the fact is calculated to prevent *greater* discouragement.

We often see fancy prices advertised by fur dealers for first-class skins ; but when the furs are sent, only a few are selected as "*prime*," the rest being rejected as worthless, or perhaps meeting with a meagre offer far below the regular rates. In this way the dealers have the opportunity of choice selection without incurring any risk. Many a young trapper has been thus disappointed, and has seen his small anticipated fortune dwindle down to very small proportions.

The fur trade is supplied through regular professional channels ; and in giving our advice to the novice, we would recommend as the most satisfactory and profitable plan that he should make his sales to some local hunter or trapper, who has had experience with the fur trade, and who is satisfied to pay a fair price for the various skins with the probability of selling at an advance, and thus realizing a profit.

In nearly every trapping locality such men are to be found, and although the prices earned may be below the market rates, the amateur takes none of the speculative risks of the business, and should be willing to take lower prices on this account.

AMERICAN FUR SKINS—THEIR USES AT HOME AND ABROAD.

In the early history of fur apparel, its use was determined by *climate ;* to-day, and especially in this country, it is regulated by the caprice of *fashion.* The mink for many years took the lead in the list of fashionable furs, but has of late been superseded by the introduction of the fur seal. The most choice and costly of our American furs at the present day is the Silver Fox. When highly dressed they are worth from 10 to 50 guineas each in the European market. They are principally bought by the Russians and Chinese.

The skins of the Red Fox are purchased by the Chinese, Greeks, Persians, and other Oriental nations. They are made into linings for robes, etc., and ornamented with the black fur of the paws which is set on in spots or waves. The fur of the

Beaver was formerly highly prized in the manufacture of hats, and yielded a large portion of the profits of the Fur Companies, constituting the largest item in value among furs. Cheaper materials have since been substituted in making hats, and the demand for this purpose has been greatly reduced. By a new process the skin is now prepared as a handsome fur for collars and gauntlets, and its fine silky wool has been successfully woven. The soft, white fur from the belly of the animal, is largely used in France for bonnets.

Raccoon skins are the great staple for Russia and Germany, where, on account of their durability and cheapness, they are in demand for linings for coats, etc. Among the Bear skins, those of the black and grizzly are extensively used for military caps, housings, holsters, sleigh robes, etc.

The fur of the Lynx is soft, warm and light, and is commonly dyed of a beautiful shining black. It is used for the facings and linings of cloaks, chiefly in America.

The Fisher yields a dark and full fur which is largely used in fashionable winter apparel.

The skin of the Marten, is richly dyed and utilized in choice furs and trimmings.

The Mink, like the two foregoing, belongs to the same genus as the Russian Sable, and its fur so much resembles the latter as to be sometimes mistaken for it. It is one of fashion's furs, and the hair of the tail is sometimes used in the manufacture of artist's pencils.

The Muskrat produces the fur most worn by the masses, and is largely exported into Germany, France and England. It is estimated that over six millions of muskrat skins are annually taken in America, and of that number one-half are used in Germany alone.

The skin of the Otter is at present classed among the leading fashionable furs in this country. They are dyed of a deep purplish black color, and are made into sacques, muffs, etc. It is also used by the Russians, Greeks and Chinese. It is mostly an American product, but is also procured to some extent in the British Isles from a smaller variety of the species.

The skins of the Wolf are chiefly used for sleigh robes and such purposes. The fur of the Rabbit is mainly employed in the manufacture of felt, and is also utilized for lining and trimming. The business of breeding rabbits for their fur has been introduced into the United States, and large numbers have been successfully raised in Danbury, Conn., for felting purposes connected with the manufacture of hats.

The fur of the Wolverine or Glutton, finds a market for the most part in Germany, where it is used for trimmings and cloak linings.

The Skunk furnishes the fur known as Alaska Sable, which forms one of our staple pelts, many thousands being annually exported to Poland and the adjacent provinces.

The Badger yields a valuable and fashionable fur, which is also extensively used in the manufacture of artist's brushes; a good " badger blender " forming a valuable accessory to a painter's outfit. Shaving brushes by the thousand are annually made from the variegated hair of the badger.

The Opossum yields a fur in very common use among the masses, and the skins of the domestic Cat are utilized to a considerable extent in the manufacture of robes, mats, etc. The fur of the Puma and Wild Cat are also employed in this form, and may often be seen handsomely mounted and hanging on the backs of sleighs on our fashionable thoroughfares. Among the small game the skins of Squirrels are used for linings, and the soft, velvety fur of the Mole is manufactured into light robes, and very fine hats, and in theatrical paraphernalia is sometimes employed for artificial eyebrows.

Full descriptions of the color of the various furs will be found in our lengthy illustrated chapter on our American animals.

THE END.

INDEX

A

Adirondack experiences with mosquitoes, 256.

Advice to the Novice on the sale of Furs, 283.

Air-tight Jar, for butter, &c., 236.

Alaska Sable, 286.—See also Skunk.

Alcohol, its use and abuse, 257.

Alum—used in waterproofing, 249.

"Amateur Trapping," 225.

AMBER, OIL OF, used in the art of Trapping, 152.

AMERICAN FUR SKINS.—Table of values, 284.

Their uses at Home and Abroad, 284.

American Lion.—See Puma.

Amputation, self inflicted, as a means of escape with captured animals, 144.

To prevent, 144, 145.

Ancient uses of Furs, 278.

ANISE, OIL OF.—

Its use in the art of trapping, 152.

As bait for fish, 240.

Annual yield of Furs throughout the world, 281.

Apparatus for stretching skins, 273.

Arrows, poisoned, 26.

Arrow Traps, 23, 25.

Artificial Eyebrows of Mole Fur, 286.

ART OF TRAPPING, 148.

ASSAFŒTIDA.—

Its use by the Trapper, 151.

As scent bait for fish, 240.

ASTOR, JOHN JACOB, and the Fur Trade, 281.

Astringent Preparations, use of, in drying Skins, 273, 276.

B

BADGER, THE.—

Nature and habits of, 175.

Skinning the, 177.

Trapping the, 175.

Uses of Fur, 286.

Value of Fur, 284.

Bags, Waterproof, for food, 236.

Baiting the Steel Trap, 143.

Baits for fishing, 240.

Baits, scent, 149.

Bait, Trapping without, 148.

BARK SHANTY.—

Hints on, 266.

Details of construction, 245.

Bark-Stone.—See Castoreum.

Bark-Stone composition.—See Castoreum.

"Barque."—See Birch Bark Canoe.

Barrel Hoops used in canoe building, 264.

BARREL TRAPS, 125, 127, 133.

Basket for the shoulders, 234, 236.

Basswood-bark canoes, 264.

Bateaux, 264.

BAT FOWLING NET, 70.

Baking, recipe for, 253.

Bay Lynx.—See Wild Cat.

Beans as food, 235.

BEAR.—

Nature and habits of, 168, 227.

Trapping the, 168.

Traps for, 17, 29, 143.

Various species of, 168.

Directions for removing skin, 172.

Use of skin, 285.

Value of skin, 284.

"Bear Tamer," 137, 142.

"Bear Chasing," dangers of the sport, 170.

Bear Grease, 171.
Bear Meat, to roast, 233.
 "   "   to dry, 237.
BEAVER.—
    Nature and habits of, 177.
    Trapping the, 177.
    Skinning the, 182.
    Skin, to tan, 277.
    Use of fur, 285.
    Value of skin, 284.
BEDS AND BEDDING, 248.
Bed, spring, 248.
 " hammock, swinging, 249.
Bed clothes, 249.
BIG HORN, the, 220.
    As food, 220, 238.
    Nature and habits of, 220.
    Trapping the, 220.
BIRCH BARK CANOE, remarks on, 226.
    Directions for making, 261.
Bird-Catching Net, 70.
BIRD LIME, 97.
    Masticated Wheat used as, 99.
    Recipe for making, 98.
    Used in capture of Puma, 35.
    Used for capture of Humming Bird,
      99.
    Used in making Fly-paper, 136.
    Used with an Owl as decoy, 98.
    With paper cone, as a Crow trap, 96.
BIRD TRAPS, 65.
 "   Box, 88, 90, 91.
BIRD WHISTLE, 72.
BISON.—See Buffalo.
Black Fly.—See " Punkey."
Blanket, woollen, 250.
    Rubber, 236.
    Use of, 250.
Block-tin, used for kettles, &c., 235.
Blossom, utilized as a trap, 99.
Blow-gun, used in the capture of Hum-
    ing Bird, 99.
BOARD FLAP, the, 130.
BOARD STRETCHERS, 273.
BOATS, remarks on, 226.
    Manufacture of. 259.
    The dug-out, or log canoe, 259.
    The birch-bark canoe, 261.
    The bateau, 264.
    The scow, 267.
    The flat-bottomed boat, 267.
Boiled Mush, 232.
 "   to fry, 232.
Boiling water used in bending wood, 268,
    272.
Book I. TRAPS FOR LARGE GAME, 17.
      II. SNARES OR NOOSE TRAPS, 39.
     III. TRAPS FOR FEATHERED GAME,
            65.

   IV. MISCELLANEOUS TRAPS, 103.
    V. HOUSEHOLD TRAPS, 125.
   VI. STEEL TRAPS AND THE ART OF
            TRAPPING, 137.
  VII. THE CAMPAIGN, 225.
 VIII. THE TRAPPER'S MISCELLANY,
            255.
Boots, hints on, 228.
    Grease for, 228.
Bottle Lantern, 241.
 "   Match Safe, 234.
Bow STRETCHER, for skins, 274.
Bow Traps, 23, 25, 116.
BOWL TRAPS, 135, 136.
Box Bird Traps, 55, 88, 90, 91.
Box DEAD FALL, 128.
Box Hut, used in Pickerel fishing, 241.
Box OWL TRAP, 88.
Box PIT-FALL, 131.
Box SNARES, 55, 56.
Box TRAP, the, 103
    Two modes of setting, 105.
Box Traps, 55, 56, 88, 90, 91, 103, 106,
    109, 110.
Box TRAP, pendent, 91.
Brandy on a trapping campaign, 257
Brass wire nooses, 41.
Brick Trap, 66.
Broiling, recipes for, 233.
Brook Trout, fishing through the ice, 240.
 "   To cook deliciously, 232.
Bruises, ointment for, 255.
Buckskin gloves, in handling traps, 149.
Building the camp fire, 233.
Buffalo, the, 220.
    As food, 221, 238.
    How hunted and trapped, 221.
Building boats, 259.
Butternut log, for canoe, 239.
Butter, to keep on a campaign, 236.

               C

Cage traps for birds, 76.
 "   "   mice, 134.
Call Birds, how used, 72.
CAMPAIGN LIFE IN THE WILDERNESS,
    225.
CAMPAIGN, PLAN OF, 225.
Camp fire, 228.
    To build, 233.
Camp Kettle, 235.
 "   Knife, 235.
 "   Stove, 228, 235.
Canada Grouse, 238.
 "   Lynx.—See Lynx.
 "   Moose.—See Moose.
Candles, in camp, 227.
 "   Novel way of using, 218.

Canned vegetables, 236.
CANOES, remarks on, 226.
" Basswood-bark, 264.
" Birch-bark, directions for building, 261.
" Hemlock bark, 264.
" Log.—See Dug-out.
" Spruce bark, 264.
Canton flannel bags, for bed clothes, 249.
Canvass-back Duck, as food, 239.
Canvas bags, waterproof, 236.
Caps, percussion, used in lighting fire, 234.
CAPTURE OF ANIMALS, 154.
CARPETING TENTS, 250.
CASTOREUM, or Barkstone, 150.
How obtained, 150.
How used.—See Beaver.
CASTOREUM COMPOSITION, 150.
Cat, domestic, use of skin, 285.
Value of skin, 284.
Cat, wild.—See Wild Cat.
Caulking boats, 261, 266.
Caution in baiting steel traps, 143.
Caution in handling steel traps, 149.
Chill, remedy for, 257.
Chimney-fire in log shanty, 245.
Chip as a plate, 232.
Chip, for a frying pan, 230, 232.
Chloride of Lime, as an antidote, 152.
Choosing a trapping ground, 225.
Cicely, Sweet, as scent bait in fishing, 240.
Cities built up by the fur trade, 281.
CLAP NET, 72.
Clearing tents and shanties from insects, 230.
Climate and fur apparel, 284.
CLOG, THE, 146.
Cloth for tent making, 247.
" Waterproof preparation for, 247.
Clothing, hints on, 228.
Coasting on the Indian sled, 270.
Cock of the plains, 238.
Coffee, 236.
Coffee-pot, 235.
Cold, remedy for, 257.
Combination camp-knife, 235.
COMMON BOX TRAP, 103.
Compass, pocket, 227.
Compound scent-bait, 150, 153.
Concealing steel traps, 22).
Cone of paper as a trap, 96.
Corrall, African trap, 34.
COOKING UTENSILS FOR A CAMPAIGN, 230, 235.
Coon.—See Raccoon.
COOP TRAP, 67.
" For large game, 33.
Cotton drilling, used for making tents, 247.
" Waterproof preparation for, 247.

" Cotton Tail."—See Rabbit.
Cougar.—See Puma.
Cow's udder, as fish bait, 240.
Crackers as food, 236.
Crow trap, 96.
CUMMIN, used in trapping, 152.
Cup, portable, 231.
CURING SKINS, 272.
Current price list of American furs, 284.

D

Dark lantern, used by bird catchers, 71.
Deer hunters, 217.
DEAD-FALLS, 17, 29, 107, 111, 113.
" Box, 128.
" For large game, 17.
" How set for the fox, 113.
" Stone, 29.
" Weighted harpoon, 26.
" With figure four trap, 114.
Dead fish, valuable in making trails, 153.
Decoys, 72, 76, 94.
Decoy traps, 72, 76, 94.
" Whistle, 74.
" Owl used as, 98.
DEER, 214.
As food, 233, 237, 238.
How to skin the, 219.
Hunting at night, 217, 218.
Luminosity of eyes at night, 217, 218.
Natural characteristics of, 214.
Salt as bait for, 218.
Season for hunting, 218.
Trapping the, 214, 215.
Various modes of hunting, 217.
Various species of, 215.
Deer lick, the, 215.
Deer meat, to dry, 237.
Deer meat, to roast, 233.
Delmonico outdone, 232.
Detecting the direction of the wind by the finger, 217.
Devices used in connection with the steel trap, 144, 147.
Devils' Lantern, 241.
Diet of the Trapper, 230.
"DOUBLE ENDER," the, 107.
Double traps, 57, 109, 110, 129.
DOWN FALL, the, 26.
Dressing for fur skins, 273, 276.
Dressing for leather, 228.
Dressing skins for market, 272.
" Home use, 276.
Dried fish, 237.
Dried venison, 237.
Drilling, as tent material, 247.
" Waterproof preparation for, 247.

Drinking cup, portable, 231.
Drying skins, 272, 273, 276.
Ducks, various species of, 239.
   As food, 239
   To cook deliciously, 233.
DUCK TRAPS, 94, 95.
"DUG-OUT," THE, hints on, 226.
   Detailed directions for making, 259.

E

Eels, oil prepared from, 151.
Elk.—See Moose.
"Ephraim."—See Bear.
Escaping from the mosquitoes, 255.
Exports of furs, 281, 285.
Extemporized frying pan, 232.
"Toaster," 233.
Extract of beef, Liebig's, 236.
Extravagance in fur apparel, 279.

F

False bottom traps, 127, 131, 133.
Fashion and fur, 279, 283, 285.
FEATHERED GAME, TRAPS FOR, 65.
Felt, use of rabbit-fur in making, 286.
FENNEL, OIL OF, used in trapping, 152.
FENUGREEK, OIL OF, used in trapping, 152.
FIGURE FOUR SNARE, 61.
FIGURE FOUR TRAP, 107.
   " Used with Dead-Fall, 114.
Finger, as a weather vane, 217.
Fire, to build, 227.
   " To light without matches, 234.
   " With powder and cap, 234.
   " Without "anything," 235.
Fire arms, 227.
   " Oil for, 227.
Fire bottle, 241.
Fire Hat for night hunting, 218.
Fire-proof preparations for tents, 247.
Fish, to bake, 232.
   To dry, 237.
   To fry, 233.
FISHER MARTEN.—
   How to trap the animal, 194.
   Its nature and habits, 194.
   Its common mode of release from capture, 144.
   Method of skinning, 195.
   Use of skin, 285.
   Value of skin, 284.
FISH-HOOK, trap for ducks, 95.
Fishing, hints on, 239.
   At night, 239.

Through the ice, 240.
   Various baits, 240.
   With tip-ups 240.
   For pickerel, 240.
Fishing tackle, 227, 240, 241.
Fish lantern, 241.
FISH OIL, used in the art of trapping, 151.
   How obtained, 151.
Fish, scent baits for, 240.
   Spearing, 239.
Fish traps, 120, 241.
Flat bottomed boats, 264, 267.
Flat bottomed sled.—See Toboggan
Flat stone, as a frying pan, 232.
Flower, converted into a trap, 99.
Fly, black.—See "Punkey."
FLY-PAPER, to make, 136.
Fly Tent, the, 246.
Fly traps, 136.
Food, portable, 230.
FOOD AND COOKING UTENSILS, 230.
"FOOLS' CAP" TRAP FOR CROWS, 96.
Forks, 235.
Fortunes founded on peltry, 281.
FOWLING NET, the, 70.
FOX.—
   Nature and habits of, 154.
   Trapping the, 154.
   Trapped by a dead-fall, 111, 113
   Varieties of, 154.
   Directions for skinning, 158.—See also Red and Silver Fox.
"Fox fire," used in capture of deer, 218.
Fritters, pork, to cook, 231.
Frying pan, 231, 235.
   " An extemporized, 232.
Fur Market, eccentricities of, 283.
Furs, ancient uses of, 278.
   Annual yield throughout the world, 281.
Furs, best season for, 147.
   " Home," 281.
   Sale of, by Hudson's Bay Company 281.
   " Shipping," 281.
   Table of market values, 282.
Fur skins, to cure for market, 272.
   To tan, 276.
   Hints on selling for profit, 283.
   Various uses of, 285.
FUR TRADE, OBSERVATIONS ON, 278.
   Immensity of, 281.

G

Game, protected from wolves, 237.
GAROTTE TRAP, 114.
Gloves to be used in trapping, 149.
Glutton.—See Wolverine.

Gnats, 230, 256.
  Painful effects of their bites, 256.
  Remedies for their bites, 255.
  Driven away by the "Smudge," 230.
Gnat, black.—See "Punkey."
Goose trap, 75.
GOPHER.—
  Nature and habits of, 205.
  Trapping the, 205.
  Traps for, 119, 120, 140.
  Directions for skinning, 206.
Grappling iron, the, 146.
Grease for boots and shoes, 228.
"Great Bear Tamer," the, 142.
GRIZZLY BEAR.—
  Nature and habits of, 169.
  Trapping the, 169.
  Traps for, 17, 142.
  Use of fur, 285.
Ground plan of trapping lines, 228.
Ground, selection for trapping, 225.
GROUND SNARES, 44.
Grouse, as food, 233, 238.
  Bait for, 42.
  Oil of, for fire arms, 227.
  Peculiarities of, 42.
  Snares for, 39.
  To cook deliciously, 233.
  Various species of, 238.
GUN TRAP, 20.

H

Hair Nooses, 41.
Half tent, 246.
Hammocks, 250.
Hammock bed, 249,
Handling steel traps, caution in, 149.
Hanging bed, 249,
Hare.—See Rabbit.
HARPOON TRAP of Africa, 26.
Hat Brim, portable, 258.
  Netting attachment for, 258.
Hat lantern for night hunting, 218.
Hawk snare, 43.
HAWK TRAP, 93.
Head lantern used in deer hunting, 218.
HEAD NET, 257.
HEDGE NOOSES, 41.
Hemlock bark canoes, 264.
Hemlock boughs, as bedding, 250.
Hemp, used in caulking boats, 261, 266.
"Hiding" steel traps, 229.
High top boots, 228.
Hints on baiting the steel trap, 143.
Hints on selection of trapping ground, 225.

Hints on skinning animals, 272.
Hints on trapping, 148.
Hints on plans of trapping lines, 228.
Hints on sale of furs, 283.
Hippopotamus trap, 26.
Historical items relating to furs and the fur trade, 278.
Hoe cake, to cook, 232.
Hogs carried off by bears, 170.
Hog's liver used as fish bait, 240.
"Home Furs," 281.
HOME-MADE BOAT, 264.
Honey as bait, 19, 31, 170.
Hook trap for ducks, 95.
Hopo, African trap, 34.
Hoop nooses, 40.
HOOP STRETCHER for skins, 275.
Horse hair nooses, to make, 41.
Hot drink for chills, 257.
HOUSEHOLD TRAPS, 125.
House Tent, 247,
How to select a steel trap, 138.
HOW TO TRAP, 153.
Hudson Bay Company, origin of, 280.
  Sales of, 281, 282.
Humming bird, killed by concussion, 99.
  " Snare, 99.
  " Trap, 99.
  " Various modes of capture, 99.
Hunting the deer, 217.
Hunting from trees, 218.
HUT, LOG.—See Log Shanty.

I

Implements required on a trapping campaign, 227.
Improved springle, 60.
INDIAN CANOE.-See BIRCH BARK CANOE.
Indian meal, as food, 231.
INDIAN SLEDGE.— See Toboggan.
INDIAN SNOW SHOE, 268.
India-rubber blanket, 236.
  How used, 250.
INSECT OINTMENTS, 255.
Insect bites, remedies for, 255.
  " Sores resulting from, 257.
Insects, to drive out from tent or shanty, 230, 256.
Intemperance, 257.

J

Jack knife, a valuable tool, 227.
Jar, as a trap, 135.

Jar, air-tight, for butter, 236.
"Jerked Venison," 237.
JOHN JACOB ASTOR, and the fur trade, 281.
Johnny cake, to cook, 232.

K

Kettle, camp, 235.
Knapsack, 234.
    Directions for making, 236.
Knife, a necessary implement, 227.
Knife, the combination camp, 235.
Knives, table, 235.

L

Lake trout, fishing for, 240.
    To cook deliciously, 232.
Lantern for the head, used by deer hunters, 218.
Lantern used by bird catchers, 71.
Lantern trap for fish, 241.
Large game, traps for, 17.
LAVENDER, used in the art of trapping, 152.
Leather preservative, 228.
"Le Chat."—See Lynx.
Lemonade, 236.
Lens, to light fire with, 234.
Lever for setting large steel traps, 142.
Liebig's extract of beef, 236.
Light, the trapper's, 227.
Light for the head in night hunting, 218.
Light home-made boat, 264.
Lime, chloride of, as a disinfectant, 152.
Liniment for wounds and bruises, 255.
    "Insect bites, 255.
Linseed oil, used as bird lime, 98.
Lion, American.—See Puma.
LIST OF PRICES OF AMERICAN FURS, 284.
Liver, as fish bait, 240.
LOG CABIN.—See Log Shanty.
Log Canoe.—See Dug-Out.
LOG COOP TRAP, 33.
LOG SHANTY, hints on, 226, 229.
    Detailed directions for building, 244.
    Site for building, 244, 287.
    To clear of gnats and mosquitoes, 230.
Lucifer Matches.—See Matches.
"Luxuries," 234.
LYNX, THE CANADIAN, 164.
    Natural characteristics of, 164.
    Trapping the, 164.
    Traps for, 17, 20, 23, 29, 33, 35, 141.

LYNX.—
    Directions for skinning, 166.
    Use of skin, 285.
    Value of skin, 284.

M

Mackinaw and the Fur Trade, 281.
Mallard Duck as food, 239.
    " to Cook.—See Duck.
MARKET VALUE OF FUR SKINS, 281.
Marmot.—See Woodchuck.
MARTEN :—
    Nature and habits of, 192.
    Trapping the, 192.
    Its common mode of escape, 144.
    Directions for removing skin, 194.
    How to tan the Skin, 277.
    Value and use of skin, 284, 285.
Mastic Varnish used in water-proofing, 234
MATCHES, 227.
    Bottle used for carrying, 234.
    To render water-proof, 234.
Meal, Indian, as food, 231.
Meat, to dry, 237
"MEDICINES," OR SCENT BAITS, 149.
Menagerie Whistle, 74.
Merganser, the, as food, 239.
    To cook.—See Duck.
MIDGETS, 256.
    Painful effect of their bites, 256.
    Driven away by the "Smudge," 230
    Ointments for bites, 255.
    Serious effects of bites on the intemperate, 257.
MINK :—
    Nature and habits of, 189.
    Trapping the, 189.
    Traps for, 43, 141.
    Its common mode of escape from the steel trap, 144.
    Directions for skinning, 191.
    To tan skin of, 277.
    Extensive use of skins in America, 281.
    Uses of skin, 285.
    Value of skin, 284.
MISCELLANEOUS hints on trapping, 148.
MISCELLANY, the Trapper's, 255.
MISCELLANEOUS TRAPS, 103.
MOLE, 207.
    Beauty of fur, 209, 211.
    Life and habits of, 207.
    Trapping the, 110. 210.
    Traps for, 119, 120, 140.
    Varieties of, 211.
    Directions for skinning.—See Gopher.
    Use of fur, 286.

Montreal and the Fur Trade, 281.
Moose :—
    Nature and habits of, 219.
    Trapping the, 220.
    "Yards," 220.
    Flesh as food, 220, 223, 238.
    How to skin the animal, 220.
Moose meat, to roast, 233.
" Meat to dry, 237.
Mosquitoes, 230.
    Painful effects of their bites, 257.
    Ointments for bites, 255.
    Driven away by the " Smudge," 230.
    Adirondack experiences with, 255,
        256.
    Head-net, 257.
    Serious effects of bites on the intem-
        perate, 257.
Mouse Traps, 124, 130, 131, 134, 135.
Mud Stick or Pusher, 267.
Mush, to boil, 232.
    to fry, 232.
Musk :—
    Its use in the art of trapping, 151.
    How obtained, 151.
Muskrat :—
    Nature and habits of, 182.
    Pit-fall Trap for, 133.
    Spearing the, 183.
    Trapping the, 182.
    Traps for, 43, 107, 110, 111, 114, 133,
        141.
    Its common mode of release, 144.
    Extensive use of skins in America,
        281.
    Skin, to remove, 185.
        To tan, 277.
        Use of, 286.
        Value of, 284.
Muscovy Duck as food, 239.
        To cook.—See Duck.
Musquaw.—See Bear.

N

Natural Advantages utilized by the Trap-
    per, 149.
Natural History.
    Necessity of its study in the art of
        Trapping, 148.
Neatsfoot Oil for Fire Arms, 227.
Net :—
    " Bat fowling, 70.
    " Bird catching, 70.
    " Clap, 72.
    " Decoy, 72.
    " Fish, use of, 241.

Net for the head, 257.
    " Fowling, 70.
Net traps, 70, 73, 75, 80, 83, 85.
        For Tiger, Puma, or Wild Cat,
            35.
        Spring, 80.
        The upright, 85.
        Wild Duck, 94.
        Wild Goose, 75.
Netting attachment for Hat brim 258.
Newhouse Trap, the, 138.
Night-hunting, 217, 218.
Night-fishing, 239.
Nooses :—
        Horse hair, 41.
        In hedge, 42.
        On hoops, 40.
        On string, 40.
Noose Traps, 39.
Nooses, wire, 41.
Northwest Fur Company, 280.
Nutting in Mid-winter, 212.

O

Oar-locks, simple, 266.
Oat-meal as food, 236.
Observations on the History of Furs
    and the Fur Trade, 278.
Oil, Fish.—
        Used in trapping, 151.
        How obtained, 151.
Oil of Amber.—
        Used in the art of trapping, 152.
Oil of Ambergris.—
        Used in the art of trapping, 152.
Oil of Anise :—
        Its use in the art of trapping, 152.
Oil of Cinnamon :—
        Its use in the art of trapping, 152.
Oil of Fennel :—
        Its use in the art of trapping, 152.
Oil of Fenugreek :—
        Its use in the art of trapping, 152.
Oil of Lavender :—
        Its use in the art of trapping, 152.
Oil of Rhodium :—
        Its use by trappers, 151.
Oil of Skunk :—
        Its use by trappers, 151.
Oil :—
        For fire arms, 227.
        For light, 227.
Oil of Partridge :—
        Its use, 227.
Oil of Pennyroyal :—
        For insect bites, 255.

Ointment for Bruises and Wounds, 255.
OINTMENT FOR INSECT BITES, 255.
OLD-FASHIONED SPRINGLE, 58.
Olive Oil in cooking, 236.
OPOSSUM, 201.
    Nature and habits of, 202
    Trapping the, 201.
    Hunting the, 202.
    Directions for skinning,
    Uses of skin, 286.
    Value of skin, 284.
OTTER :—
    Nature and habits of,
    Trapping the, 186.
    Directions for skinning, 189.
    How to tan the skin, 277.
    Use of skin, 286.
    Value of skin, 284.
OWL TRAP, 88.
Owl :—
    Used in connection with bird lime as
    decoy, 98.

P

Paint as a water-proof covering, 236,
Painter, the.—See Puma.
Panther, the.—See Puma.
Paper Cone used as a trap, 96.
Partridge, 42, 238.
    As food, 238.
    Fat for fire arms, 227.
    Snares, 39, etc.
    To cook deliciously, 233.
Peltry :—
    Fortunes founded on, 281.
    Cities built up on, 281.
PENDENT BOX, BIRD TRAP, 91.
Pennyroyal for insect bites, 255.
Pepper Tea as a remedy, 257.
Percussion Cap used in lighting fire, 234.
Peshoo, the.—See Lynx.
Phosphorescent wood used in night-hunt-
    ing, 218.
Phosphorus lantern for catching fish, 241.
Pickerel fishing, 240.
    " Spearing, 241.
    " Trap for, 121.
    " To cook, 233.
Pigeon Net-trap, 72.
Pigs carried off by Bears, 170.
Pine Log Canoe.—See Dug-out.
Pinnated Grouse, 238.
Pitch for stopping leaks, 261, 264, 266.
PIT-FALL TRAPS.—
    For large game, 31.
    For small game, 125, 127, 131.
    Barrel, 127.
    Box, 131.
    For Muskrat, 133.

PLAN OF TRAPPING CAMPAIGN, 225.
Plates, substitutes for, 232, 235.
Platform snare, 61.
Poachers, or trap robbers, 249.
POACHER'S SNARE, 48.
Pocket compass, 227.
POCKET HAT BRIM, 258.
    " Sun-glass, 234.
Poisoned arrows, 26.
POISONING, 222.
Pop-corn as bait for Quail, 54.
Portable boats, 259.
Portable food & cooking utensils, 230, 235.
Portable drinking cup, 231.
    Hat brim, 258.
    " With netting attached, 258.
    Snares, 50, 52.
    Stove, 228, 235.
Pork as food, 231.
    " Fritters, 251.
    " " To make, 232.
" Possum."—See Opossum.
Potatoes as food, 235.
Pouched Rat.—See Gopher.
Powder used in lighting fire, 234.
Prairie Hen, 238.
Prairie Whistle, 74
Precautions in handling steel traps, 156.
PREFACE, 3.
Preparation of skins for market, 272.
Preserve jar used as trap, 135.
Price Current of American Furs, 284.
Prime fur, best season for, 147.
Prof. Blot outdone in cooking, 232.
Profit in selling furs, 233.
PRONGHORN Antelope, 221.
    Nature and habits of, 221.
    How hunted and trapped, 221, 238.
Provisions, to protect from Wolves, 237.
Ptarmigan, to cook, 233.
    Trap for, 75.
    How hunted and trapped, 239.
    Various species of, 230.
PUMA :—
    Bait for, 20, 31, 32, 163.
    Nature and habits of, 161.
    Peculiarities of, 20.
    Traps for, 17, 20, 23, 29, 31, 33, 141.
    Trapping the, 161.
    Directions for skinning, 164.
    Use of skin, 286.
    Value of skin, 284.
Pumice Stone, used in finishing skins, 276.
" PUNKEY."—
    Description of the Insect, 256.
    Severity of bites, 256.
    Ointment for bites, 255.
    Serious effects of bites on the intem-
    perate, 257.

Punk Tinder. used in lighting fire, 234.
" Pusher."—See Mud stick.
Putty, for stopping leaks, 261.

Q

Quail, bait for, 40, 54.
" Snares, 39, 40, 41, etc.
To cook deliciously, 233.
Quotations of the Fur Market, 284.

R

RABBIT :—
    As food, 238.
    Bait for, 203.
    How to skin, 204.
    Nature and habits of, 203.
    Salt as bait for, 109.
    Traps for, 43, 64, 103.
    Use of fur, 286.
    Value of fur, 284.
    Varieties of, 203.
RACCOON :—
    As a pet, 173.
    Nature and habits of, 172.
    Trapping the, 172.
    Traps for, 110, 116, 141.
    Hunting the, 172.
    Directions for skinning, 175.
    How to tan the skin, 277.
    Use of the fur, 285.
    Value of the fur, 284.
Rat :—
    Snares for, 43.
    Trapping the, 125.
    Traps for, 43, 125, 127, 128, 131, 138.
Rations for a Campaign, 230.
Raw Furs.—See Furs.
Recipe for insect ointments, 255.
    Boot grease, 228.
    For cooking, 230.
    For curing skins, 272.
    For tanning skins, 276.
Red Fox.— See Fox.
Red Fox.—
    Value of skin, 284.
    Use of skin, 285.
Red Pepper Tea as a remedy, 257.
Red Squirrel.—See Squirrel.
Remedies for insect bites, 255.
    For chills, 257.
Requisites of a good steel trap, 138.
    " For snaring, 39.
    " For a good trapping ground, 225.
    " For a trapping campaign, 227.

Revolver, 227.
Reynard outwitted by a dead-fall, 111, 113.
RHODIUM, Oil of :—
    Its use by the trapper, 151.
Rice as food, 236.
Rifle and Shot Gun combined, 227.
    Oil for, 227.
RIFLE TRAP, 20.
Roasting, recipes for, 233.
Rocky Mountain Sheep.—See Big Horn.
" Roughing it," 230.
Rubber blanket, 236.
    How used, 250.
Ruffed Grouse.—See Partridge.
Rum on a trapping campaign, 257.

S

Sage Cock, the, 238.
Sale of furs by the Hudson's Bay Company, 282.
Salmon, spearing, 239.
    " Spear, 239.
Salmon Trout, spearing, 239.
Salmon, to cook deliciously, 232.
Salt as bait for Deer, 218.
    As bait for Rabbit, 109.
Salt Lick, the, 218.
Sandpaper used in softening skins, 276.
Salt Pork as food, 231.
SCENT BAITS, 149.
    " Compound, 150, 153.
Scented baits for birds, 240.
Scented baits for fish, 240.
Season for Deer hunting, 218.
SCOW, 267.
Season for trapping, 147.
Selection of trapping ground, 225.
Self-amputation as a means of escape with captured animals, 144.
Self-amputation, to prevent, 144, 145.
Self-raising flour, 235.
SELF-SETTING TRAPS, 110, 125, 127, 131.
SHANTY :—
    Bark.—See Bark Shanty.
    " Home."—See Log Shanty.
    Log.—See Log Shanty.
Sheeting as tent material, 247.
    Water-proof, preparation for, 247.
Shellac Varnish used in water-proofing, 234.
SHELTER :—The trapper's remarks on, 226.
Shelter tent, 247.
    Details of construction, 242.
Shingle stretchers for skins, 274.

"Shipping furs," 281.
SHOOTING AND POISONING, 222.
Shot-gun Trap, 20.
Shot-gun combined with rifle, 267.
Shoulder basket, 234, 226.
SIEVE TRAP, 65.
Silver Fox, 154.
    Value of skin, 284, 285.
Skinning animals, hints on, 272.
Skins :—
    Stretchers for, 273.
    To dry, 272, 276.
    To soften, 276, 277.
    To tan, 276.
    Value of, 284.
    Use of, 285.
SKUNK, 195.
    Adventure with, 196,
    As food, 238.
    Nature and habits of, 195.
    Trapping the, 195.
    Traps for, 43, 111, 114, 141.
    To eradicate odor of, 152, 198.
    Oil of, used in trapping, 151.
    Directions for skinning, 198.
    Use of skin, 286.
    Value of skin, 284.
Sled, Indian.—See Toboggan.
SLIDING POLE, 145.
Slippery Elm used for bird-lime, 98.
"Small Game" as food, 237.
Smell, acute sense of, in animals, 148.
Smoking the steel trap, 128.
Smouldering birch bark to drive away insects, 230.
Smudge, the, 230, 256.
SNARE.—
    Box, 55.
    Double box, 56.
    Fig. Four, 62.
    Hawk, 43.
    Hedge, 42.
    Hoop, 40.
    Humming-bird, 99.
    Knotted string, 52, 53, 54.
    Pasteboard box, 56.
    Platform, 61.
    Poacher's, 48.
    Portable, 48, 50, 52.
    Quail, 53.
    Rat, 43.
    "Simplest," 52.
    Springle, 58, 60.
    Stovepipe, 120.
    Tree, 42.
    Triangle, 42.
    Twitchup, 43.
    Wood Chuck, 43.
SNARES, OR NOOSE TRAPS, 39.

Snaring, requisites for, 39.
Snow Grouse, the, 238.
SNOW-SHOES, 267.
Snow-shoe race, 267.
Softening skins, 276, 277.
Sores resulting from insect bites, 217.
Soups, recipes for, 236.
Spearing fish, 239, 241.
Spearing Muskrats, 183.
Spider for cooking, 233.
Spoons, 235.
Spring-bed, 249.
SPRINGLE, 58, 60.
Spring-net Traps, 80.
Spring-pole, the, 144.
Spring, to temper, 84.
Spruce Bark Canoes, 264.
Spruce boughs as bedding, 250.
Spruce Grouse, 238.
SQUIRRELS, 211.
    As food, 238.
    Nature and habits of, 211.
    Traps for, 43, 103, 106, 107, 110, 116, 128, 140.
    Various species of, 213.
    To cook, 233.
    Use of skins, 286.
STEEL TRAPS, 137.
    Caution in handling, 149.
    Concealing in the woods, 229.
    Various modes of setting, 144.
    Requisite number for a campaign, 227.
    To set for rats, 128.
    To select judiciously, 138.
    Requisites of, 138.
    Hints on baiting, 143.
Steel Trap spring, to set with lever, 142.
STEEL TRAPS AND THE ART OF TRAPPING, 137.
Still hunting, 217.
Stimulants, 257.
Stone Dead-fall, 29.
Storing traps in the woods, 229,
Stove, portable, 228, 235.
Stovepipe fish-trap, 120.
St. Paul, Minn., and the Fur Trade, 281.
STRETCHERS FOR SKINS, 273.
Strychnine poisoning, 222.
Sucker wire nooses, 41.
Sugar of lead used in water-proofing, 247.
Sun-glass, 234, 235.
Sweet Cicely as bait for fish, 240.
SWEET FENNEL.—
    Oil used in trapping, 152.
Sweet Oil and Tar Ointment for insect bites, 255.
Swinging bed, 249.

T

Table knife and bowl trap, 135.
Table showing sale of furs by Hudson
    Bay Company, 282.
Tallow, mutton, as ointment, 255.
Tame Geese as decoys, 75.
TANNING SKINS, 276.
    Mixtures, 276, 277, 278.
    With the hair on, 276.
    Simple, 278.
Tar and Sweet Oil ointment for insect
    bites, 255.
Tar for water-proofing, 264.
Tea, 236.
    " Red pepper, as a remedy, 257.
Teal Ducks as food, 239.
    To cook.—See Duck.
"Telescope" Drinking Cup, 231.
Tempering iron spring, 84.
TENTS, 246.
    House-tent, 246.
    Fly-tent, 247.
    Half-tent, 247.
    Shelter-tent, 247.
    Materials, 247.
    Water-proof preparation for, 247.
    Fire-proof preparation for, 247.
    To carpet with spruce, 250.
    To clear of gnats and musquitoes,
        230.
TENT CARPETING, 250.
Thimble used with bowl as Mouse trap,
    136.
Tiger captured with bird lime, 35.
Tiger trap, 31.
Tinder, 234.
Tip-ups, 240.
Toaster, an extemporized, 233.
TOBOGGAN, OR INDIAN SLEDGE, 269.
Tools required on a trapping campaign,
    227.
Tools required for canoe building, 259.
Torch for the head, used in night hunting,
    218.
"Touch-wood" used in lighting fire, 234.
Trail, The.—
    Its value to the trapper, 153.
    Various modes of making, 153.
TRAP.—
    Arrow, 23, 25.
    Barrel, 125, 127.
    Bird, 65, 70, 73, 75, 88, 90, 91, 96.
    Bow, 23, 25, 116.
    Bowl, 135.
    Box, 55, 56, 88, 90, 91, 103, 106, 109,
        110.

Brick, 66.
Cage, 76, 134.
Cob house, 67.
Coon, 110, 116, 141.
Coop, 33, 67, 70.
Crow, 96.
Dead-fall, 17, 107, 111.
Decoy, 72, 76, 94.
Double ender, 109.
Down-fall, 26.
Duck, 94, 95.
Fish, 120.
Fish hook, 95.
Fly, 136.
Fool's-cap, 96.
Garotte, 114.
Gun, 20.
Harpoon, 26.
Hawk, 42, 93.
Hook, 95.
Jar, 135.
Mole, 119, 120.
Mouse, 130, 131, 134, 135.
Net, 70, 73, 75, 80, 83, 85.
Owl, 88.
Partridge, 43, etc.
Pendent Box, 91.
Pitfall, 11, 125, 127, 131.
Ptarmigan, 75.
Quail, 39, 40, 41, 53.
Rabbit, 43, 64, 103.
Rat, 43, 125, 127, 128, 131, 138.
Rifle, 20.
Self-setting, 110, 125, 127, 131.
Sieve, 65.
Spring net, 80, 83, 85.
Steel, 140.
The "Newhouse," 140.
Tree, 42, 91.
Upright net, 85.
Wild Duck, 94, 95.
Wild Goose. 75.
Woodchuck, 43.
Trapper's beds and bedding, 248.
    "   Cooking utensils, 230.
    "   Diet, 230.
TRAPPER'S MISCELLANY, 255,
    "   Shelter, 226, 242.
    "   Sled.—See Toboggan.
TRAPPING, art of, 148.
    Season for, 147.
    Miscellaneous hints on, 148.
    Campaign, plan of, 225.
        Tools and other requisites, 227.
        Ground, selection of, 225.
    Valuable suggestions on, 228.
Trapping Lines, 226.
Trap robbers, 229.
Traps for large game, 17.

FOR FEATHERED GAME, 65.
  HOUSEHOLD, 125.
Tree hunting, 218.
Tree snare, 42.
  " Traps, 42, 91.
TRIANGLE SNARE, 42.
Trout, to cook deliciously, 232.
Trumpet Creeper flower used as a trap, 99.
Tumbler fly-trap, 136.
Twitch-up, 43, 62.
    Poacher's, 48.
    Portable, 50.
    " Simplest," 52.

U

UPRIGHT NET TRAP, 85.
    "   Snares 44, 58.
Use and abuse of Alcohol, 257.
Uses of fur skins, 285.
Utensils for cooking, 230, 235.

V

Value of fur skins, table of, 262.
Various uses of fur skins, 285.
Varnish water-proof preparation for preserving matches, 234.
Vegetables for food on a campaign, 235.
    "   Canned, 236.
Venison as food, 233, 237.
    To roast, 233,
    To preserve, 237,
    " Jerked," 237.
    Dried, 237.

W

Walking on the snow, 267.
War in the fur trade, 281.
Watch crystal as sun glass, 287
Water fowl as food, 239.
Water-proof application for boats, 261, 264, 266.
    " Canvas bags, for food, 236.
Match safe, 234.
    " Preparation, 236, 247, 266.
    " Varnish for matches, 234.
Water traps, 110, 120.
Wedge stretcher for skins, 274.
Weighted harpoon trap, 26.
Wheaten grits as trappers' food, 236.
Wheat flour as food, 235.
    " Self-raising, 235.

Wheel form of trapping lines, 229.
Whiskey on a trapping campaign, 257.
Whip lashes from Woodchuck hide, 204.
Whistlebird, 74.
White Birch Canoe, 261.
White-wood log for Dug-out, 259.
Widgeon, the, as food, 239.
    To cook.—See Duck.
WILD CAT :—
    Nature and habits of, 167.
    Snares for, 43.
    Trapping the, 166.
    Skinning the, 168.
    Uses of skin, 286.
    Value of skin, 284.
Wild Duck, to cook. 233.
Wild Duck, traps, 94, 95.
Wild Goose as food, 239.
Wild Goose to cook, 233.
Wild Goose trap, 75.
Wind, direction of, to detect by the finger 217.
Winged vermin, 255.
Winter fishing, 240.
Wire cage trap for birds, 76.
    "   "   For mice, 134.
Wire nooses, 41.
WOLF.—
    Nature and habits of, 158.
    Trapping the, 158.
    Poisoning the, 222.
    Traps for, 20, 141.
    To protect provisions from, 237.
    Varieties of, 158.
    Directions for skinning, 161.
    Use of skin, 286.
    Value of skin, 284.
WOLVERINE :—
    Nature and habits of, 199, 238.
    Trapping the, 199.
    Natural enemy to the Beaver, 20
    Directions for skinning, 201.
    Use of skin, 286.
    Value of skin, 284.
WOODCHUCK, 204.
    As food, 238.
    Nature and habits of, 204.
    Snare, 205.
    Trapping the, 204.
    Use of skin, 204.
    Smoked from its burrow, 205.
    Removing skin of, 205.
Woodcock, to cook, 233.
Wood Duck as food, 239.
    To cook.—See Duck.
Woodland beds and bedding, 249.
Wounds, ointment for, 255.

A CATALOG OF SELECTED
DOVER BOOKS
IN ALL FIELDS OF INTEREST

A CATALOG OF SELECTED DOVER
BOOKS IN ALL FIELDS OF INTEREST

100 BEST-LOVED POEMS, Edited by Philip Smith. "The Passionate Shepherd to His Love," "Shall I compare thee to a summer's day?" "Death, be not proud," "The Raven," "The Road Not Taken," plus works by Blake, Wordsworth, Byron, Shelley, Keats, many others. 96pp. 5³⁄₁₆ x 8¼. 0-486-28553-7

100 SMALL HOUSES OF THE THIRTIES, Brown-Blodgett Company. Exterior photographs and floor plans for 100 charming structures. Illustrations of models accompanied by descriptions of interiors, color schemes, closet space, and other amenities. 200 illustrations. 112pp. 8⅜ x 11. 0-486-44131-8

1000 TURN-OF-THE-CENTURY HOUSES: With Illustrations and Floor Plans, Herbert C. Chivers. Reproduced from a rare edition, this showcase of homes ranges from cottages and bungalows to sprawling mansions. Each house is meticulously illustrated and accompanied by complete floor plans. 256pp. 9⅜ x 12¼.
0-486-45596-3

101 GREAT AMERICAN POEMS, Edited by The American Poetry & Literacy Project. Rich treasury of verse from the 19th and 20th centuries includes works by Edgar Allan Poe, Robert Frost, Walt Whitman, Langston Hughes, Emily Dickinson, T. S. Eliot, other notables. 96pp. 5³⁄₁₆ x 8¼. 0-486-40158-8

101 GREAT SAMURAI PRINTS, Utagawa Kuniyoshi. Kuniyoshi was a master of the warrior woodblock print — and these 18th-century illustrations represent the pinnacle of his craft. Full-color portraits of renowned Japanese samurais pulse with movement, passion, and remarkably fine detail. 112pp. 8⅜ x 11. 0-486-46523-3

ABC OF BALLET, Janet Grosser. Clearly worded, abundantly illustrated little guide defines basic ballet-related terms: arabesque, battement, pas de chat, relevé, sissonne, many others. Pronunciation guide included. Excellent primer. 48pp. 4³⁄₁₆ x 5¾.
0-486-40871-X

ACCESSORIES OF DRESS: An Illustrated Encyclopedia, Katherine Lester and Bess Viola Oerke. Illustrations of hats, veils, wigs, cravats, shawls, shoes, gloves, and other accessories enhance an engaging commentary that reveals the humor and charm of the many-sided story of accessorized apparel. 644 figures and 59 plates. 608pp. 6 ⅛ x 9¼.
0-486-43378-1

ADVENTURES OF HUCKLEBERRY FINN, Mark Twain. Join Huck and Jim as their boyhood adventures along the Mississippi River lead them into a world of excitement, danger, and self-discovery. Humorous narrative, lyrical descriptions of the Mississippi valley, and memorable characters. 224pp. 5³⁄₁₆ x 8¼. 0-486-28061-6

ALICE STARMORE'S BOOK OF FAIR ISLE KNITTING, Alice Starmore. A noted designer from the region of Scotland's Fair Isle explores the history and techniques of this distinctive, stranded-color knitting style and provides copious illustrated instructions for 14 original knitwear designs. 208pp. 8⅜ x 10⅞. 0-486-47218-3

Browse over 9,000 books at www.doverpublications.com

ALICE'S ADVENTURES IN WONDERLAND, Lewis Carroll. Beloved classic about a little girl lost in a topsy-turvy land and her encounters with the White Rabbit, March Hare, Mad Hatter, Cheshire Cat, and other delightfully improbable characters. 42 illustrations by Sir John Tenniel. 96pp. 5³⁄₁₆ x 8¼. 0-486-27543-4

AMERICA'S LIGHTHOUSES: An Illustrated History, Francis Ross Holland. Profusely illustrated fact-filled survey of American lighthouses since 1716. Over 200 stations — East, Gulf, and West coasts, Great Lakes, Hawaii, Alaska, Puerto Rico, the Virgin Islands, and the Mississippi and St. Lawrence Rivers. 240pp. 8 x 10¾. 0-486-25576-X

AN ENCYCLOPEDIA OF THE VIOLIN, Alberto Bachmann. Translated by Frederick H. Martens. Introduction by Eugene Ysaye. First published in 1925, this renowned reference remains unsurpassed as a source of essential information, from construction and evolution to repertoire and technique. Includes a glossary and 73 illustrations. 496pp. 6½ x 9¼. 0-486-46618-3

ANIMALS: 1,419 Copyright-Free Illustrations of Mammals, Birds, Fish, Insects, etc., Selected by Jim Harter. Selected for its visual impact and ease of use, this outstanding collection of wood engravings presents over 1,000 species of animals in extremely lifelike poses. Includes mammals, birds, reptiles, amphibians, fish, insects, and other invertebrates. 284pp. 9 x 12. 0-486-23766-4

THE ANNALS, Tacitus. Translated by Alfred John Church and William Jackson Brodribb. This vital chronicle of Imperial Rome, written by the era's great historian, spans A.D. 14-68 and paints incisive psychological portraits of major figures, from Tiberius to Nero. 416pp. 5³⁄₁₆ x 8¼. 0-486-45236-0

ANTIGONE, Sophocles. Filled with passionate speeches and sensitive probing of moral and philosophical issues, this powerful and often-performed Greek drama reveals the grim fate that befalls the children of Oedipus. Footnotes. 64pp. 5³⁄₁₆ x 8 ¼. 0-486-27804-2

ART DECO DECORATIVE PATTERNS IN FULL COLOR, Christian Stoll. Reprinted from a rare 1910 portfolio, 160 sensuous and exotic images depict a breathtaking array of florals, geometrics, and abstracts — all elegant in their stark simplicity. 64pp. 8⅜ x 11. 0-486-44862-2

THE ARTHUR RACKHAM TREASURY: 86 Full-Color Illustrations, Arthur Rackham. Selected and Edited by Jeff A. Menges. A stunning treasury of 86 full-page plates span the famed English artist's career, from *Rip Van Winkle* (1905) to masterworks such as *Undine, A Midsummer Night's Dream,* and *Wind in the Willows* (1939). 96pp. 8⅜ x 11. 0-486-44685-9

THE AUTHENTIC GILBERT & SULLIVAN SONGBOOK, W. S. Gilbert and A. S. Sullivan. The most comprehensive collection available, this songbook includes selections from every one of Gilbert and Sullivan's light operas. Ninety-two numbers are presented uncut and unedited, and in their original keys. 410pp. 9 x 12. 0-486-23482-7

THE AWAKENING, Kate Chopin. First published in 1899, this controversial novel of a New Orleans wife's search for love outside a stifling marriage shocked readers. Today, it remains a first-rate narrative with superb characterization. New introductory Note. 128pp. 5³⁄₁₆ x 8¼. 0-486-27786-0

BASIC DRAWING, Louis Priscilla. Beginning with perspective, this commonsense manual progresses to the figure in movement, light and shade, anatomy, drapery, composition, trees and landscape, and outdoor sketching. Black-and-white illustrations throughout. 128pp. 8⅜ x 11. 0-486-45815-6

Browse over 9,000 books at www.doverpublications.com

A CHRISTMAS CAROL, Charles Dickens. This engrossing tale relates Ebenezer Scrooge's ghostly journeys through Christmases past, present, and future and his ultimate transformation from a harsh and grasping old miser to a charitable and compassionate human being. 80pp. 5³⁄₁₆ x 8¼. 0-486-26865-9

COMMON SENSE, Thomas Paine. First published in January of 1776, this highly influential landmark document clearly and persuasively argued for American separation from Great Britain and paved the way for the Declaration of Independence. 64pp. 5³⁄₁₆ x 8¼. 0-486-29602-4

THE COMPLETE SHORT STORIES OF OSCAR WILDE, Oscar Wilde. Complete texts of "The Happy Prince and Other Tales," "A House of Pomegranates," "Lord Arthur Savile's Crime and Other Stories," "Poems in Prose," and "The Portrait of Mr. W. H." 208pp. 5³⁄₁₆ x 8¼. 0-486-45216-6

COMPLETE SONNETS, William Shakespeare. Over 150 exquisite poems deal with love, friendship, the tyranny of time, beauty's evanescence, death, and other themes in language of remarkable power, precision, and beauty. Glossary of archaic terms. 80pp. 5³⁄₁₆ x 8¼. 0-486-26686-9

THE COUNT OF MONTE CRISTO: Abridged Edition, Alexandre Dumas. Falsely accused of treason, Edmond Dantès is imprisoned in the bleak Chateau d'If. After a hair-raising escape, he launches an elaborate plot to extract a bitter revenge against those who betrayed him. 448pp. 5³⁄₁₆ x 8¼. 0-486-45643-9

CRAFTSMAN BUNGALOWS: Designs from the Pacific Northwest, Yoho & Merritt. This reprint of a rare catalog, showcasing the charming simplicity and cozy style of Craftsman bungalows, is filled with photos of completed homes, plus floor plans and estimated costs. An indispensable resource for architects, historians, and illustrators. 112pp. 10 x 7. 0-486-46875-5

CRAFTSMAN BUNGALOWS: 59 Homes from "The Craftsman," Edited by Gustav Stickley. Best and most attractive designs from Arts and Crafts Movement publication — 1903–1916 — includes sketches, photographs of homes, floor plans, descriptive text. 128pp. 8¼ x 11. 0-486-25829-7

CRIME AND PUNISHMENT, Fyodor Dostoyevsky. Translated by Constance Garnett. Supreme masterpiece tells the story of Raskolnikov, a student tormented by his own thoughts after he murders an old woman. Overwhelmed by guilt and terror, he confesses and goes to prison. 480pp. 5³⁄₁₆ x 8¼. 0-486-41587-2

THE DECLARATION OF INDEPENDENCE AND OTHER GREAT DOCUMENTS OF AMERICAN HISTORY: 1775-1865, Edited by John Grafton. Thirteen compelling and influential documents: Henry's "Give Me Liberty or Give Me Death," Declaration of Independence, The Constitution, Washington's First Inaugural Address, The Monroe Doctrine, The Emancipation Proclamation, Gettysburg Address, more. 64pp. 5³⁄₁₆ x 8¼. 0-486-41124-9

THE DESERT AND THE SOWN: Travels in Palestine and Syria, Gertrude Bell. "The female Lawrence of Arabia," Gertrude Bell wrote captivating, perceptive accounts of her travels in the Middle East. This intriguing narrative, accompanied by 160 photos, traces her 1905 sojourn in Lebanon, Syria, and Palestine. 368pp. 5⅜ x 8¼.
0-486-46876-3

A DOLL'S HOUSE, Henrik Ibsen. Ibsen's best-known play displays his genius for realistic prose drama. An expression of women's rights, the play climaxes when the central character, Nora, rejects a smothering marriage and life in "a doll's house." 80pp. 5³⁄₁₆ x 8¼. 0-486-27062-9

AN ENCYCLOPEDIA OF BATTLES: Accounts of Over 1,560 Battles from 1479 B.C. to the Present, David Eggenberger. Essential details of every major battle in recorded history from the first battle of Megiddo in 1479 B.C. to Grenada in 1984. List of battle maps. 99 illustrations. 544pp. 6½ x 9¼. 0-486-24913-1

ENCYCLOPEDIA OF EMBROIDERY STITCHES, INCLUDING CREWEL, Marion Nichols. Precise explanations and instructions, clearly illustrated, on how to work chain, back, cross, knotted, woven stitches, and many more — 178 in all, including Cable Outline, Whipped Satin, and Eyelet Buttonhole. Over 1400 illustrations. 219pp. 8⅜ x 11¼. 0-486-22929-7

ENTER JEEVES: 15 Early Stories, P. G. Wodehouse. Splendid collection contains first 8 stories featuring Bertie Wooster, the deliciously dim aristocrat and Jeeves, his brainy, imperturbable manservant. Also, the complete Reggie Pepper (Bertie's prototype) series. 288pp. 5⅜ x 8½. 0-486-29717-9

ERIC SLOANE'S AMERICA: Paintings in Oil, Michael Wigley. With a Foreword by Mimi Sloane. Eric Sloane's evocative oils of America's landscape and material culture shimmer with immense historical and nostalgic appeal. This original hardcover collection gathers nearly a hundred of his finest paintings, with subjects ranging from New England to the American Southwest. 128pp. 10⅝ x 9. 0-486-46525-X

ETHAN FROME, Edith Wharton. Classic story of wasted lives, set against a bleak New England background. Superbly delineated characters in a hauntingly grim tale of thwarted love. Considered by many to be Wharton's masterpiece. 96pp. 5³⁄₁₆ x 8 ¼. 0-486-26690-7

THE EVERLASTING MAN, G. K. Chesterton. Chesterton's view of Christianity — as a blend of philosophy and mythology, satisfying intellect and spirit — applies to his brilliant book, which appeals to readers' heads as well as their hearts. 288pp. 5⅜ x 8½. 0-486-46036-3

THE FIELD AND FOREST HANDY BOOK, Daniel Beard. Written by a co-founder of the Boy Scouts, this appealing guide offers illustrated instructions for building kites, birdhouses, boats, igloos, and other fun projects, plus numerous helpful tips for campers. 448pp. 5³⁄₁₆ x 8¼. 0-486-46191-2

FINDING YOUR WAY WITHOUT MAP OR COMPASS, Harold Gatty. Useful, instructive manual shows would-be explorers, hikers, bikers, scouts, sailors, and survivalists how to find their way outdoors by observing animals, weather patterns, shifting sands, and other elements of nature. 288pp. 5⅜ x 8½. 0-486-40613-X

FIRST FRENCH READER: A Beginner's Dual-Language Book, Edited and Translated by Stanley Appelbaum. This anthology introduces 50 legendary writers — Voltaire, Balzac, Baudelaire, Proust, more — through passages from *The Red and the Black, Les Misérables, Madame Bovary,* and other classics. Original French text plus English translation on facing pages. 240pp. 5⅜ x 8½. 0-486-46178-5

FIRST GERMAN READER: A Beginner's Dual-Language Book, Edited by Harry Steinhauer. Specially chosen for their power to evoke German life and culture, these short, simple readings include poems, stories, essays, and anecdotes by Goethe, Hesse, Heine, Schiller, and others. 224pp. 5⅜ x 8½. 0-486-46179-3

FIRST SPANISH READER: A Beginner's Dual-Language Book, Angel Flores. Delightful stories, other material based on works of Don Juan Manuel, Luis Taboada, Ricardo Palma, other noted writers. Complete faithful English translations on facing pages. Exercises. 176pp. 5⅜ x 8½. 0-486-25810-6

HEART OF DARKNESS, Joseph Conrad. Dark allegory of a journey up the Congo River and the narrator's encounter with the mysterious Mr. Kurtz. Masterly blend of adventure, character study, psychological penetration. For many, Conrad's finest, most enigmatic story. 80pp. 5³⁄₁₆ x 8¼. 0-486-26464-5

HENSON AT THE NORTH POLE, Matthew A. Henson. This thrilling memoir by the heroic African-American who was Peary's companion through two decades of Arctic exploration recounts a tale of danger, courage, and determination. "Fascinating and exciting." — *Commonweal*. 128pp. 5⅜ x 8½. 0-486-45472-X

HISTORIC COSTUMES AND HOW TO MAKE THEM, Mary Fernald and E. Shenton. Practical, informative guidebook shows how to create everything from short tunics worn by Saxon men in the fifth century to a lady's bustle dress of the late 1800s. 81 illustrations. 176pp. 5⅜ x 8½. 0-486-44906-8

THE HOUND OF THE BASKERVILLES, Arthur Conan Doyle. A deadly curse in the form of a legendary ferocious beast continues to claim its victims from the Baskerville family until Holmes and Watson intervene. Often called the best detective story ever written. 128pp. 5³⁄₁₆ x 8¼. 0-486-28214-7

THE HOUSE BEHIND THE CEDARS, Charles W. Chesnutt. Originally published in 1900, this groundbreaking novel by a distinguished African-American author recounts the drama of a brother and sister who "pass for white" during the dangerous days of Reconstruction. 208pp. 5⅜ x 8½. 0-486-46144-0

THE HUMAN FIGURE IN MOTION, Eadweard Muybridge. The 4,789 photographs in this definitive selection show the human figure — models almost all undraped — engaged in over 160 different types of action: running, climbing stairs, etc. 390pp. 7⅞ x 10⅝. 0-486-20204-6

THE IMPORTANCE OF BEING EARNEST, Oscar Wilde. Wilde's witty and buoyant comedy of manners, filled with some of literature's most famous epigrams, reprinted from an authoritative British edition. Considered Wilde's most perfect work. 64pp. 5³⁄₁₆ x 8¼. 0-486-26478-5

THE INFERNO, Dante Alighieri. Translated and with notes by Henry Wadsworth Longfellow. The first stop on Dante's famous journey from Hell to Purgatory to Paradise, this 14th-century allegorical poem blends vivid and shocking imagery with graceful lyricism. Translated by the beloved 19th-century poet, Henry Wadsworth Longfellow. 256pp. 5³⁄₁₆ x 8¼. 0-486-44288-8

JANE EYRE, Charlotte Brontë. Written in 1847, *Jane Eyre* tells the tale of an orphan girl's progress from the custody of cruel relatives to an oppressive boarding school and its culmination in a troubled career as a governess. 448pp. 5³⁄₁₆ x 8¼. 0-486-42449-9

JAPANESE WOODBLOCK FLOWER PRINTS, Tanigami Kônan. Extraordinary collection of Japanese woodblock prints by a well-known artist features 120 plates in brilliant color. Realistic images from a rare edition include daffodils, tulips, and other familiar and unusual flowers. 128pp. 11 x 8¼. 0-486-46442-3

JEWELRY MAKING AND DESIGN, Augustus F. Rose and Antonio Cirino. Professional secrets of jewelry making are revealed in a thorough, practical guide. Over 200 illustrations. 306pp. 5⅜ x 8½. 0-486-21750-7

JULIUS CAESAR, William Shakespeare. Great tragedy based on Plutarch's account of the lives of Brutus, Julius Caesar and Mark Antony. Evil plotting, ringing oratory, high tragedy with Shakespeare's incomparable insight, dramatic power. Explanatory footnotes. 96pp. 5³⁄₁₆ x 8¼. 0-486-26876-4

Browse over 9,000 books at www.doverpublications.com

THE METAMORPHOSIS AND OTHER STORIES, Franz Kafka. Excellent new English translations of title story (considered by many critics Kafka's most perfect work), plus "The Judgment," "In the Penal Colony," "A Country Doctor," and "A Report to an Academy." Note. 96pp. 5⅜₆ x 8¼. 0-486-29030-1

MICROSCOPIC ART FORMS FROM THE PLANT WORLD, R. Anheisser. From undulating curves to complex geometrics, a world of fascinating images abound in this classic, illustrated survey of microscopic plants. Features 400 detailed illustrations of nature's minute but magnificent handiwork. The accompanying CD-ROM includes all of the images in the book. 128pp. 9 x 9. 0-486-46013-4

A MIDSUMMER NIGHT'S DREAM, William Shakespeare. Among the most popular of Shakespeare's comedies, this enchanting play humorously celebrates the vagaries of love as it focuses upon the intertwined romances of several pairs of lovers. Explanatory footnotes. 80pp. 5⅜₆ x 8¼. 0-486-27067-X

THE MONEY CHANGERS, Upton Sinclair. Originally published in 1908, this cautionary novel from the author of *The Jungle* explores corruption within the American system as a group of power brokers joins forces for personal gain, triggering a crash on Wall Street. 192pp. 5⅜ x 8½. 0-486-46917-4

THE MOST POPULAR HOMES OF THE TWENTIES, William A. Radford. With a New Introduction by Daniel D. Reiff. Based on a rare 1925 catalog, this architectural showcase features floor plans, construction details, and photos of 26 homes, plus articles on entrances, porches, garages, and more. 250 illustrations, 21 color plates. 176pp. 8⅜ x 11. 0-486-47028-8

MY 66 YEARS IN THE BIG LEAGUES, Connie Mack. With a New Introduction by Rich Westcott. A Founding Father of modern baseball, Mack holds the record for most wins — and losses — by a major league manager. Enhanced by 70 photographs, this warmhearted autobiography is populated by many legends of the game. 288pp. 5⅜ x 8½. 0-486-47184-5

NARRATIVE OF THE LIFE OF FREDERICK DOUGLASS, Frederick Douglass. Douglass's graphic depictions of slavery, harrowing escape to freedom, and life as a newspaper editor, eloquent orator, and impassioned abolitionist. 96pp. 5⅜₆ x 8¼. 0-486-28499-9

THE NIGHTLESS CITY: Geisha and Courtesan Life in Old Tokyo, J. E. de Becker. This unsurpassed study from 100 years ago ventured into Tokyo's red-light district to survey geisha and courtesan life and offer meticulous descriptions of training, dress, social hierarchy, and erotic practices. 49 black-and-white illustrations; 2 maps. 496pp. 5⅜ x 8½. 0-486-45563-7

THE ODYSSEY, Homer. Excellent prose translation of ancient epic recounts adventures of the homeward-bound Odysseus. Fantastic cast of gods, giants, cannibals, sirens, other supernatural creatures — true classic of Western literature. 256pp. 5⅜₆ x 8¼. 0-486-40654-7

OEDIPUS REX, Sophocles. Landmark of Western drama concerns the catastrophe that ensues when King Oedipus discovers he has inadvertently killed his father and married his mother. Masterly construction, dramatic irony. Explanatory footnotes. 64pp. 5⅜₆ x 8¼. 0-486-26877-2

ONCE UPON A TIME: The Way America Was, Eric Sloane. Nostalgic text and drawings brim with gentle philosophies and descriptions of how we used to live — self-sufficiently — on the land, in homes, and among the things built by hand. 44 line illustrations. 64pp. 8⅜ x 11. 0-486-44411-2

Browse over 9,000 books at www.doverpublications.com